Ministry
to
Turbulent
America

A HISTORY OF THE AMERICAN BAPTIST
HOME MISSION SOCIETY COVERING ITS
FIFTH QUARTER CENTURY, 1932-1957

by **G. Pitt Beers**

THE JUDSON PRESS

Philadelphia   Chicago   Los Angeles

MINISTRY TO TURBULENT AMERICA

© The Judson Press 1957

All rights in this book are reserved. No part of the book may be reproduced in any manner without permission in writing from the publisher, except in the case of brief quotations included in a review of the book in a magazine or newspaper.

FIRST EDITION

LIBRARY OF CONGRESS CATALOG CARD NO. 57-7919

PRINTED IN THE U.S.A.

Dedicated to
ALICE T. BEERS

*whose sacrificial cooperation in service
made possible the writing of this book*

Preface

THE AMERICAN BAPTIST HOME MISSION SOCIETY has been pursuing its motto, "North America for Christ," for a hundred and twenty-five years. The history of the first one hundred years was ably written by Dr. Charles L. White, long the Executive Secretary of the Society, and bears the title, *A Century of Faith*.[1] The present author, having served the Society as Executive Secretary for eighteen and a half years, was requested by the Board of Managers to bring the story down to the end of its fifth quarter of a century.

In doing this, the writer has carefully reread all of the minutes of the Society and its Board of Managers, the annual reports of the Board of Managers to the Society, the reports of the missionaries of the Society, and the reports of the state and city secretaries in regard to cooperative work. He has reread many of the reports of conferences and committees as they are found in the files of the Society. He has refreshed his memory of the period by rereading also his own diary. References to these sources have been omitted from the body of the text as seeming to be unduly pedantic. Undoubtedly many books read during the period of service are reflected in this account, but it is impossible to single them out for individual mention.

In presenting this material it has seemed better to tell the story of each department throughout the period, rather than to describe the whole work year by year. This plan will require the reader to retrace the entire quarter century in most of the

[1] Published in 1932 by The Judson Press, Philadelphia, Pa.

chapters. Whatever the disadvantages of so doing, they seem less than those connected with any other plan of organization.

It may be noted that this is primarily an account of The American Baptist Home Mission Society, for the integration with the Woman's American Baptist Home Mission Society did not take place until 1955. The writer, however, has been glad to note at numerous points the cooperation there has been between the General Society and the Woman's Society, and he has endeavored to indicate those changes of relationship which the integration of these two Societies has now brought about.

Perhaps one matter of terminology should be noted. The Northern Baptist Convention, meeting in Boston, Mass., in 1950, voted to change its name to the American Baptist Convention. The writer has endeavored to use the term "Northern" in connection with all events prior to that date and the term "American" in connection with all events since then.

The writer wishes to thank the secretaries of the departments of the integrated Boards of Managers who aided him in securing many details and in insuring the accuracy of the statements. He is grateful to Dr. Robert G. Torbet, who read the entire manuscript and made many valuable suggestions, and especially to Dr. Theron Chastain, the Executive Secretary of the Society, who gave the fullest cooperation at all times.

Table of Contents

		PAGE
Preface		7
Introduction		11

CHAPTER

I	Turbulent America	17
II	Advance Against Odds	25
III	Ministry to Youth in Military Service	34
IV	Meeting the Postwar Situation	43
V	Churches for New Communities	49
VI	The Challenge of Urban Growth	58
VII	Mission to Village and Rural America	90
VIII	Ministry to the Original Americans	104
IX	Ministry to Latin America Part 1: Mexico, Cuba, Puerto Rico	115
X	Ministry to Latin America (Continued) Part 2: El Salvador, Nicaragua, Haiti	142
XI	A Developing Evangelism	164
XII	Building New Churches	183
XIII	Philanthropic Institutions and Services	189
XIV	Administering Emergency Aid	195
XV	Undergirding the Work	202
XVI	Developing Relationships	213
XVII	North America for Christ	233

APPENDICES

PAGE

A   The First One Hundred Years............... 244

B   Presidents of the A. B. H. M. S............... 249

C   Chairmen of the Board of Managers........... 250

D   Board Members of the A. B. H. M. S........... 251

     Index 254

Introduction

IN THE SUMMER OF 1931 staid New Englanders rubbed their eyes and stared again. No, it had not vanished. There was the covered wagon of their great-grandfathers' day rolling down the main streets of their cities! It was a curious version of the covered wagon, however, for it was drawn not by oxen but by an automobile.

Thus did The American Baptist Home Mission Society announce to the world that it had been preaching the gospel to the pioneers for a hundred years. The most dramatic part of that centennial celebration was the trip of the automobile-drawn covered wagon from coast to coast. It left Brockton, Mass., June 20, 1931, and, on September 9 of that same year, arrived at the West Union Baptist Church in Oregon, the oldest Baptist church west of the Rockies. On the way it had traveled five thousand miles and had been the center of sixty-three meetings in seventeen states. Directing the tour was Dr. Coe Hayne, one of the secretaries of The American Baptist Home Mission Society. With him was Dr. G. Clifford Cress, himself a pioneer missionary of the Society. Dr. Cress had served the Society as state superintendent in Montana, had been employed by *The Baptist*[1] as field editor, and had been a representative of the Board of Promotion of the Northern Baptist Convention. At the time, he was associate secretary of The Ministers and Missionaries Benefit Board of the Northern Baptist Convention. That Board very graciously had released him to the Home Mission Society to make his contribution to this celebration. He was the principal speaker at most of the rallies; his subject being, "The Spirit of the Pioneer." William Turkington, then a graduate student at Eastern Baptist Theological Seminary, went along with

[1] A denominational weekly published in Chicago for a number of years.

his cornet and accordion to lead the singing. Don Hayne, son of Dr. and Mrs. Coe Hayne, also went along to drive the car and to perform those many services that sometimes are little honored but are essential to such a trip. Don Hayne, later, earned the degree of Doctor of Philosophy at the University of Michigan, and became a member of the faculty at Michigan State University at East Lansing.

In many places the rallies drew large crowds. Sometimes more than a thousand persons were present. Some of the rallies were sponsored by large and well-known churches; others were sponsored by small and little-known churches. For example, a rally was held in Central Baptist Church, Hartford, Conn., Dr. John Lackey, pastor; and another, in the same state, at a little church used only on special occasions, but which had a historic connection with John Mason Peck, the Father of Home Missions. There was a great Sunday evening gathering at the First Baptist Church, Syracuse, N. Y., where Dr. Bernard C. Clausen was pastor, and another at Amenia, N. Y., where Peck once had been pastor. A rally was held in the Delaware Avenue Church at Buffalo, N. Y., Dr. Earl F. Adams, pastor, and one on the nearby Cattaraugus Indian Reservation, where Rev. David Owl was the missionary, under joint appointment of the New York State Convention and The American Baptist Home Mission Society. Delegations came by train, bus, and private car to such centers along the route as Granville, Ohio, and Fort Wayne, Ind. In Michigan the party not only held a rally at Kalamazoo, but also met a group at the grave of Rev. Thomas W. Merrill, the first missionary of the Society.

Over a thousand persons gathered for the meeting at Alton, Ill., seat of Shurtleff College, founded by John Mason Peck. The presence of two of his granddaughters, Mrs. Ida Jett of Odin, Ill., and Mrs. Sarah C. Mitchell of Salem, Ill., together with two great-great-granddaughters and two great-great-great-grandsons, made the occasion a notable one. From there the covered wagon went to Rock Springs, Ill., where the old home of John

Mason Peck was still standing. In attendance there was Mr. Charles B. Dorram, 92 years old, who had been a student in Peck's old Rock Springs Seminary, and who remembered Peck very well. At Kansas City, Mo., a thousand people gathered for an impressive religious service in Penn Park, at the foot of the statue of the Pioneer Mother.

Everywhere the covered wagon received special honors. In many places it was escorted by police, brass bands, and Boy Scouts. Mayors were regularly on the platform, and several governors and senators participated in the programs. It was an enthusiastic recognition of one hundred years of pioneer service and a pledge of cooperation for the future.

In addition to this main tour, the covered wagon, with different personnel, traveled up and down the West Coast to a large number of enthusiastic and well-attended meetings. It was on exhibition also at the sessions of the Northern Baptist Convention in San Francisco.

When the wagon came to its final resting place at the West Union Baptist Church in Oregon, there ended what was perhaps the most dramatic presentation of home missions that had ever been made. At least twenty thousand people had been present at the meetings across the country, and several thousand additional persons had attended the meetings on the West Coast and at the Convention. Local newspapers everywhere gave the meetings good publicity, and Dr. Cress' "Diary of the Covered Wagon" was published in *Missions*. A deep impression was made on the denomination and on the general public.

Other phases of the celebration were centered largely upon a memorial honoring John Mason Peck, undoubtedly the main personal influence in the founding of the Home Mission Society.[1] A service commemorating his conversion was held at Litchfield, Conn., his childhood home. Because Peck originally was a

---

[1] Biographies of John Mason Peck are: *Memoir of John Mason Peck,* edited by Rufus Babcock; *Vanguard of the Caravans,* by Coe Hayne; *John Mason Peck and One Hundred Years of Home Missions, 1817-1917,* by A. K. deBlois and L. C. Barnes; and *John Mason Peck,* by Matthew Lawrence.

Congregationalist, the Congregationalists joined with the Baptists in the service. A Board Meeting and a rally were held near Catskill, N. Y., where Peck began his ministry. Another was held in the First Baptist Church of Shelbyville, Ky., with the wholehearted cooperation of the pastor, the church, and other Southern Baptists. This gathering commemorated the historic conference of John Mason Peck and Jonathan Going in September, 1831, at which they decided that a Home Mission Society should be organized and laid plans accordingly. There was a special centenary program at the Northern Baptist Convention under the leadership of Dr. Austin K. deBlois, for many years a member of the Board of Managers of the Society. Centennial Sunday was observed in the churches May 1, 1932, and a booklet, *Memorial and Pioneer Programs,* was provided by the Society for this purpose.

Another feature of the celebration was the publication of a centenary history, entitled *A Century of Faith,* written by Dr. Charles L. White, the Executive Secretary of the Society from 1917 to 1929. Before that, he had served as associate corresponding secretary from 1908 to 1917. Thus he had been on the staff of the Society for twenty-one years. A memorial volume had been published in 1882, but *A Century of Faith* was the first formal account of the Society's history and achievements.

What was expected to be the most tangible result of this celebration never came to pass. The Convention had given permission to undertake the raising of $1,500,000 to $2,500,000, but the celebration had been held against a very dark backdrop. The depression, which began with the stock-market crash in October, 1929, reached its greatest depth in 1932. While general conditions thereafter began to improve slightly, gifts to the missionary budget continued to decrease until 1939. As a result, the raising of this fund for the work of the Society was postponed from time to time, until, as the minutes state, it was "indefinitely postponed." It is not referred to again.

Thus was celebrated the completion of a century of service by The American Baptist Home Mission Society. The new century was begun under very trying conditions, but with high courage and great hope. The story of the first quarter of this *second* century is related in this book.

I

Turbulent America

W HILE THE AMERICAN BAPTIST HOME MISSION
Society was thus joyfully celebrating one hundred years of
achievement and laying bold plans for the future, it really was
working against great odds. America and the world were in the
grip of the longest and severest depression known in modern
times. Although the leaders of the Society in 1932 could not
foresee it, that condition would continue, though in mitigated
form, until it ended in the most widespread and destructive war
mankind had ever seen. That war was followed by an uneasy
peace, interrupted by a "police action" in Korea not easily distinguishable from war. Furthermore, the entire period following
World War II has been characterized by the "cold war" with
Communist Russia, which, in 1956, still showed no sign of coming to an end. It has been indeed a turbulent era in America's life.

The great depression which began in 1929, and was at its
worst in 1932, was the darkest financial experience this nation
has ever known.[1] Even in the boom year of 1929 there had
been 1,800,000 unemployed, and from that time on unemploy-
ment increased until in February, 1934, 8,000,000 households,
representing 28,000,000 persons, were on relief. Many of those
employed were working only part time and at greatly reduced
wages. The national income between the years 1929 and 1932
dropped from $81,000,000,000 to $41,000,000,000. There were
85,000 business failures; 5,000 banks suspended payments,
9,000,000 savings accounts were wiped out. From 1928 to 1933

---

[1] In the writing of this chapter the author has received much help from *The Age of the
Great Depression 1929-1941*, by Dixon Wecter, the MacMillan Co.; and *From Versailles to the
New Deal*, by Harold U. Faulkner, in the *Chronicles of America* series, Yale University Press.

17

construction of residential property dropped 95 per cent, while expenditures for repairs dropped 90 per cent. In 1932 alone, 273,000 home owners lost their homes. Wages dropped by some $26,000,000,000. Joblessness and poverty became acute social problems with which private charity, even with the help of state and local relief agencies, was totally unable to cope. Bread lines lengthened; soup kitchens were opened; the unemployed rioted. Barter came back into use in many local areas. The number of admissions to hospitals for mental cases from 1930 to 1932 was almost three times that for the years 1922 to 1929. The years 1932 and 1933 showed an abrupt rise in the ratio of hospital admissions to population. The suicide rate rose steadily until 1932, then gradually subsided until 1936, when it was only slightly higher than in 1929. Deaths from accident, disease, and general collapse also increased markedly, due in considerable measure to malnutrition.

In agriculture the situation was in some respects even darker. The decline in value of farm produce came within two years after World War I. In those two years the price of corn dropped one-third, and that of wheat and cotton dropped one-half.

To meet the demands of World War I for food and fiber, agriculture had expanded more rapidly than ever before. Marginal and even submarginal land had been brought under cultivation. A vast amount of farm machinery had been bought on credit, greatly increasing the production per man. At the same time, better methods of agriculture had greatly increased the yield per acre. Three generations earlier it had taken about one-half of the labor force of America to meet the demand for food and textiles. By 1955 only 14 per cent of the population was on farms, and only 13 per cent of the labor force was working on farms. And yet this reduced force was producing substantially more than could be sold, either in America or abroad.[1]

When the demand dropped sharply with the close of the war, agriculture could not reduce production as rapidly as the

[1] Editorial, *New York Times*, January 22, 1955.

situation demanded. The marginal and submarginal land which had been brought under cultivation during the war should have gone back to grass, but for the individual farmer that change was difficult or impossible. Land had been bought on credit at highly inflated prices, and the mortgage payments had to be made, even though under the changed conditions the farms could not produce enough to pay the interest. Machinery had been bought on credit and still had to be paid for.

Then came the drop in the purchasing power of America because of the depression. From 1919 to 1932 the farm income of America dropped from $12,000,000,000 to $5,020,000,000. At the same time there was no lessening in the demands for payments on mortgages and farm machinery. Wages to labor, taxes, and the price of commodities did not decrease. Freight rates increased. The year 1932, therefore, was the darkest hour the American farmer had ever known.

From 1919 to 1929 mortgage indebtedness increased almost $2,000,000,000. From 1930 to 1935, 750,000 farms were lost through foreclosure and bankruptcy sales. As a result, the proportion of tenant farmers rose from about 25 per cent to about 40 per cent. The significance of this increase is best seen in the light of the fact that it came in sections of the country where the rate of tenancy previously had been below the average. Moreover, tenancy, once a step up the ladder from laborer to tenant to owner, had largely become a dead end. The cost of farms and machinery had risen to such an extent that it was practically impossible for the renter to accumulate enough money to become an owner.

As though these difficulties were not enough, in 1933 came drouth and storm on an unprecedented scale. That winter and the next the wind stripped the soil from vast stretches of farm-land from the Dakotas to Oklahoma. The dust darkened the sky at noon and found its way into the tightest buildings; it buried fences and farm implements, and thousands of families were ruined financially.

It is estimated that a million persons took to the road. Many walked, taking with them what possessions they could in wheelbarrows or baby carriages. Others drove autos of ancient design. They became migrants, always looking for work and a place where they could settle down or where they could get relief. In the four years from 1935 to 1938 inclusive, 350,000 farmers, fleeing from the dust bowl, moved into California. For the most part they were employed at starvation wages by the large-scale operators who constituted less than 3,000 of the 150,000 farmers in California. The CIO attempted to organize the workers and improve their wages, but accomplished little.

Such is the picture of America in the great depression. What brought it about? Some are disposed to say that it was the result of forces beyond man's control. Probably that is true only in the sense that man was either too blind to see what was causing his distress in time to do anything about it, or too greedy for individual advantage to do what the common weal required. We can recognize at least some of the elements that produced it.

The orgy of gambling on the stock market is usually named as a primary cause. The mad buying which forced prices of stock up—buying not because of the value in the stocks or for investment, but buying on the narrowest possible margin in the hope of a quick profit through the rise in prices—could only end in collapse. However, all through that period of wild speculation, those who should have been competent advisors were assuring the public that all was sound. Some saw the evil day coming and withdrew from all risk, but many of the speculators lost all they had.

This was an immediate cause of the depression, but back of it lay other things that probably would have produced the same result sooner or later. In the decade after World War I the efficiency experts had increased the production of labor by more than one-third, but wages had gone up only 12 per cent between 1923 and 1928, and prices had not come down. No less a conservative than President Hoover said, "When we fully understand the economic history of the twenties we shall find that the debacle which terminated another apparently highly prosperous period was largely contributed by the failure of industry to pass its improvements (through labor-saving devices) on to the consumer." [1] Probably mention should be made also of the failure to increase wages more rapidly. On this matter, Wecter has this to say: "The basic cause of the depression was 'selfish blindness to the bond between group welfare and the satisfaction of the individual.' " [1]

One effect of World War I was to make America a creditor nation. America had never played that role before and was unprepared for it. Both government and business operated in the field of international trade on the old assumptions. In a time when the markets of the world were needed as never before, they acted as though one could sell indefinitely without ever buying, even though the world already was in one's debt. The destruction of property by war in those nations where America hoped to sell surpassed anything before known. A large percentage of their young men had been killed. They were heavily in debt to America and she was pressing for payment. America seemed to be totally unconscious of the significance of this total situation. The Hawley-Smoot tariff bill of 1930 was only one example of that attitude. The reaction abroad was such that by 1932 twenty-five nations had set up retaliatory regulations that cut American foreign trade in half.

Another element in the situation was the fact that the frontier, with free or cheap good land, was gone. In former times of financial stress many had solved their problems by moving west and homesteading land. By 1930 that outlet was closed. Probably this is the only element in the situation that could not have been prevented by man, if he had been sufficiently foresighted to see the demand of the common welfare and sufficiently unselfish to meet it.

[1] Quoted by Wecter, *The Age of the Great Depression,* p. 11.
[1] *Ibid.* p. 24.

Some Effects on American Life

This depression resulted in a bloodless revolution in American life. As in all revolutions, some regarded it as a blessing, while others regarded it as a curse; but none could deny the event. Government moved into the life of its citizens to an unprecedented degree. This was the first time that masses of people had thought of the Federal Government as influencing their personal lives, except in time of war. Thousands of people came to look to the Federal Government for protection and help. Others hated the trend and strove in every way to stop it. But all were well aware that the change had occurred.

In President Hoover's administration the Government began to take measures to relieve the distress of the people. Through President Roosevelt's administration until the coming of World War II, relief was one of the most conspicuous activities of the Federal Government, for relief had become too great a load for states and smaller units of government to handle. Social Security, so new an idea in 1936, was extended to almost everyone in 1956. Public works were carried out for the avowed purpose of making jobs for the unemployed. The Federal Government provided credit to save homes and farms, and guaranteed the security of deposits in banks and other savings institutions. Many measures were carried out for the public health. Taxation became a means of equalizing somewhat the incomes of the American people. Slums were cleared and housing was provided for low-income groups, although much of it was still largely beyond the reach of the neediest. For the first time in American history there was a slight decline in the growth of slums. The welfare of the individual citizen had become a concern of the Federal Government.

All of this led to a change in the attitude of the Federal Government toward debt. It became an accepted policy to spend without regard to immediate resources and to borrow without provision for repayment. During the years of unprecedented prosperity following World War II the national debt steadily increased. After 1950, there was a popular demand for tax reduction even though the government was operating at a deficit. In 1956 the basic debate in Congress with regard to taxes and the budget was whether to balance the national budget and possibly reduce the national debt by an infinitesimal amount, or to reduce taxes and continue to increase the debt.

World War II

As has been stated, the Great Depression lasted, though with declining force, till the outbreak of World War II. At the outset, America took a neutral position, but it soon found itself becoming more and more an ally of Britain and France. War materials were provided under varying plans for some time. The equipment of this country to produce for war was built up. There was abundant work and high pay. The people moved rapidly to settle around the new industrial plants.

On December 7, 1941, Japan attacked Pearl Harbor, and America was brought into the war. The pressure then was not to find jobs, but to find the manpower to do the work that needed to be done. Women took their place in industry to a greater extent than ever before. Women also were inducted into the armed services. Millions of youth were withdrawn from education and industry for military service.

One effect of the war was a great increase in the number of marriages and a consequent increase in the birth rate. The decade of the 1930's was the period when population growth in America was at its lowest, and many prophesied at that time that the population would level off and stabilize. But the 1940's saw the greatest numerical growth in population America had ever had. That growth continued each year down to 1955, the last year for which figures are available at this writing. This growth in population and the movement of people to the new factories, together with other minor factors, led to an unprecedented development of new communities of large size. These new conditions became a dominant element in the planning and work of all home mission societies.

When the war closed it was followed by an insecure peace. The steady pressure of Russia to extend her power left the Western World no choice but to remain armed. This kept large numbers of youth in the armed services, and made large demands on the country's industrial plants, thus continuing employment at a high level. The "police action" in Korea—distinguishable from war only in name and technicalities—was followed by a series of conflicts throughout the Far East and Near East. Although the United States was not militarily involved in these, the situation called for an elaborate and expensive preparedness. In 1955 one of the debates that raged in Washington was whether the expenditures for defense could be reduced.

Truly, it had been a turbulent era, and the work of the Home Mission Society during those twenty-five years had been a *Ministry to Turbulent America.*

II

Advance Against Odds

THE AMERICAN BAPTIST HOME MISSION SOCIETY, when it began its second century of service in 1932, was feeling the full impact of the depression. In the fiscal year May 1, 1924, to April 30, 1925, the budget of the Society had been $1,100,000. By 1932-33 it had dropped to $600,512. The budget continued to decline until 1941-42, when it was only $453,528. This situation was made more desperate by the fact that there was an accumulated deficit. In 1926-27 it had amounted to $282,329. By 1932 it had been reduced to $159,426, and it was finally wiped out in 1941-42. Thus, out of a reduced income, the Society was paying off a deficit accumulated in earlier and more prosperous years.

In that period the churches also were in a desperate plight. In the prosperous decade of the 1920's many of them had contracted large debts to erect buildings. In the depression years they could not meet the payments on the mortgages and were in danger of losing their buildings. Pastors' salaries were reduced. One of the richest churches in one of the large industrial cities dismissed all of its staff except the pastor and reduced his salary to a fraction of what it had been. Students graduated from seminaries and found no churches wanting them at any salary. Some of them went to small rural fields for the sake of a parsonage in which to live and such other support as the people could give. Distress was everywhere.

The effect of all this on the work of the Society may be readily imagined. With a budget reduced to less than half of what it once had been, and with a deficit instead of reserves with

25

which to cushion the shock, the only course of action open to the Society was a systematic reduction of the amount of work being done and of the salaries being paid to the workers. The effort was to conduct the retreat in a statesmanlike way, so as to do as little permanent damage to the work as possible and to bring as little suffering to the workers as might be.

Society salaries were twice reduced by ten per cent. However, a scale of adjustments was used so that the largest percentage of reduction fell on those with the larger salaries, rather than on those with the smaller salaries. This reduction applied to the secretaries and field workers on the same basis as to the missionaries.

Workers, however, were not dismissed because of reduced budgets. Instead, the Society withdrew from those phases of the work that were showing the least results. Usually, when workers died, retired, or resigned, they were not replaced; and the normal changes in personnel were rapid enough to keep the number employed within the limit that could be paid from the reduced budget.

Buildings were allowed to go without any but the most necessary repairs. This was not long-range economy, but it saved immediate expenditures and for several years was the only course that could be followed. No new buildings were erected except where the people themselves by their own labor were able to build them. The effect of these economies on the work and on the morale of the workers was bad, but this was inescapable.

Many of the services that had made the workers more effective had to be discontinued. Conferences that had meant much to the missionaries were not held, were shortened in time, or were held less frequently. Yet those were times when the mutual encouragement that came from such meetings was sorely needed. The men themselves could not afford the expense of attendance, and the Society had no funds for the purpose. When the situation was somewhat relieved, the resumption of such conferences marked a first step in improvement.

The spirit of the missionaries in all of this was highly praiseworthy. The annual report of the Society for 1932 states, "Our missionaries have displayed a superb courage, sharing the sacrifices of their members, feeding and clothing the needy, serving community relief organizations, and proclaiming a high spiritual ideal." Many of the mission churches and Christian Centers became agencies for the distribution of relief. In them the needy frequently were able to secure aid not available through other organizations. Some Christian Centers, notably Brooks House in Hammond, Ind., obtained the free use of vacant land and organized a garden program for all who would co-operate. Many tons of food were produced—food that otherwise could not have been grown and that cost the growers practically nothing. Brooks House also secured a large unused building and provided shelter and nourishment for homeless men. Many work projects were set up by various other Christian Centers, and by means of them the hungry were able to earn at least some food.

The effect of the depression was plainly visible at the head-quarters of the Society. A Society that in better days had employed about twenty secretaries and field men under various titles, in 1932 employed only eight. The office staff was reduced in a corresponding degree. For almost four years there was no executive secretary. When officers died or retired, they were not replaced and their work was assigned to others in addition to their former responsibilities. The Secretary for Latin America became also Secretary of Evangelism. The Secretary for Missions in the United States became also Secretary for Education. The Department of Edifice Funds and Building Counsel, which at one time employed the services of three persons of secretarial rank, in 1932 had only one. Field workers were not replaced, and secretaries were left to carry on the work as best they could. The Treasurer did the work of the Executive Secretary in the office, and the Secretary for Missions in the United States (who was also responsible for the Department of Education) represented the Society on the field. Under all of these handicaps the program inevitably slowed down. The Board of Managers felt frustrated, and everyone was sorely perplexed as to what the future might hold. The opening sentence of one section of the annual report of the Board of Managers in 1933 was: "The Home Mission enterprise, as indeed the whole Christian Church, finds itself in a day of confusion."

This was the situation, then, when The American Baptist Home Mission Society in 1932 began its second century of work. The Board of Managers faced a problem for which there was no precedent, but they faced it with such courage and statesmanship that they built thereafter a large and effective work. At no time during the first quarter of the second century did the nation enjoy both prosperity and peace. Furthermore, the period witnessed the greatest uprooting of the American people ever known. Yet the twenty-five years was a time of steady advance and growth, not so much in spite of hostile circumstances, as by reason of harnessing them and making them labor for the advancement of the kingdom of God.

Decision to Advance

Retrenchment necessarily had been the policy of the Home Mission Society since the death of its Executive Secretary, Dr. Charles A. Brooks, on January 11, 1931. Declining income and the pressure of accumulated debt left no alternative. In 1934, however, the Board decided that this policy must be changed if the Society was to take any significant part in the work of the denomination.

The first step in this direction was to rebuild the administrative staff. Accordingly Rev. G. Pitt Beers, D.D., then pastor of the First Baptist Church of Paterson, N. J., was called as Executive Secretary. He took office October 1, 1934. Under his direction more than a year was spent in studying the needs of the field and in determining the best adjustment of staff personnel to meet those needs in view of the limited financial resources. As a result of the study, in 1936, three steps were taken. Dr.

Walter E. Woodbury was called as Secretary of Evangelism, and began his work September 1, 1936. He had been pastor of the First Baptist Church of Melrose, Mass., and later had served several years as Director of Promotion in Southern California. It was decided, also, that a specialist was needed in the field of city work and also one in the field of town and country work. Accordingly the Department of Missions in the United States was divided into the Department of Cities and the Department of Town and Country. Dr. Frank A. Smith, who was approaching his time of retirement, headed both departments, and an associate was called to each department that they might be in training to succeed him. On July 25, 1936, Rev. John W. Thomas, pastor of the Oaklyn Baptist Church, Oaklyn, N. J., came as Field Representative in the Department of Cities; and on October 1, 1936, Rev. Ellsworth M. Smith, of the faculty of Andover Newton Theological Institution, became Field Representative in the Department of Town and Country.

Dr. Frank A. Smith retired August 31, 1936. Because neither Mr. Thomas nor Mr. Ellsworth Smith had had time to become sufficiently familiar with his duties to take full charge of a department, the Executive Secretary was asked to direct both departments with their assistance. This arrangement continued in the Department of Cities until June 16, 1941, when Mr. Thomas was elected secretary and officially assumed the responsibilities which he had actually been carrying under varying titles for some time. In the Department of Town and Country, Mr. Smith resigned September 30, 1938. Rev. Mark Rich, Ph.D., was called to succeed him, and on September 1, 1938, began work as Field Representative. June 15, 1942, he was elected Secretary for Town and Country and assumed full responsibility for the work of that department.

These staff changes greatly strengthened the planning and the administering of the work. They raised the morale of the missionaries, who were assured thereby that the Board of Managers intended to go forward. Likewise, they strengthened the position of the Society in the denomination by indicating a clear purpose and plan to advance.

Another bold step was taken near the beginning of this period in transferring to the Board of Education of the Northern Baptist Convention the schools for Negroes in the South which had been founded and fostered by the Society.[1] In 1917 the Society was aiding ten secondary schools and thirteen schools of higher grade. Up to that time it had invested several million dollars in the operation and equipment of these institutions. This work, however, reached a turning point in 1934. Southern Baptists were manifesting increased interest in education for Negroes. Although some of the schools had not prospered, others had become accredited colleges and were leaders in their field. Their advance had so changed their status that it seemed wise to have them administered by a body dealing mainly with educational matters, rather than by one dealing mainly with missionary matters. The decreased income of the Society had forced a substantial cut in the amount of support given to these schools, and it was hoped that an appeal on their behalf through educational channels would bring them wider support.

After some informal conversations the Society made an official approach to the Baptist Board of Education in the spring of 1934. Having carefully discussed all that would be involved, the two Boards agreed to enter upon a three years' experiment. On June 1, 1935, the Board of Education took over the administration of the schools, while the Society continued to finance them, paying the money to the Board of Education to be distributed at their discretion. It was agreed that the Society would provide "a slightly larger amount of money than it would have paid had it retained their supervision, thus enabling the Board of Education to deal equitably with them."

Morehouse College at Atlanta, Ga., was not involved in this transfer. It had become a strong institution, closely coordinated

[1] The Home Mission Society's long and honorable history in the education of Negroes is fully recounted in *A Century of Faith*, by Charles L. White.

with Spelman College, a Baptist college for women, and with Atlanta University, a Congregational institution. The three were exchanging professors, were using common administration, dining-hall facilities, and libraries, and had a coordinated athletic program. In conference with the General Education Board,[1] it was decided that the time had come for Morehouse College to be an entirely independent institution. Arrangements then were made to make the trustees of Atlanta University and the trustees of Morehouse College identical in personnel. The property of Morehouse College that was held by the Home Mission Society was transferred to this Board of Trustees under strict reversionary conditions. The endowment funds held by the Society for Morehouse College were transferred to the trustees for the use of that school, and the Society gave $100,000 from its John D. Rockefeller Fund to the endowment fund. It was agreed that in doing this the Society had fulfilled all of its obligations to the college and would not be asked to provide any further support. Thus Morehouse College was not involved in the transfer of the schools to the Board of Education.

The year that the transfer was made, Virginia Union University, in Richmond, Va., had successfully completed a campaign for $600,000 for its endowment fund. Of this sum the General Education Board contributed $350,000. Benedict College, in Columbia, S. C., had completed a new gymnasium and had an excellent offer toward a new library which would be used not only by the students there, but also by a Methodist college nearby and by the community at large.

The three-year experimental period was carried through very satisfactorily. May 1, 1937, the money for the schools for Negroes was transferred by the Finance Committee of the Northern Baptist Convention from the budget of the Home Mission Society to that of the Board of Education. The amount thus transferred was $26,850. At the same time, $11,000 of

[1] The General Education Board was endowed by Mr. John D. Rockefeller, Sr. It had as its stated object, "promoting education within the United States, without distinction of race, sex, or creed." This Board contributed large sums to the Baptist schools for Negroes. Many of these contributions were matched by The American Baptist Home Mission Society.

income from funds designated for the education of Negroes was transferred. The Board of Education received a somewhat larger amount from the unified budget, enabling it to make some advances in the support of the schools.

It was agreed that, upon the transfer of the schools, the Home Mission Society should retain title to the property to which it already had title and also continue to hold the endowment funds of these schools. In view of this fact, it was agreed that the Society permanently should have a member on the Board of Trustees of each school. That position, since it has to do mainly with financial affairs, has always been held by the Treasurer of the Society. The period of transition was difficult, but the outcome has fully justified the course taken. Under this plan the colleges have steadily increased their resources, and today they are filling a large place in the life of the Negro people.

This transfer of the colleges for Negroes to the Board of Education on June 1, 1935, left the Department of Education of the Home Mission Society with only three schools to administer. Bacone College held a crucial place in the total missionary program among the Indians. International Seminary, at East Orange, N. J., had for years trained most of the leaders for the bilingual churches. It was approaching a critical period in this work, but it was still rendering important service. The Spanish-American Baptist Seminary in Los Angeles was providing all of the trained leaders for the Spanish-speaking Baptist churches in the United States and some leaders also for the Latin-American fields. The Murrow Indian Orphans' Home,[1] located on the campus of Bacone College, was also administered by the Department of Education because of its close relation to Bacone College. Although it was an independent corporation, the president of the college was the manager of the Home, and the college carried the deficit of the Home. The Society, of course, ultimately guaranteed both budgets.

[1] The school was incorporated under this name. It is now more frequently called the Murrow Children's Home.

These three schools, with the Murrow Children's Home, constituted the remaining responsibilities of the Department of Education. Since the retirement of Dr. George R. Hovey in 1930, Dr. Frank A. Smith had administered that department in addition to his other duties. Upon Dr. Smith's retirement in 1936, Dr. Charles A. Detweiler, Secretary of the Department of Missions in Latin America, was asked to assume those duties. He continued to administer the Department of Education until September 18, 1946, when the department was abolished. Bacone College and the Murrow Children's Home were then assigned to the division of Indian work in the Department of Town and Country. The International Seminary and the Spanish-American Baptist Seminary were transferred to the Department of Cities, since they trained leadership for churches administered by that department. In May, 1941, the International Seminary discontinued classes in its building in East Orange, N. J., and began using its funds as scholarships for students of foreign-language background attending other seminaries. Ultimately, this meant chiefly the Spanish-American Seminary.

When the work of The American Baptist Home Mission Society and the Woman's American Baptist Home Mission Society was integrated in 1955, Bacone College and the Murrow Children's Home were placed in the new Department of Alaska, Indian Work, and Schools in the United States. The Spanish-American Baptist Seminary was left in the Department of Cities.

With the coming of World War II, the modest program of advance undertaken in 1934 turned into a desperate effort to meet the needs of the changed situation. Service to the armed forces, establishing churches in the new communities, and the program for juvenile delinquents were possibly the most conspicuous of the many new demands. Traditional methods and approaches were no longer adequate, and the Board of Managers and the staff found it necessary to make frequent adjustments. At the same time, the increased prosperity provided greater resources with which to meet these demands.

III

Ministry to Youth in Military Service

THE SECOND WORLD WAR brought to The American Baptist Home Mission Society a new set of responsibilities in connection with the young people in the armed services. Demanding immediate attention was the work with chaplains carried on through the interdenominational General Commission on Army and Navy Chaplains, later known as the General Commission on Chaplains. This commission had been established at the request of chaplains during World War I. After that war, however, it became but little more than a paper organization. Representation was from the Home Mission Society, rather than from the Northern Baptist Convention. It met once or twice a year, transacted very little business, and was poorly attended. But when war came again and large numbers of young people entered the armed services, there was an urgent call to the churches to provide an adequate ministry to them. Many more chaplains were needed, and the demands on the Commission became much heavier.

The Commission, therefore, was reorganized. It became a body made up of representatives of the denominations, rather than of denominational agencies. Its membership was increased, the range of its duties was broadened, and a much larger budget was required. The Northern Baptist Convention appointed a Committee on Chaplains, the members of which became the Convention's representatives on the Commission. This committee had responsibility for recruiting, screening, and endorsing pastors who applied for appointment as chaplains. It conferred with the Home Mission Society as to its work with chaplains, and it represented the denomination in related matters. The Executive Secre-

34

tary of the Home Mission Society and the secretary of the Department of Christian Ministry to Service Personnel were ex-officio members of this committee.[1]

As the need for a ministry to service personnel became critical, several agencies in the denomination came to feel that they had a responsibility in the matter. Up to that time the Home Mission Society had done this work and had furnished all the funds. To avoid confusion and duplication of effort, the matter was taken to the General Council. After carefully considering all that was involved, the General Council assigned to the Home Mission Society the responsibility for the ministry to service personnel; and it advised the Finance Committee of the Convention to assign whatever money could be provided for this work to the budget of that Society. Provision was made by the Society for conference relationship with several agencies involved in particular matters, but the budget and the administration have remained entirely with the Home Mission Society.

With this clear assignment of responsibility, the Board of Managers, seeing the tremendous growth of the work both with chaplains and with service personnel in the civilian communities, organized in 1942 the Department of Christian Ministry to Service Personnel. Money for the work of the department was provided through the World Emergency Fund, set up by the Convention in May, 1941. In the beginning, the funds for the department amounted annually to $100,000, but eventually they amounted annually to $200,000. A part of this sum was assigned to the Woman's American Baptist Home Mission Society, but a single unified program was carried on. At first it was believed that this work would be of a temporary nature and could be done on a part-time basis. For that reason the Board of Managers did not think it wise to add a new man to the staff. It was decided, therefore, to ask Dr. M. E. Bratcher, who had been representing the Society on the West Coast for several years, to give half of his time to the work with service personnel.

---

[1] This was the status in 1956. It is not important to record the intermediate steps.

The story of its chaplains in World War II and in the later Korean conflict is one of which the American Baptist Convention can be proud. The Convention furnished more than its full quota of chaplains. At the close of hostilities there were 564 Northern Baptist chaplains in the armed services. Altogether the Convention had furnished 976 chaplains, more than any other denomination with the exception of the Methodist. The record of these chaplains was an honorable one. Ten lost their lives in action or otherwise died on duty from service-related causes.[1] Twenty-five were returned to civilian life, largely on the basis of physical disability. Many received decorations for various services. The chaplains baptized thousands of young people, many of whom had no relation to the church or Sunday school before going into the service. Some chaplains, laboring "beyond the call of duty," started orphanages in Korea; others, with the aid of their men, gave a great deal of assistance to similar institutions.

At the same time that the work with chaplains was developing, a call came from many civilian communities for help in ministering to the service men and women stationed in their area. These young people spent considerable time in the towns and cities adjacent to their military stations. In 1945 it was reported that there were over 13,000,000 men and women in the services. The chaplains were responsible for all the work in the camps, and civilians (unlike the situation in previous wars) were not allowed to render service there, except on the invitation and under the direction of the chaplain in charge. On the other hand, when the men were on leave, the chaplains had no responsibility. Whatever was done for them then had to be done by the churches in the community. Even in larger cities it was not always easy for the churches to devise an effective plan of service. When the need fell on a small city in which there was only one Baptist church, it became difficult indeed for that church to serve adequately even those men who sought it out.

[1] The names of those who died in service are: Charles S. Blakeney, William Dawson, Edwin U. Monroe, Erle F. Rounds, David H. Youngdahl, John R. Kilbert, William H. Turner, Gustav T. Lutz, Chester P. Hansen, Kenneth L. Thompson.

The Home Mission Society accordingly undertook to aid these churches in formulating and executing a suitable program. Some funds were provided for this work. Sometimes it was the salary of a full-time worker; sometimes it was a modest allowance for actual expenses involved in a program carried on by volunteers. During the time that Dr. Bratcher administered this work, there came to be as many as 175 service men's centers. Many of them handled from 8,000 to 10,000 men per month. One of the interdenominational centers in which the Society cooperated reported that it had had an attendance of more than 25,000 in one month.

By 1944 the work with chaplains, in service men's centers, and in local churches had grown to such an extent that it needed someone who could give it his entire attention. Dr. Bratcher was so valuable to the Society as its West Coast representative that it was felt that he should give his full time to the work there. Accordingly, Rev. Ernest C. Witham, pastor of the First Baptist Church of Decatur, Ill., was called to direct the work with service personnel. He began his duties July 1, 1944.

At the same time that this program was being developed, these problems were being approached interdenominationally. The Federal Council of the Churches of Christ in America, in cooperation with the Home Missions Council, set up the Christian Commission in Camp and Defense Communities. The American Baptist Home Mission Society participated in this effort, and its Executive Secretary was chairman of the Commission. The Commission undertook to minister not only to service personnel in the civilian communities, but also to the new industrial communities that were springing up. It finally assigned this latter work to the Home Missions Council and made basic readjustments in its work for service personnel. Shortly after this the war closed, and the work of the Commission with service personnel was discontinued.

Before that, however, the people had begun to look ahead to the close of the war and to give thought to the situation which would exist when the men began to return to their homes in large numbers. Enough already had returned to make people realize that they would be confronted with a difficult task of readjustment—one which would require the best of the men themselves, of the communities, of the families, and of the churches. There arose a demand for leadership in preparing the churches for this task.

In 1945 the Northern Baptist Convention launched the Christian Life Crusade as the denominational program for the year. Approximately two hundred training conferences were held across the country. To each conference were brought six representatives from each church in the area. They were the church's chairmen for service men's work, for evangelism, for missions, for Christian education, for Christian social progress, and for stewardship. These conferences were led by pastors who had been coached the preceding summer at a training conference at Green Lake, Wis.—sixty for each subject—and who had agreed to give two weeks to leading the local conferences. So far as service personnel was concerned, attention was given almost entirely to preparing the churches for the returning service men. A handbook was prepared to guide the churches and 22,000 copies of it were distributed. These conferences and this handbook probably constituted the largest contribution made to an effective ministry to the returning service personnel.

The close of the war brought another heavy responsibility to this department of the Society. What could be done to help the chaplains released from service to get back into pastorates? There still were unhappy memories of the difficulties experienced by some chaplains at the close of World War I. It was clearly understood by all that these men had gone into the service voluntarily and that the denomination had assumed no responsibility for them. Nevertheless, it was felt that it would be best for the denomination, as well as for the chaplains, if the change from military life to civilian life could be made in a way that would conserve their leadership for the denomination. The Convention assigned to the Home Mission Society funds from the World Mission Crusade to aid chaplains in making this transition.

Most of the chaplains went into pastorates. Some of them entered general service in the denomination. Others returned to school for refresher courses, meanwhile looking for permanent positions. The government encouraged the latter course by providing $90 a month to each one who continued his studies. However, this was hardly adequate for a man and wife, usually with children. The Society, therefore, made available an additional $60 a month for each ex-chaplain while in school. For those who were looking for permanent settlement, the Society provided $150 a month while they were without employment, up to six months. Very few required aid for the full time, for usually they found employment quickly. About 350 chaplains received some financial assistance.

To facilitate placement in churches needing their services, the chaplains were urged to notify the department at the earliest opportunity regarding the date of their release. Each was requested to state also the part of the country in which he desired to locate and the kind of church which he would prefer to serve. With this information in hand, the department communicated with state secretaries and aided their placement in all possible ways. The result was that all the chaplains found pastorates or some other denominational service without any of the strain which followed World War I.

A totally different phase of the responsibility of this department was in connection with the conscientious objectors, of whom there was a substantial number in the Northern Baptist Convention. The military authorities recognized their rights as they had not done in previous wars. The historic peace churches (Friends, Brethren, and Mennonites) set up a system of work camps to which conscientious objectors could be assigned for specified service during terms corresponding to the period of their military obligation. They welcomed the cooperation of other churches, and the Board of Managers of the Home Mission Society voted to assist in the movement, contribute to the expense, and serve these young people in any way they could. The Northern Baptist Convention approved the plan, but allowed the use only of money designated by the donors for this specific purpose. The amount so designated, although much larger than might have been expected in a denomination that had no tradition of work of this kind, fell considerably short of the amount needed. The historic peace churches were the mainstay of this program.

During the war there were at least 150 Northern Baptists in these camps. When the war was over and these men were released, the department rendered all possible aid in getting them back into civilian life and work. A few young men who took a more extreme stand—one which put them beyond reach of this assistance—were sentenced to prison. In the case of these men, the Society could do nothing except pray for them and keep them under pastoral care.

The Department of Christian Ministry to Service Personnel administered this work, but Rev. John W. Thomas, secretary of the Department of Cities, did much of it. His personal contacts with the peace churches and with the conscientious objectors made his services invaluable. He gave a great deal of time to this program. The Council on Christian Social Progress also assisted materially.

Mr. Witham continued in charge of this work until April 30, 1949. In 1946 he had been asked to give part time to a new Department of Personnel serving all of the Associated Home Mission Agencies, but administered by the Home Mission Society. The experiment was so successful that on May 1, 1949, he was asked to give his whole time to the new department. In 1948, Rev. Joseph H. Heartberg, pastor of the First Baptist Church of Webster City, Iowa, had been called to be secretary of the Department of Rural and Indian Missions. When Mr. Witham was transferred to the Department of Personnel, it was decided that the work with service men and women could be handled in conjunction with another department, if a field man were provided who could give his whole time to the field work of each department. Accordingly, on May 1, 1949, Mr. Heartberg, already secretary of the Department of Rural and Indian Missions, became also secretary of the Department of Christian Ministry to Service Personnel. Having been a chaplain in World War II, Mr. Heartberg had a background of military experience which neither Dr. Bratcher nor Mr. Witham had possessed. He has been a conspicuously useful man in this endeavor.

Because of the new world situation and the position which America has taken in world affairs, this department is not likely to decline to the minor position it held between the two world wars. It will remain a major enterprise far into the future. In 1949 it was reported that there were 130 Northern Baptist chaplains on active duty. An interdenominational service men's center was opened in Newport, R. I., where the Atlantic Fleet is based. There were then seven such centers in which the Home Mission Society was participating, four of them on the Pacific Coast. The interdenominational center in Seattle, Wash., reported that it was reaching more men each weekend than it had during the war. The center at Tacoma, Wash., was ministering to more than 3,000 men each weekend; the center at Oakland, Calif., was ministering to more than 1,000 men per day. The center in San Diego reported (1954-1955) a monthy attendance of over 10,000, with 7,000 attending church services. In 1956 the number of chaplains had risen to two hundred. There were eleven service personnel centers in the United States and the Society was cooperating financially in several centers in the Pacific Far East.

Several churches enlarged their buildings to take care of this work and the result was an increase in attendance at the worship services. Often, in these cases, the service men have aided materially in defraying the cost of the enlargement. When service men returning from the Pacific theater were delayed on the West Coast at Christmas time, the Home Mission Society wired credit up to $500 to each of six centers to take care of the situation. Thirty-seven university pastors either had assistants paid by the Home Mission Society or were aided in other ways to minister to the G.I.'s in their student bodies.

Mr. Harvey Kester of Denver gives his full time to the chaplains and the service men's centers as a field representative of the Department. Mr. Heartberg visited the chaplains in the Pacific theater in 1953 and those in Europe and Africa in 1955. Mr. Kester visited the Pacific theater in 1956. A number of pastors have visited the camps, conducting preaching missions or spiritual retreats, under the auspices of the General Commission on Chaplains or of the Chief of Chaplains. Among them were Dr. Clarence W. Cranford, Dr. Lee J. Beynon, Dr. G. Eugene Bartlett, and Dr. Ralph C. Walker. This constant contact with the chaplains has proved to be a fruitful ministry.

The importance of this work will be seen when it is noted that in 1953 the armed services were "graduating" one million per year, more than twice as many as obtain degrees from all of the colleges, universities, and technical schools in the country. Not only have these young people rendered their military service, but they have received an education with a certain slant as to moral standards, outlook on life, and the philosophy of relations with other nations. They have been subjected to a combination of powerful temptations which few of them would have encountered in civilian life. It is extremely important that the call to Christian living be kept clearly before them and that they be given all possible encouragement in the maintenance of their ideals. Such, then, is the enduring significance of the work of this department, of the chaplains, and of the service men's centers. So far as one can foresee, this will continue to be a responsibility.

IV

Meeting the Postwar Situation

IN THE MIDST of the wartime tasks arose the question, "Will the denomination be ready to meet the postwar situation when it comes?" It was recognized that probably it would come with little warning and would present a totally new set of responsibilities. Would the agencies be prepared to meet them? Mr. E. H. Rhoades, Jr., technical advisor of the Budget Research Committee, urged the denomination to begin at once to plan for that day. The General Council, on June 6, 1943, authorized the appointment of a Postwar Planning Commission to be composed of representatives of all of the agencies of the Convention, as well as of pastors, laymen, and women. President Joseph C. Robbins appointed the commission at once, and it was approved at the next session of the Convention, held in Atlantic City, N. J., in 1944.

Immediately on appointment this commission began its study of the probable postwar situation and what should be done to meet it. A serious job of research was carried out through two or three years, and much of what was accomplished later was due to the foresight and statesmanship exhibited by this commission.

The World Mission Crusade

One important outcome of the commission's work was the World Mission Crusade. When the commission began to face its task, it immediately perceived that in every phase of the work the needs would be tremendous. On most of the foreign fields the disruption of the work and the destruction of property were

43

such that, financially, only a major expenditure would be effective. On the home field, the unprecedented uprooting of people, the unexpected growth in population, and the deplorable breakdown of morals and laws, combined to produce a situation that demanded attention. In education, the condition was extremely critical. When the various agencies tabulated their financial needs, the total came to more than $50,000,000, but it was felt that it was quite out of the question to raise so large an amount. There were many different views as to what the denomination should do. Some believed that the agencies should state their total need, ask for all of it, and raise whatever they could. Others believed that the denomination should not attempt to raise so much.

For several years the churches had contributed, in addition to the unified budget, to a World Emergency Forward Fund. (Other names were used at different times.) In the first year, beginning in May, 1941, the Convention voted to raise $600,000; in the last year of the Fund about $1,500,000 was raised. Some felt the denomination should simply continue along this line. Others advocated a middle course. After very careful study and thorough discussion, it was recommended that the Convention undertake to raise a fund of $14,000,000. In 1945 the General Council, acting for the Convention in a year when it did not meet, adopted the plan.

A committee was set up for this purpose, of which Dr. C. Oscar Johnson, pastor of the Third Baptist Church of St. Louis, was the chairman. Dr. Luther Wesley Smith, Executive Secretary of the Board of Education and Publication, was called as director of the campaign, and his Board generously released him for this service. Marts & Lundy were retained as counselors. The campaign extended through two years. The final report was made to the Convention at its meeting in Atlantic City, N. J., in 1947. The campaign, due in large measure to the great ability and devotion of Dr. Johnson and Dr. Smith, was remarkably successful. The pledges totaled $16,163,601, and the total amount collected was $15,212,355.

From the World Mission Crusade the Home Mission Society received $1,206,884.65. Part of this was to be used for current operations called "recurring items." The rest was for "non-recurring items," principally expenses related to property. It was the expectation that the amount for current operations would be sufficient for a two-year period, and that by the end of that time the unified budget would be so increased that the work could continue permanently on that level. This expectation was only partially realized, with the result that the level of work established through this fund had to be reduced to the great distress of both the Board and the missionaries on the field. The Society drew upon its accumulated reserves to make this adjustment less drastic, so that at the worst of this period the level of the work was higher than at any time prior to the World Mission Crusade. That movement not only raised $14,000,000 for the work, but it permanently improved the denomination's support of its missionary enterprise. Although the unified budget was not raised the first year, it was not long before the goal was attained. The World Mission Crusade had started this upward movement.

Juvenile Protection

Out of the work of the Postwar Planning Commission came a totally new task. The war had brought an alarming increase in juvenile crime. The average age of the criminals was lower and the violence of their crimes was greater. This fact focused attention on something with which neither the Convention nor its agencies had ever dealt directly, and with which no other church body, so far as could be discovered, had attempted to deal. The commission felt that some direct approach to this problem should be found. The American Baptist Home Mission Society obviously was closest to the center of any such work, but other agencies also had a contribution to make.

At the Convention in Atlantic City in 1944, a committee was set up composed of representatives of all of the national agencies. Rev. John W. Thomas, secretary of the Department of

Cities, represented the Home Mission Society and was largely influential in shaping its studies and conclusions. The committee worked out a very promising line of experimentation. But the Finance Committee of the Convention reported that no money could be provided until the next year's budget had been set up, and it could give no promise that there would be any funds then. All felt, however, that the work could not wait, and the Home Mission Board agreed to advance up to $6,000 in order that the committee might proceed with its experiment. It was understood that if funds were made available to the committee later, the sum would be returned. This agreement was fulfilled.

The committee carried out experimental projects in twenty-eight states. These comprised surveys of local delinquency conditions, assistance to churches desiring to set up programs for the youth of their communities, the training of recreational leaders, and the establishing of a camping program as a means of rehabilitating youth who were delinquent or pre-delinquent. The following year money was provided for the committee out of the World Emergency Forward Fund, to be administered by the Home Mission Society. The program proved so successful that it was agreed that it should be continued, and that increased support should be provided for it.

At this point the question arose as to which agency should accept permanent responsibility for the work. All agreed that a new agency should not be established. The work could have been related to any one of three or four agencies, but after careful study, the committee decided that it would be best to relate it to the Home Mission Society, both because it seemed to be a part of that ministry, and because it then could be closely related to the Christian Centers which the Society conducted. Accordingly, upon action by the Board of Managers, the Home Mission Society accepted the responsibility for the work. The administration of it was assigned to the Department of Cities, and an advisory committee was set up representing all groups having a direct interest in the program.

Rev. Emil Kontz, pastor of the Lincoln Park Baptist Church of Cincinnati, Ohio, was called to be the director of the program, and an office was opened in Chicago. Two field workers were appointed, and an extensive program was developed. Later, Mr. Kontz resigned to return to the pastorate; and Rev. Clifford G. Hansen, pastor of the First Baptist Church of Milwaukee, Wis., was appointed as director. He began his work February 2, 1948. At the same time the office was moved to New York so that there could be more effective administration. When Mr. Hansen became secretary of the Department of Public Relations, September 1, 1951, Rev. Edward D. Rapp, pastor of the First Baptist Church of Winterset, Iowa, was appointed director. About this time the work of Juvenile Protection was brought into closer relationship with the Christian Centers, and Mr. Rapp became the director of both programs. In 1956, however, it was decided to separate the two. Rev. Lawrence H. Janssen was made director of Juvenile Protection.

The Juvenile Protection program has taken a rather definite form. Each year at the request of local churches, surveys are made of their cities or of sections of their cities. These surveys undertake to discover what the delinquency situation is, what is being done about it, and what resources are available in the community to meet it. With these facts in hand, the department counsels with the churches about setting up programs to help the youth of their communities.

Such a program in a local church requires specially trained recreational leaders. To meet this need the division set up a national recreation laboratory at Green Lake, Wis., to which men and women from all over the Convention come for training. Later several local recreation laboratories of shorter duration were set up, as many as seven being held in some years. By this means a larger number of recreational leaders were trained for the churches.

In addition to these preventive measures, it was felt that something should be done toward reclaiming the youth already in difficulty. Accordingly, an experimental Junior Citizens' Camp was held at Camp Okalona in Indiana in the summer of 1945. The youth who attended the camp were recommended and their expenses provided by the social agencies, juvenile courts, the police, and the schools. A case history of each boy and girl was made available. The staff of the camp was made up of specially trained persons. Before opening day, they studied carefully these case histories, noted special needs, and made specific plans for dealing with each individual.

These experiments were so successful that the program was enlarged, and as many as nine Junior Citizens' Camps have been held in a summer. The results in the lives of the campers were very gratifying. Practically all of them went back to their communities with their activities given a better direction. A large portion of them were brought into the church schools and finally into church membership. Boys and girls with criminal records became law-abiding, constructive citizens. To be sure, the number reached was dishearteningly small in the face of the great need, but the approach had proved itself and it could be made more widely effective as others became willing to take up the task.

The demand for help in the Juvenile Protection program has grown steadily. As a result, in September, 1955, when Rev. Paul O. Madsen, secretary of the Department of Cities, reported to the Board of Managers that the calls for Juvenile Protection work were far beyond what the staff could meet, another field worker was appointed. At the same time, Mr. Madsen reported that the requests for Junior Citizens' Camps for 1956 were twice the number it would be possible to conduct.

The integration of the two Societies has not affected the administration of this work. It has remained in the Department of Cities, where it has been from its inception.

V

Churches for New Communities

LONG BEFORE PEARL HARBOR, December 7, 1941, the United States had begun to feel the impact of World War II. Prior to Pearl Harbor, it had been manufacturing material for the allied countries, as well as making preparation for its own probable involvement. This meant that industry had been stepped up beyond anything ever known before. Older factories were abandoned as inadequate and new ones were built, often in the open country. It became necessary to provide new housing for the workers thus drawn together, and sometimes complete cities were built where before there had been not even a village. All of this building had been done as rapidly as possible. Many thousands of the workers were still housed in trailers, and the first houses were constructed for temporary use.

Out of this demand of industry for labor came one of the greatest migrations of people ever known. In one three-year period, half of the people in the United States moved. There was another period of several years in which one-fifth of the population moved each year. Within a year or two cities of thirty-five thousand grew up in open country areas. Villages became cities, and cities in some cases multiplied their population fivefold.

This movement of population to the industrial centers greatly augmented the population changes already in progress. Masses of these people came from the rural areas, thus increasing the long-continued flow of population from rural areas to urban areas. The movement from the center of the city to the suburbs likewise was stepped up, and the result was an unprecedented

49

development. The thousands of young men taken into the armed services increased the demand for goods, and at the same time reduced the labor supply at the very point where it was usually recruited. The fact that women were brought into industry more largely than ever before caused a great disruption of home life. While their parents were working, many children were left largely to their own devices.

This situation laid a great task at the door of all home mission agencies, a task for which they were not prepared. All of these new or enlarged communities needed churches. In such communities there was little on which to build. The people all had a sense of transiency. At one time the bus companies of Richmond, Calif., reported that they were carrying out about the same number of persons they were bringing in, namely, about 3,000 per month. This meant that the people there had no roots, a condition that militated against the building of churches and all other permanent institutions. There was potential leadership in those communities, but very little chance for it to assert itself. Some of the industrial concerns did what they could, but they could not do much. Moral standards deteriorated rapidly. Hundreds of thousands of children were growing up without any of those stabilizing influences which, in the older established communities, helped parents to mold their lives for good; and the parents themselves all too frequently succumbed to the demoralizing influences around them. It was evident that churches would not spring up of themselves. Yet churches were desperately needed.

The Home Mission agencies had never before faced a situation of this kind and magnitude. In the pioneer days the Home Mission Society had built churches in the frontier towns, but those communities had been small and the problems had been comparatively simple. For these new conditions, the financial resources were inadequate. The country was only beginning to come out of the depression. The income of the missionary agencies had not yet recovered to any considerable extent. Edifice funds were entirely too small, and the cost of building was mounting rapidly.

However, steps were taken through the Department of Cities to meet the need as fully as possible. Home Mission workers were sent into those new communities to which they already had some access and so some prospect of success. Sometimes homes were used for starting the work; sometimes recreation halls built by industry could be utilized or other temporary arrangements could be made. The work was started as quickly as workers and money could be withdrawn from other projects and put into these crucial spots. Later, additional support was provided through the World Emergency Fund and the scope of this work was considerably enlarged. Some of these projects were conducted interdenominationally through the Home Missions Council. Frequently it seemed necessary to act denominationally because of the time required for the interdenominational process to function. In all cases, however, such projects were undertaken under comity agreements, thereby avoiding duplication of effort and consequent waste of resources both of men and of money.

During this period of wartime emergency, it was the common opinion that these communities were only temporary, and that when the war was over the people would go back to their former homes. This made it necessary to conduct the work as a temporary service to meet a temporary need. The people were slow in awakening to the likelihood that these communities would become permanent. This, however, proved to be the case. After the war, these plants found their place in the ongoing industrial life of the nation, and usually most of the people remained. In fact, there was a constant, if smaller, stream of new people coming in. This meant that the work started by the missionary became a permanent church. Consequently the end of the fighting did not bring release from responsibility in these communities, but rather resulted in many new demands for further help in order that these growing communities might be adequately churched.

During this emergency period, the Home Mission Society was aiding from sixty to eighty such projects at any given time. Some served a temporary need and passed out of existence when that need was met. But many have become strong churches and have taken places of leadership in the missionary outreach of the denomination.

What had begun as an attempt to meet an emergency situation became in time a permanent responsibility which the Home Mission Society needed to face realistically. Evangelizing new communities and building churches in them had been the basic task of the Society in its first century of existence. In the twenties and thirties, however, there had grown up a feeling that this work was largely finished, and that in the future the organizing of churches in new communities would require less attention. Immigration had practically stopped, and the rate of population growth was decreasing. Although the cities continued to grow at the expense of the rural sections, and the suburbs at the expense of the inner city, neither was considered to present a serious home mission problem.

With the approach of World War II this whole situation changed. Providing churches for new communities became a major enterprise with all denominations. Not only had millions migrated to the new cities, but the population of the nation began to grow at an unprecedented rate. The calling of young men into the service and the substantial rise in prosperity led to the largest number of marriages ever recorded in this country. The birth rate increased proportionately. The net gain in population in the decade from 1940 to 1950 was the greatest our country had ever seen. Moreover, it was a natural growth, not the result of immigration as the growth so largely had been in the past. After 1950, the rate of growth not only continued but even increased.

Other factors contributed to the magnitude of this task. In the Columbia River Basin, and elsewhere, large areas were brought under irrigation. Oil was discovered in new areas, one being in North Dakota. Great atomic energy plants were built, of which the one in Richland, Wash., is an example. Uranium ore was discovered in Utah and Colorado.

All of these forces combined to produce more totally unchurched communities of large size than ever before had been in America. One survey in 1953 indicated there were at least seven thousand such communities, most of them with a population of over twenty-five hundred persons. In them there was no place of worship of any kind. It was apparent that they presented the greatest evangelistic responsibility the churches of America had ever faced. The churches that ministered to these people would be increasingly significant in the life of the nation; those that turned their backs on this great need would steadily decline in influence. It was the hour of destiny.

Unless the home mission agencies gave leadership, few if any churches would be organized. Churches do not often spring up from local leadership alone. There is an impression that churches started that way in the pioneer days, but a study of the record will show that much more frequently they were started as a result of the efforts of home missionaries. Certainly, in these new communities it was unlikely that many churches would be organized through the unaided initiative of the people. They lived in an atmosphere of transiency. There was no sense of community, no community organization. Usually the women, as well as the men, were employed. The hours of work left very little leisure or energy for voluntary activities. The living conditions were not conducive to the far-sighted planning necessary for starting a church.

Though this was a task that must be done, no one had adequate finances for it. The first step taken was to withdraw funds from other work wherever that could be done without undue damage. The amount that could be provided in this way, however, was pitifully small. The American Baptist Home Mission Society had some money from the World Mission Crusade that could be used for this purpose, but it would make only a meager beginning. It was apparent that a large sum must be raised, if the situation was to be met in any adequate way.

Churches for New Frontiers

As early as 1944, the need for church extension had been recognized, and there had been requests from states and cities as well as from the Home Mission Society for permission to raise a fund of several million dollars for this purpose. The outcome of that movement was to place a comparatively small amount for church extension in the World Emergency Forward Fund. It was administered jointly by a committee representing the states, the cities, and the Home Mission Society. This method of administration proved to be unsatisfactory. Although some churches were started, the fund was soon exhausted.

The city, state, and national Home Mission executives, meeting in conference at Green Lake, Wis., in the summer of 1951, declared that church extension was the chief responsibility of the times and that wherever possible, money should be diverted from other work to that end. In December, 1951, the need had become so pressing that the Home Mission Society proposed in the meeting of the Associated Home Mission Agencies that permission be requested to raise an adequate fund for this purpose. After much discussion, the amount was set at $8,000,000. This request was presented to the Finance Committee of the Convention and to the General Council. It was thoroughly discussed, and finally in May, 1952, the General Council recommended to the Convention meeting in Chicago that such a fund be raised and that a committee be appointed to bring definite plans to the Convention the next year. This was done and the Convention, meeting in Denver, Colo., in 1953, adopted the proposed plans and launched the campaign.

The committee of twenty-five appointed to conduct the campaign represented all the interests in the denomination, but particularly those most directly involved in the work of church extension. Dr. Finley Keech, pastor of the First Baptist Church of Fall River, Mass., was the chairman. The project was named "Churches for New Frontiers." The amount was set at $8,350,000, the $350,000 being needed to replace the America for Christ offering for the two Home Mission Societies and the Board of Education and Publication, since that offering could not be taken during the campaign. The Executive Committee which directed the campaign consisted of Dr. Theron Chastain, Executive Secretary of The American Baptist Home Mission Society; Dr. Reuben E. Nelson, General Secretary of the American Baptist Convention; and Dr. Ralph M. Johnson, director of the Council on Missionary Cooperation. Dr. Chastain was chairman of the committee and in that capacity was practically the director of the campaign. Ketchum, Inc., was retained for financial counsel.

The active campaign was carried on from May, 1953, to December 31, 1954. The final report was made to the American Baptist Convention in 1955 in Atlantic City, N. J. The total amount raised was much less than the goal. However, it provided more additional money for church building than all agencies of the denomination had ever had before. One-third of this amount was administered by the states and cities in which it was raised, so far as they had approved church extension projects. Accordingly, such projects were begun in all parts of the country. The remaining two-thirds was administered by the Home Mission Society under the agreement that one-half of the money received from each state and city would be used, in the first instance, in that state or city if it had approved projects requiring its use.

It was also agreed that up to 20 per cent of the amount received by each agency might be used for salaries of pastors in church extension projects, if the agency believed it wise. The remainder should be used for buildings, entirely on the basis of loans, with longer than the usual time for repayment when that seemed to be in the best interests of the project, and at lower than the usual rate of interest when it seemed necessary for the success of the project. Up to the time of this writing, the Home Mission

Society had used about 90 per cent of its portion for buildings. In this way the Home Mission Society will add approximately $2,500,000 to its Edifice Funds available for church extension purposes. Thus, this campaign did more than meet an immediate emergency; it provided a partial solution for what appears likely to be a permanent need.

One of the direct benefits of the campaign was that the states and cities gained substantial funds of their own for erecting new churches. There had been attempts in the past to raise such funds, but in most states they had produced little. In 1922 the Home Mission Society, to aid the states in this matter, assigned $996,250 to the states and cities in contingent mortgages with the understanding that any money received from them should be held as a "Home Mission Edifice Fund" to be used by the state or city for church edifice purposes. Some of the agencies acquired very useful sums of money in this way. However, very few states or cities had any substantial edifice funds before this campaign. From the Churches for New Frontiers campaign they will receive approximately $1,250,000. This is not evenly distributed among them, but all of them (with one possible exception)[1] will have some additional funds, and most of them quite substantial sums.

By 1955, the Society, because of this fund, had been able to help in starting 119 new churches. Most of them grew rapidly. A considerable number of them have become self-supporting, and are contributing generously to the unified budget of the denomination.

With the raising of this fund in prospect, the work of church extension assumed such importance that it seemed wise to the Board of the Society to set up a Department of Church Extension. This was done in 1953. Dr. Lincoln B. Wadsworth, secretary of the Department of Cities, was transferred to the Department of Church Extension, and Rev. Paul O. Madsen,

[1] Vermont had no church extension projects and so retained none of the money raised in that state. In spite of that fact, Vermont made a very energetic campaign and raised a very creditable amount.

pastor of the First Baptist Church of Boulder, Colo., was called to be secretary of the Department of Cities.

When the two Home Mission Societies integrated their staffs and work, the administration of the department was unchanged and Dr. Wadsworth was continued as secretary.

VI

The Challenge of Urban Growth

THE AMERICAN CITY has had a tremendous growth. Whereas in 1920 less than half of the people in the United States lived in cities, in 1956 two-thirds of the population was listed as urban. Much of this urban growth has come about through migration from the rural areas. At the same time, there have been great changes within the city. As already mentioned, successive waves of population have swept over sections of the inner city, and the movement from the inner city to the suburbs has been greatly accelerated. As a group became more prosperous it moved to a more desirable section, and a less prosperous group moved in. Throughout this process, the number of people in the inner city steadily increased. Large one-family houses were made into several apartments. Because the property steadily deteriorated, such a district ultimately became a slum. Then a movement for slum clearance began. Old buildings were cleared away and new ones were put up. Some of these housing developments were subsidized by the government to make possible a rental that people with low incomes could pay. In other cases, expensive apartment houses were built by commercial firms and correspondingly higher rents were charged, bringing in tenants with larger incomes.

All of these changes in the urban scene had their effect on the work of The American Baptist Home Mission Society. The expanding suburbs needed churches, and the Society shared with the city societies and the state conventions the responsibility for establishing them. The successive waves of population which passed over sections of the inner city largely were indifferent or even hostile to the Protestant faith. If a few were friendly, they were not able financially to do much toward maintaining the existing churches. For the most part, the people did not respond to the traditional program of church worship. Yet they were persons who needed the gospel. Furthermore, they were citizens and had a large, often dominant, share in determining what kind of government the city as well as the nation should have. Methods needed to be devised whereby they could be reached for Christ.

The bilingual churches had been founded in the midst of colonies of people whose mother tongue was not English. As the population of the area changed, these churches often found themselves in the midst of people of a different tongue and occasionally they were entirely deserted by the people whom they originally served. These churches needed the help of the Home Mission Society, if they were to cope with the changed situation. Sometimes the rehabilitation of a slum demanded a new church, or a radical shift in the program of an existing one. Even those areas that had an especially bad record of crime and delinquency could not be passed by. Some way had to be found to minister to the people there. To meet these varied needs the Society developed several different types of work. But first, a fuller account of the bilingual churches.

The Bilingual Churches

During the later years of the nineteenth century and the first thirteen years of the twentieth century, immigration was a dominant element in the growth of the population of America. In some years over one million people came to America. They came from many different European countries. Very naturally, they tended to settle in colonies, partly because relatives and friends wished to remain near each other and partly because they preferred to stay among those who spoke their own language. It sometimes came about that there were more people of a certain nationality in a single American city than there were in any city in the homeland. In a tour of New York city one could hear all the languages of Europe and several of Asia. In 1937, 11 per cent of the population of America was foreign born and 22 per cent had at least one foreign-born parent. In certain sections of some cities as high as 87 per cent of the youth sixteen to twenty-four years of age were either foreign born or had at least one foreign-born parent.

Here was an opportunity to preach the gospel to these newcomers in their native language, and this work became for the Home Mission Society a major undertaking. Some groups were predominantly Protestant, others were predominantly Catholic, but on most of those in these groups these religious relationships rested very lightly. Thousands had no personal faith and needed to be evangelized. Fortunately, the new situation made many of them more susceptible to the gospel than they had been at home. They were in a new land and were ready for new ways. They were lonely and appreciated friendliness. After hearing an unfamiliar language on every side, when they heard someone preaching the gospel in the familiar language of their homeland, they would stop to listen to its music, if for no other reason. This interest in the language led many to an interest in the message.

Apparently the first work was among the Welsh in 1836, and a number of Welsh churches were established. Very early, however, these churches took full responsibility for their work and the Society had no further connection with them. In 1839 Conrad Fleischman began work among the Germans in Philadelphia, and from that beginning a strong German work spread across the United States and Canada. The next group was made up of the Scandinavian peoples. As other groups came to America in considerable numbers, the gospel was taken to them in their own language.

When this work was at its height, the gospel was being preached in twenty-five languages other than English. As a result, there were in 1939, the centennial year, more than a thousand churches related to the Northern Baptist Convention that were a direct outgrowth of this work. This number included the German and the Swedish churches which at that time had not severed their connection with the Northern Baptist Convention. It takes no account of those churches which were founded, did an honorable work for the Master, and then, because of changed conditions, were no longer needed. Neither does it take account of the many persons who became Christians, then went back to the homeland, many of them to establish churches there. Besides these, a very large number transferred from these churches into the English-speaking churches of the Convention. There is no way to tell what that number was, but to scan the membership rolls of the churches or to read the list of ministers in the American Baptist Convention is to be impressed with the fact that it must have been very large. At one time four of the ten members of the Headquarters Council of The American Baptist Home Mission Society had come out of bilingual churches.

By the opening of the second century of the Society's history, however, conditions had changed greatly. World War I practically stopped immigration, and afterward a series of restrictive laws held it to a negligible number. From that time on the number of foreign born steadily declined, and their children became increasingly "American." During the depression, many of the foreign born returned to their home country and a large percentage of them remained there. Those going to Europe in several of the depression years outnumbered those coming from Europe. This meant that the growth of the foreign-language churches largely ceased. The German and the Swedish churches had become self-supporting or were aided only by their own people. Many churches of the other groups had also attained self-support. Others found themselves with a dwindling constituency using their native language, and accordingly changed their program to one wholly in English. Thereafter they received as members anyone from the community who desired fellowship with them.

World War II produced further changes. It largely broke up the large foreign-language colonies through the demand for labor in other areas. In 1932 the young people of the bilingual groups for the most part stayed with the parental groups even though they themselves used the native tongue very little and often only with difficulty. By 1950 a growing number of these young people, and often of their parents, were coming into the English-speaking churches. Even the foreign born, more and more, used the English language. Young men preparing for the ministry tended to go to the English-speaking colleges and seminaries rather than to the schools which prepared specifically for bilingual work. The temper of the age was for the disappearance of anything with a foreign name.

These changes led to a steady falling-off in the results of the bilingual work, and so to a decrease in the amount of support the Home Mission Society was justified in providing for it. At one time the Society shared in the support of about two hundred bilingual pastors. In 1956, after the integration of the Societies, the Department of Cities reported sixteen pastors in bilingual churches and five women missionaries. Some of this decrease, however, actually represented the attainment of strength and self-support by these churches. Some of it indicated that the bilingual churches had completed their task. In some instances they had become the English-speaking churches of the community. Every effort was made to handle the withdrawal of support in such a way that the work of the bilingual churches would be completely conserved.

In 1938, a conference on bilingual work was held in Cleveland. City, state, and national societies were represented. An attempt was made to appraise the situation as it was then. But this conference was largely under the leadership of those who had been in the work when it was at its highest usefulness, and some of them did not recognize the dawn of a new day.

The results of the conference were mainly two: the first, undoubtedly, was to raise the morale of those who were engaged in the work; the second was an attempt to tie the bilingual conferences more closely to the Northern Baptist Convention. Each language group of churches was organized as a conference whose unity was based on a common language and culture. Before the use of the mother tongue had become unimportant, they had developed an organizational self-consciousness, a co-operative program, and a sense of separateness that eventually led some of them to withdraw from the Convention.

As a further step in the direction of closer fellowship, the Cleveland conference recommended to the Northern Baptist Convention that it establish a new category of organizations related to it, to be called "Associated Organizations." The national societies were called "Co-operating Organizations." The state conventions and city societies were called "Affiliating Organizations." It was the hope that the bilingual conferences would become members of the Convention as Associated Organizations. For a long time the German Conference and the Swedish Conference had each been drawing apart to itself. Every possible effort was being made to hold them in the fellowship of the Northern Baptist Convention, and it was hoped that this new category of relationship might contribute to this end. Some of the leaders in the German Conference who were present in the meeting expressed the hope that this step would be acceptable to their conference. Events, however, proved otherwise. Not many years afterward both groups formally withdrew from the Northern Baptist Convention. Each set itself up as an independent denomination. The other conferences all maintain a good relationship with the American Baptist Convention and the Home Mission Society. In 1954 the Norwegian Conference held its final meeting, voted to disband, and recommended that the churches relate themselves to the American Baptist Convention and to the associations and state conventions in which they are located.

In 1943, a serious attempt to re-evaluate this work was begun, and it continued over the next few years. As a basis of study, a questionnaire was prepared with the assistance of Dr. H. Paul Douglas, director of Cooperative Field Research of the Federal Council of the Churches of Christ in America. A committee was set up in each standard city. After the committee had made its local study, a representative of the Home Mission Society visited that city for extended consultation. Rev. Emil Kontz, pastor of the Lincoln Park Baptist Church in Cincinnati, was released to the Society for a year to conduct these conferences. As a result of these surveys, it became clear that each church should carefully study its field to determine what it should do. Several courses were open to these churches. None of them could continue long as foreign-language congregations and expect to grow. Some of them could unite with a nearby English-speaking church. The bilingual church had been started because of the need to use a non-English language. That need had passed, and the two churches could unite. The bilingual church as a unit would disappear, but the work would continue more strongly than before. It was a case of losing one's life to find it. Another possibility was that the bilingual church should begin to minister to the entire community around it, particularly where it was the only Baptist church in the community. This meant that the services must be entirely in English, with perhaps a Bible class in the mother tongue for older persons who still were not fully at home in the English language. Usually where this was tried the name was changed, dropping the indication of nationality. The pastor needed to speak English and "think American" sufficiently well to be acceptable to persons of other nationalities and also to the native American stock. These, then, were the three major possibilities, though there may have been variants in individual cases.

In 1951, city, state, and national home mission executives, together with some board members and others, held a conference at Green Lake, Wis., to consider the entire home mission situation. They were sorely pressed by the demands for churches in the many new communities. It was obvious that this was the greatest opportunity to advance that the denomination would have for many years, and that the future lay with those who took advantage of it. On the other hand, there was little money available for this work. Although funds had increased during the past few years, they still were inadequate for the work in which these agencies were already engaged and for the new lines of endeavor growing out of the war situation. Much of the discussion, therefore, revolved around the question, "What money can be withdrawn from other work and be put into starting these new churches?" Everyone was agreed that every dollar possible must be transferred to this new opportunity. After long consideration it was decided that in the main the money then being put into bilingual work was not justified in the light of this other need. Accordingly, the conference voted that all the agencies should do everything possible to make the bilingual churches self-supporting within five years.

Every effort was made to carry out this decision in such a way as to make this change, not a defeat, but a real advance for the bilingual churches. The Department of Cities of the Home Mission Society set apart Rev. Edward Catlos to give practically his whole time to visiting each bilingual pastor and church to explain the meaning of this action and to point out what could best be done in their particular situation. As a result of his excellent work and of the high confidence in which he was held, pastors and people almost unanimously accepted these plans in the best possible spirit and set about making them effective. Never did they show their appreciation of the total Christian cause in this land more clearly than in their acceptance of this drastic move. Thus, this quarter of a century almost completes the final chapter of the glorious story of foreign-language work on American soil.

Three language groups have not been included in the above account. The Spanish-speaking work is growing rapidly and will be presented separately. The work among the Japanese and the Chinese also calls for separate treatment.

While these changes were taking place in the work of the bilingual churches, a corresponding change was taking place in the training of their ministers. In the beginning it had been necessary to train the ministers from each group in their mother tongue. The Germans established a seminary in Rochester, N. Y. The Swedes established Bethel Seminary in St. Paul, Minn. A Danish-Norwegian seminary was established in Morgan Park, Ill., and a Hungarian one in Scranton, Pa. A Slavic training school was opened in Chicago and a Russian training school in New York. There was a French department in Newton Theological Institution and an Italian department in Colgate Theological Seminary, then located in Hamilton, N. Y. In 1920 the International Seminary was organized in East Orange, N. J., by combining the Slavic and Russian training schools. Dr. Frank L. Anderson, executive secretary of the Chicago Baptist Association, was made president, and he held that position until his death in 1935. Dr. Frederick Lent, president of Elmira College in Elmira, N. Y., then became president. Many nationalities were trained in that school, including Russian, Polish, Hungarian, Czechoslovak, Roumanian, Italian, Lithuanian, and Latvian.

This school was maintained until the use of English became general in what had been bilingual churches. It then was better for the young men who were preparing for the ministry to attend English-speaking colleges and seminaries. The seminary finally discontinued classes in May, 1941, but the corporation was continued to handle the income of funds designated for its use. The court decreed that the corporation could use this money for the support of foreign-language students in other schools, and that has been the practice since that time. In 1955, 13 students in two seminaries were receiving scholarships from this income.

The Spanish-Speaking Work

The Spanish-speaking people in the United States constitute the one exception to all of the general statements in the preceding pages about foreign-language groups. Their number in the

United States has steadily increased. The work among them is done mainly in the Spanish language, and they are responding to the gospel in an encouraging way. The Society has worked among them, with some interruptions, for more than a hundred years, and there have been large returns from the work.

It is interesting to note that in *A Century of Faith,* Dr. White refers only to work among the Mexicans. At the time when he wrote, the number of Puerto Ricans coming into New York city had not yet become so large as to be a matter of special concern. Since that time the situation has completely changed. In 1955 there were 450,000 Puerto Ricans in that city and 109,000 in other parts of the country. This number was increasing rapidly. Of the large number of Spanish-speaking Protestant churches in New York, many were Pentecostal. There were nine Spanish-speaking Baptist churches connected with the work of the City Societies of New York and Brooklyn, and three independent Spanish-speaking Baptist churches. Most of them had large Sunday schools. Many of these people knew of the work of the Home Mission Society in Puerto Rico, and so were familiar with Baptist churches even though they were not members.

The other main stream of Spanish immigration was from Mexico. The greater number of Mexicans settled in the southwest, but they are to be found in all parts of the country. Many settled in such industrial centers as Chicago and Detroit. The Society has worked among these Mexicans for many years.

The Society has helped the Spanish-speaking groups to support their pastors, has aided them in securing buildings, has provided a general worker to advise them and assist them with their problems, and has maintained the Spanish-American Baptist Seminary in Los Angeles for the training of their ministers. In 1938 the Society reported that it was supporting "over fifty" pastors and four colporters. In 1956 the integrated Societies were aiding sixteen churches in the support of their pastors. Two women missionaries were working among Spanish-speaking people. This decrease in support by the Society represents the attainment of self-support by a number of the churches. Rev. Adam Morales, the general worker, reported in a recent year that he had visited seventy-three Spanish-speaking congregations. There were at least one hundred and three such churches and missions known and probably others of which there is no record.

Because the stream of immigration from both Mexico and Puerto Rico continues, the end of this work is not in sight, and the Spanish language will continue to be used. This is one of the great evangelizing responsibilities before the Society.

A general worker has been maintained to give assistance ever since the appointment of Rev. Edwin R. Brown in 1918 "as an evangelist, an organizer, and a guide for the expanding work in the nation."[1] He continued in that capacity until his retirement in 1948. During the latter years of his service he gave part of his time to the Spanish-American Baptist Seminary as a professor. In 1948 he was succeeded by Rev. Adam Morales, already mentioned. Mr. Morales is a graduate of the Spanish-American Baptist Seminary and came from the pastorate of the First Mexican Baptist Church of West Los Angeles, Calif. He was heartily welcomed by the people as one of their own, and has done a very effective work both in evangelizing the people and in guiding the churches.

The Spanish-American Baptist Seminary was founded in 1921 as a branch of the International Seminary, but it was located in Los Angeles. Later it became a separate corporation with a self-perpetuating Board of Trustees, one-third of whom were nominated by the Board of Managers of The American Baptist Home Mission Society. Dr. J. F. Detweiler was appointed as dean, and later, when it became a separate school, he was made president. He filled this position very effectively until his retirement in 1943. He was succeeded by Rev. Samuel F. Nelson. Mr. Nelson was appointed to the staff of the seminary, June 16,

[1] C. L. White, in *A Century of Faith*, p. 148.

1941. He spent one year in Mexico, presenting the cause of the seminary there, assisting the churches, and familiarizing himself with the language and the life of the people. The next year he taught in the seminary, and in 1943, when Dr. Detweiler retired, he became president. He held that position until 1954 when he accepted an appointment with the American Bible Society. Rev. Benjamin Morales, pastor of the First Mexican Baptist Church at West Los Angeles, Calif., then was appointed as acting president. He had studied at the University of California in Los Angeles and was a graduate of the Spanish-American Baptist Seminary. In 1956 he was appointed as president.

This seminary is the only Protestant school in the territory of the American Baptist Convention devoted entirely to the educating of Spanish-speaking ministers, and it has made a noteworthy contribution to that work. Mainly, it has trained men for service in the Spanish-speaking churches in the United States, but it also has sent graduates to Mexico, Central America, and the West Indies. In several years one-fourth of the students have come from outside the United States. For some years it conducted a correspondence department through which it aided pastors already at their task both in the United States and in other Spanish-speaking fields. In 1955 the seminary required that entrants have a high school diploma or enroll in high school and complete their work within a year. It grants the degree of Bachelor of Theology. In 1955 it enrolled forty-three students, including two women.

During the summer of 1955 a group of students from the seminary, under the leadership of Rev. Adam Morales, traveled across the country, visiting Spanish-speaking churches and Spanish-speaking communities in which there were no churches. As a result of their efforts seven new missions were established, and the young men had an experience which contributed greatly to their preparation for the ministry. This is an example of the way evangelistic work is carried on.

Originally the seminary was supported entirely by The American Baptist Home Mission Society, but as time went on it received some support from other sources. In 1955 the seminary's budget was $60,622, of which the Home Mission Society provided slightly less than 25 per cent.

Work Among the Chinese

The work among the Chinese on the West Coast was begun by the Society in 1870, and in New York city in 1892. At the present time it is being carried on in San Francisco, Sacramento, Fresno, San Mateo, and Locke, Calif.; Portland, Ore.; and Seattle, Wash. The Society also cooperates in interdenominational work in Philadelphia, Pa., and Chicago, Ill. The work in New York continues on a self-supporting basis. Dr. Charles R. Shepherd was the general missionary from 1919 until his retirement in 1954. Before that he had been a missionary in China under the Foreign Society, and he spoke the dialect of most of the Chinese on the West Coast. Thus he was well prepared for that position.

The work has progressed well at all points. In 1955, the First Chinese Baptist Church of San Francisco was a source of special encouragement. Because the English-speaking youth had become numerous and influential, an English-speaking youth church was formed, and Rev. James Chuck was called as pastor. Mr. Chuck, a product of that church, was American born and a graduate of the Berkeley Baptist Divinity School. For a time the Chinese-speaking congregation maintained a separate pastor. When he left, they voted their confidence in Mr. Chuck, who then became pastor of the entire church. Some of the services were conducted in Chinese, but most of the work was carried on in English. This was the first Chinese Baptist church to take this step.

In New York city, the work made progress under the able leadership of Dr. Mabel Lee, and a small but very attractive church and Christian Center were built early in this period. This work was supported generously by the Baptist agencies and by members of the Baptist churches in that area, until 1954, when it became self-supporting. It is interesting to note that the nearby Mariners' Temple was ministering to a considerable number of Chinese, using only the English language.

A particularly bright expression of the Christian spirit was the attitude of the Chinese Christians toward the Japanese Christians during the invasion of China by Japan. In a conference of home missionaries held in Seattle, Wash., a Chinese pastor led the devotions. Instead of manifesting the resentment against the Japanese that might have been expected, he took pains to assure the Japanese pastor who was present of his good will and later called on him to lead in prayer. The undoubted genuineness of this action touched the hearts of all who were in attendance.

Chung Mei Home for Chinese boys has had an important part in the work with the Chinese. This Home was opened in October, 1923. At that time it was a common practice for a Chinese man to bring his sons to America with him, leaving his wife and daughters in China. It was his hope that the boys would have the benefit of an American education, but too often it turned out that he worked such long hours and lived under such conditions that the boys became delinquents. Too, some boys were left orphans, and there was no institution that would receive them. This need lay heavily on Dr. Shepherd's heart, and he overcame tremendous difficulties in order to establish a place for them. He got the money for a building and for part of the operating budget from the Home Mission Society. The Chinese people, following the lead of the Chinese Baptist Church of San Francisco, gave money for the furnishings. The San Francisco Bay Cities Union provided most of the operating cost and some extras that were needed. Dr. Shepherd was paid by the Home Mission Society and gave most of his time to the Home.

This Home was opened in a dilapidated building in an unsavory section of Oakland, Calif., with seven boys. The number soon rose to fifty, the outside limit that the Department of Public Welfare could approve for the building. And yet there were more boys that needed such a home. Under Dr. Shepherd's leadership the boys themselves undertook to raise money for a larger building. They ran a woodyard; they cut the logs in a burned-over tract into firewood; they worked in the summer for nearby farmers; they formed a band and gave concerts; and they presented a black-faced Chinese minstrel show (probably the only one of its kind ever known). The programs were presented in the churches and brought good offerings. Altogether, the boys raised $10,000, and they pledged themselves to raise $20,000 more. And they did it!

Meanwhile, the San Francisco-Oakland Bridge was being built and the land on which Chung Mei stood was needed for the Oakland approach. In 1933 the California State Highway Commission bought the property for a fair price. They allowed the boys to stay in the Home, however, until the land was needed. This extension of time proved to be eighteen months.

Of course, this meant that a new building had to be secured at once—and this was when the depression was at its worst! However, the Home Mission Society gave $15,000, the San Francisco Bay Cities Union gave $7,000, and the Woman's American Baptist Home Mission Society gave $4,000. Various individuals made gifts ranging from $1,000 to $5,000 each. The Chinese contributed liberally, for by this time they had come to know the worth of this institution. The large part taken by the boys themselves has already been mentioned. The result was that Sunday, June 30, 1935, the new Chung Mei building in El Cerito, Calif., was dedicated and a new period in the history of the Home was begun.

There is not space to tell the stories of the boys who became happy and useful citizens instead of juvenile delinquents through the ministry of this home, but there were many. The boys attended the public schools, had an excellent reputation, and made a good record. On May 19, 1934, Edward Hing Tong received the degree of Bachelor of Arts from the University of California, the first Chung Mei boy to achieve that distinction. Later "Eddie" Tong graduated from the Berkeley Baptist Divinity School with the degree of Bachelor of Divinity. In 1956 he was pastor of the First Chinese Baptist Church and director of the Chinese Christian Center in Fresno, Calif. By V-J Day, 135 sons of Chung Mei had entered the armed services. Many of the Chung Mei boys, now men, are filling places of distinction in various walks of life.

By 1954, conditions had so changed that such an institution was no longer needed. The fact that Chinese boys would be received in any home for boys, that men more commonly brought their entire families with them from China, and that Dr. Shepherd retired in 1954 were among the contributing factors. As a result, Chung Mei was closed. It had served a most worthy purpose.

Work with the Japanese

One of the incidents of World War II less to the credit of Americans was the evacuation of the Japanese-Americans from the West Coast. Seventy-one thousand of them were native-born American citizens. Of the foreign born, all but a negligible minority would have become citizens—and loyal citizens—had they been permitted to do so. Their young men were in the American Army, and were making an outstanding record for bravery, effectiveness, and loyalty. There had been no established case among them of sabotage or of communication with the enemy. The FBI assured the military that they knew the dangerous persons and had them under constant surveillance. But those who hated the Orientals had their day, and 112,000 persons, some of them Japanese, but more of them Americans of Japanese ancestry, were given very brief notice to dispose of whatever belongings they could not take with them and were sent off to crude camps designated as "relocation centers." Under this forced disposal they received five to twenty cents on the dollar for their property. Thus the savings of a lifetime were wiped out while Americans who were willing to profit at their expense took their possessions.

It is greatly to the credit of the churches on the West Coast that almost without exception they spoke out in defense of these Japanese-Americans. They gave them every possible assistance and in many practical ways demonstrated their unity with their Christian brethren.

The Home Mission Society and the Woman's Home Mission Society immediately went into action and did everything possible to assist and encourage the evacuees. All of the missionaries of both Societies stood by them, and the secretaries went to the Coast to help in finding storage for goods, assisting in sales, driving cars to take people where they had to go, caring for babies, feeding people when the feeding program broke down, in short, rendering every assistance, physical and spiritual, that was in their power. Rev. John W. Thomas, at that time secretary of the Department of Cities, stayed on the Coast throughout this period to give help, as did also certain workers of the Woman's Society.

When the people finally were removed to the relocation centers, the missionaries of both Societies went with them. Seven Nisei pastors, under appointment by the Society at that time were stationed in the centers, with the cooperation of the government agency, so that the Protestant people in each camp would have a pastor. Emery E. Andrews, the missionary in Seattle, moved to a point near the relocation center at Emmett, Idaho, and gave his whole time to serving the people there.

In the relocation centers the living conditions were extremely trying. The housing was primitive, heat was inadequate, and often two or three families were housed in one room with no privacy except such as could be gained by hanging a blanket between them. All meals were in a public dining hall. Furthermore, there was little that was constructive for these evacuees to do. The best that can be said is that most of those who supervised the relocation program did it as humanely as was possible under their orders.

The spirit of the Christians among these Japanese-Americans was remarkable. They recognized the fact that their treatment was a very natural consequence of the war and that probably Americans in Japan would not have fared any better. The pastors issued a formal apology to the American public, in which they asked forgiveness for what Japan had done in attacking Pearl Harbor. They displayed a patience and steadfast faith that humbled those who beheld it. One year, during pre-Easter season, the Nisei in one of the camps set up a series of conferences with the Buddhists. As a result of those conferences 187 persons were converted.

The churches took a genuine interest in these people in their misfortune and did what they could to sustain their spirits. One year over ten thousand Christmas packages were received in the camps and many thousands of Christmas cards. It greatly strengthened the Christians to know that they were kept in mind by their brethren outside the camps, and the Buddhists were greatly impressed by the fact that there were people in this country who cared for them in their plight.

Eventually the restrictions were lessened and the releases began. First, some students were allowed to enter colleges that would accept them. The Society's representatives and the Christian Friendliness missionaries of the Woman's Society took the lead in finding such colleges and in preparing public opinion to welcome these students. The Society also aided with their expenses. There were very few untoward incidents in this program. When others were allowed to come to certain Eastern cities to work, the Society again aided in finding housing and jobs and in preparing the public to receive them. Several hostels were opened, some by the Home Mission Society alone and some interdenominationally, to care for these people until they could find permanent housing. Although the Society guaranteed the cost of operation, each person paid for his accommodations; thus, the actual cost of each hostel to the denomination was only the salary of the director and some incidental expenses. Some of the Nisei pastors were brought to these areas to minister to the people. In the course of time, all of the people were released, and the relocation centers were closed. It is estimated that about 60 per cent went back to the West Coast, the remainder settling in the East or Midwest. The Fujin Home, operated by the Woman's Society in Seattle, Wash., became a hostel to aid those returning to that area.

After this experience, several of the Nisei pastors found themselves called to positions formerly held by Caucasians. The most conspicuous example of this is Rev. Jitsuo Morikawa, Canadian born of Japanese ancestry and a naturalized American citizen. The Home Mission Society sent him to Chicago as a pastor to the Japanese-Americans in that area. In a short time the First Baptist Church, Dr. E. L. Titus, pastor, expressed an interest in placing him on its staff with some assistance from the Home Mission Society. In a well-attended meeting and after full discussion of what was involved, he was unanimously called. It was understood that he was to serve not merely the Nisei but also the entire congregation, and this he did with complete acceptance. At first he was named assistant pastor, but soon he was made co-pastor. When Dr. Titus resigned, and the Rev. Robert Steiger became pastor, the same cooperative relationship continued. On Mr. Steiger's resignation, a committee was appointed to seek a new pastor. After careful consideration, however, they reported to the church thus: "We have a pastor and do not need any other." Mr. Morikawa, thereupon, was made pastor of that great historic church. In 1948 he received the honorary degree of Doctor of Divinity from Blackburn College.

Many feared that his going to the First Baptist Church would be detrimental to that organization, but it has proved otherwise. In 1956 there were more Caucasians attending the church than for many years, and there were about as many Nisei as Caucasians. Of the many Negroes who had moved into the neighborhood of the church, a number had been welcomed into the church membership. Furthermore, the finances of the church were found to be in better condition than they had been for several decades.

Dr. Morikawa is recognized as one of the great preachers of the denomination. He is in demand wherever a man with a great spiritual message is desired. At the Northern Baptist Convention in Boston in 1950, he gave one of the principal addresses. At its close, the people by their applause compelled him to rise for a third time, an ovation that had seldom if ever before been given in that convention. In 1956, the convention, meeting in Seattle, elected him as one of its vice presidents.[1]

Other Nisei became pastors of Caucasian churches and workers in Christian Centers. Rev. Jobu Yasamura was on the field staff of the Home Mission Society in the Department of Cities for several years and rendered a great service, particularly in the settlement of displaced persons in the days following the war.

Today many of the Japanese-Americans in the East are in Caucasian churches, but the majority of those on the West Coast are still in churches of their own group and are working on a bilingual basis.

Christian Centers

In 1932, the beginning of the second century of the life of the Home Mission Society, the oldest Christian Centers were only thirteen years old. Brooks House in Hammond, Ind., and Katherine House in Indiana Harbor, Ind., had both been dedicated in 1919. By 1932 the Christian Centers had proved themselves to be an effective approach to the crowded and often underprivileged areas of the industrial communities. They had been preceded by the "institutional churches," of which Judson Memorial Church on Washington Square in New York city was a conspicuous example. But these institutional churches had been expensive to build and operate, and they had not fulfilled all of the expectations of their founders. The Christian Center was a new approach, based on the experience of the social settlements, but with an avowedly Christian program. Whereas the extreme

---

[1] Since the writing of this account, the American Baptist Home Mission Boards have chosen Dr. Morikawa to be their Secretary of Evangelism.

social-settlement philosophy denied the validity of the religious approach, the experience of the Society fully justified it.

In 1955 the Society was participating in the program of forty Christian Centers through the Department of Cities, and two among the Indians through the Department of Town and Country. When the two Societies integrated their programs, these two Indian Centers and a similar one that had been supported by the Woman's Society were assigned to the Department of Alaska, Indian Work, and Schools in the United States.

Sometimes these Centers were organized in connection with a church already in existence; in other cases a church sometimes has developed out of the Center's work. All of the Centers have Sunday schools, Youth Fellowships, or other groups following a distinctively Christian program. Their influence, however, reaches far beyond these organizations. Whatever the nature of the community, the Center endeavors to be the helper of the churches, rather than a competitor. Many individuals have been sent back to their churches renewed in spirit and usefulness. Indeed, the life of many communities has been transformed. It is generally reported that where a Center is opened, juvenile delinquency drops markedly, poverty and crime are lessened, family life is lifted to a higher level, and large numbers of young people are led to a good purpose in life.

A major need of the Christian Center movement from the beginning has been properly trained leadership. At first there was no established program, and one had to be developed. The work called for special skills not developed by instruction in any theological seminary nor by experience in most pastorates. Workers had to train themselves through their own efforts, through observation of the work of others, and through such studies as might be related to their new duties. The Woman's American Baptist Home Mission Society early began to train women workers in the Baptist Missionary Training School in Chicago, which arranged for them clinical experience in the nearby Centers. There was no similar opportunity for the men.

The first step in this direction was the holding of a conference once a year at which the workers might share their experiences. To these meetings were brought speakers and conference leaders who could help the workers in solving their problems. The first of these conferences, held in the summer of 1938, was fostered by The American Baptist Home Mission Society for its own appointees. The second, held the following year, included the workers of both the Home Mission Societies. Later, the conferences came to include all the workers in Christian Centers who cared to come, and the state conventions and the city societies shared in the planning and financing. The programs, worked out by a committee of the workers in conference with the leaders of the Home Mission Agencies, have always been strictly practical and educational.

In 1946, a more formal training program was instituted at Brooks House, Hammond, Ind. Rev. John M. Hestenes had been the Director of Christian Centers and had largely developed the Christian Center program. He also had served as director of Brooks House throughout its history. In 1945, he was compelled by ill health to surrender his work. Rev. C. Dwight Klinck was called from the Center in Milwaukee to succeed Mr. Hestenes as director of Brooks House, with the understanding that he would establish a training program.

The plan was to select young men who were graduating from a seminary and who were interested in spending their lives in Christian Center work and to provide for them a working fellowship which would enable them to serve for a year at Brooks House under expert direction. At the same time, they could take courses related to their work in George Williams College in Chicago. They would live in Brooks House, share in all staff conferences, formulate and execute programs under the guidance of the director of Brooks House, and thus secure a practical training.

The objectives of this program, as stated in the annual report of the Society for 1947, were as follows:

"To provide orientation and introduction to Christian Center work through practical experience on the field.

"To give an orientation in the philosophy and techniques of Christian Center work through weekly seminars and discussions.

"To offer a program of reading in fields related to Center work.

"To give further training through George Williams College in Chicago."

Mr. Klinck has given this fuller account of the training program:

"Inaugurated in 1946, the Home Mission Society provides a scholarship and the House provides a room. Trainees work alongside the Center missionaries; they carry a fair share of the work and thereby gain first-hand experience in Center work. They lead clubs, supervise gym programs, teach craft classes, teach Sunday school classes, assist in worship services, share in community programs planned by the Center, attend meetings of the local ministerial association and the local Welfare Council, visit in the homes of the neighborhod, learn to write reports. They gain experience working with probation officers, school authorities, police, and social workers. This experience is invaluable in introducing the new missionary to the actual problems which are faced on the field.

"Not only does the trainee gain this actual experience, he does his work under proper supervision and with ample opportunity for the interpretation of his experiences. Each Monday afternoon is set aside for a seminar meeting at which time the philosophy and techniques of Christian Center work are outlined and discussed. Problems faced by the trainee in his groups or in his assignments are discussed and explained; written records are reviewed; opportunities for the Christian missionary to be found in many experiences of the average day's work are pointed out and suggestions are made as to how these opportunities can be used for Christian teaching and winning others to Jesus Christ.

"Each traineee attends all Brooks House staff meetings and thereby gains the experience of observing a staff of trained workers facing and meeting their problems and planning their programs. Trainees are invited to share in the discussion, but have no voice in the policy making.

"Trainees may elect (and usually do) to study further at George Williams College, Chicago, to secure more academic training in the field of Christian Center work.

"Since the trainees live in the staff residence, they steadily become a part of the staff family and participate in the fellowship of the missionaries at the House."

In 1952-53 Dr. Fred H. Willkens, Professor of Christian Education at Colgate Rochester Divinity School, during his sabbatical leave, visited most of the Christian Centers and made a careful study of their programs. He brought a very encouraging report to a joint meeting of the Boards of Managers of the two Societies and held extended conferences with the secretaries who administered the Centers. These conferences proved helpful in further developing the Christian Center program.

The Christian Centers are the best means that have been found for ministering to the neediest people in some of the neediest areas of our cities. They succeed in reaching large numbers of people who do not respond to the conventional church program. Their program can be adapted to the type of community, and when this has been done they are unsurpassed as a missionary instrument. It is interesting to note that whereas the Christian Center type of ministry was developed in an effort to serve disadvantaged areas, the technique has proved of value also in overprivileged areas. Individuals find a new life in them. Families and homes are put upon a sounder basis. The life of the entire community is lifted to a higher level.

Educational Centers

There have been Negroes in the north from colonial days. However, the period from 1914 to 1955 witnessed a tremendous increase in their number. World War I, with its demand for labor in industry, produced a flood of migration from the rural south to the industrial centers of the north. From 1917 to 1925, some 600,000 Negroes moved north. After the war, this movement slowed down but never stopped. The demand for labor opened to the Negroes an opportunity for a more abundant life than they had ever known before. World War II brought this migration to a still greater flood. There came to be large Negro populations in New York, Chicago, Detroit, Philadelphia, Pittsburgh, and other industrial centers. Harlem in New York became the largest Negro city in the world.

This migration posed a new missionary problem, and since the Negroes were predominantly Baptists it was particularly the problem of The American Baptist Home Mission Society. There was no need to start churches. In fact, churches sprang up with such rapidity that there have been no really reliable statistics as to their number. Two things, however, were necessary: buildings to house the growing congregations and an adequately trained leadership.

The problem of housing was one that the people themselves had to solve in their own way. Some of the congregations secured very satisfactory buildings, but others occupied rented stores. Some were able to buy church buildings from white congregations that were moving to new locations. Some were able to build. Some of the Negro churches became very large. In fact, the Negro Baptists in several of our larger cities far outnumbered the white Baptists. The part of the Home Mission Society in this development was to make loans from their edifice funds, just as they did to other groups. This assistance did not play a major role in housing these congregations, but in some instances it was of crucial importance.

The problem of leadership was both urgent and difficult. Seldom has a people made so long a trek sociologically as had the Negro from the share-cropper's farm in the south to the industrial city of the north. Every condition of his life was radically changed, and he was unprepared for so radical a transition. For many years the Negroes had depended for leadership on their ministers, now the ministers often were as badly lost in the new situation as were their people. Most of the ministers were poorly trained; some of them had received no schooling whatever. Soon the people came to feel that their ministers knew little or nothing about the problems of their daily life in the new environment. This attitude was particularly true of the young people in high school and college.

The Home Mission Society had no established method of dealing with a situation of this kind. Accordingly, it began a study of the problem, and it undertook some experimentation in cooperation with the New York City Society. In the course of a few years, the Educational Center was devised as a means of helping the ministers to understand and meet the demands of the new situation. The very fact that the pastors were studying, helped to restore the confidence of their people, particularly their youth. The Educational Center also helped the people to adjust their church life to the new situation. This was the greatest contribution the Society could make to the rise of the Negro people in the northern industrial cities.

The experimentation which produced the Educational Center began in 1925 when the Home Mission Society and the New York City Society cooperated in opening the first Educational Center in Harlem, with Dr. Vernon Johns as its director. The plan called for courses of training for ministers in whatever subjects they might need, ranging from reading and writing to theological studies, and also for courses for lay leaders, not only in methods of church school and youth work, but also in the responsibilities of church officers and members. At the beginning there was no precedent on which to base the program. It was a case of learning by trial and error.

In 1930 Dr. Johns resigned and Rev. Horatio S. Hill was called to the directorship. He had a Bachelor of Arts degree from Benedict College, one of the schools fostered by the Home Mission Society. He also had his Bachelor of Divinity degree from Oberlin College, and his Master of Arts degree from Yale University. More recently Benedict College conferred on him the honorary degree of Doctor of Divinity. During the years, Dr. Hill has rendered distinguished service in this field. Because of the high quality of his leadership, he has been able to draw together a remarkable teaching staff from the faculties of the colleges and universities in New York. In a single year the Educational Center in Harlem has enrolled as many as five hundred in the ministerial courses and a thousand in the lay leadership training courses. Not only did classes meet in the Educational Center, but institutes were held in churches in Westchester County and on Staten Island.

This work was carried on in a church building, with the inevitable handicaps to both the Educational Center and the church. The need for a building better suited to the work had long been recognized, and in 1955 this goal was finally attained.

In 1935 it was decided that the time had come to develop similar work in other cities having large concentrations of Negroes. Although a somewhat similar work had been carried on in Cleveland in connection with a Christian Center, no other experiments had been attempted. It was decided that the next step should be taken in Detroit. There were several reasons for this choice. Detroit had a large Negro population, the Negro leaders were eager for a Center and would lead their people to participate in it, and the city society, under the secretaryship of Dr. H. C. Gleiss, was ready to support the project. Also, some money was available for use in that city.

In 1935 Dr. Horatio S. Hill visited Detroit to study the situation. After careful planning, the Detroit Baptist Training School was opened in 1937. Rev. Franklin A. Fisher was called as the first director and the program developed rapidly. The Negro Associations shared in the management, and the Negro churches shared in the cost. This Educational Center has furnished a large number of trained lay leaders to the churches in Detroit and has aided greatly in raising the level of training of the ministers.

The Chicago Baptist Institute opened February 1, 1938, with Dr. H. M. Smith as dean, and has grown to be the largest of all. It has deviated somewhat from the usual Educational Center program. It has been the purpose of the Educational Centers to aid ministers already in the pastorate, not to become a seminary for the education of prospective ministers. That could best be done through the regular theological schools, and the Educational Centers were not prepared to enter that field. In Chicago, however, Dr. Smith felt that the situation required that some young men be trained for the ministry, and to some extent this was undertaken. This phase of the work, however, has not developed very largely.

Other Educational Centers have been established in Brooklyn, N. Y., and in Philadelphia and Pittsburgh, Pa. Most of these Educational Centers have developed some kind of interracial program in cooperation with the Caucasian churches. Each one has found additional avenues of service in its own area.

More recently there has been another development of this program. In those states where there is a considerable Negro population that is not largely concentrated in any one city, there has sometimes been appointed to the state staff, with support shared by the Home Mission Society, a person who goes from place to place holding institutes for pastors and for lay workers. This plan provides for these smaller groups the same type of training which the Educational Centers offer in the larger cities. This plan has proved very useful in West Virginia, Kansas, Iowa, and Northern California.

Work in Alaska

For many years the Woman's American Baptist Home Mission Society had maintained a Home for children in Kodiak, Alaska, with a branch at Ouzinkie. The only church program was a small chapel related to the Children's Home until the first military developments in the area began. In 1940 the General Society was asked to assume the responsibility of starting a church. Although the Society had decided many years before not to enter Alaska, a new element had now entered into the situation. World War II had begun, but America was not yet formally engaged. However, through the advances made in aviation, Alaska had become an exposed frontier; and the government was actively developing its defenses there. At Woman's Bay, eight miles from Kodiak, a naval base was being built; and Kodiak, the trading center, was growing rapidly. There was great need for work not only on behalf of the inhabitants of Kodiak, but also on behalf of the personnel at the Naval Base when off duty.

In the spring of 1940 the Society sent to Kodiak Rev. W. A. Warner, one of its missionaries, who was also a very competent builder, to study the situation. His report was such that the Board that summer sent the Executive Secretary to confer with the local people and determine a course of action. As a result, a desirable location was secured, a church was organized, and an attractive building erected. Rev. Gregory S. Morony of California was appointed as missionary to this field in December 1940.

The results were gratifying. The church and the Children's Home always cooperated closely. Because at first there was no chaplain at the Naval Base, the missionary was welcomed there to carry on such a program as his time would permit. Men from the Base were constantly in attendance at the church and were frequent visitors at the parsonage. The missionary reported that in one month there were only three meals that he and his family did not share with someone from the Base. The people in the community also welcomed the church.

Almost from the beginning, the church building was too small for the rapidly growing work. The congregation carried all of the local expenses, except the salary of the pastor-missionary, and contributed liberally to missions. Very soon it assumed responsibility for half of the pastor's salary. Then it began accumulating a building fund.

In 1950 the Society provided funds to supplement those raised in the community and sent Dr. J. B. Dahl, an ordained Baptist minister and a successful church builder, to erect an educational building. While he was in Kodiak, Rev. R. N. Wilkinson, who was then the missionary, was on furlough, and Dr. Dahl served as pastor as well as builder. When the educational unit was completed, the Society in its report for 1951, boasted: "Today we have at Kodiak one of the most ample facilities for Christian ministry in Alaska." The following year the church reported 136 members, with an average attendance at the morning service of 137, and a church school with an average attendance of 140. In 1952 the church secured time on the radio, and this radio ministry has become a permanent feature of its work. By 1955 the building was again entirely too small. The church school reported 350 present, with all the rooms in the parsonage being used for classes.

For some time the Society had considered extending its work to the mainland. In 1949 there came an opportunity to take over a community hospital in Cordova, Alaska, together with a church already established there. Both were having difficulties. The hospital, with its twenty beds, was housed in a rented building not well suited for such a purpose, and had lost much of its standing. The church, to a large extent, had lost contact with the community. But it was believed that with proper management the situation could be improved.

In December, 1949, a satisfactory agreement was reached, and the Society began its administration May 1, 1950. At that time Rev. Howard E. May was sent to Cordova as pastor of the church and business manager of the hospital. Several missionary nurses also were appointed. The local doctors were employed directly by the patients, and the facilities of the hospital were put at their disposal.

In October, 1951, a disastrous fire destroyed the entire central area of the town. Two of the doctors lost their offices and two of the directors of the hospital lost their businesses. While one of the nurses was busy at the hospital caring for those who had been injured in the fire, her own apartment, with all its contents, was destroyed. The heroic work of the doctors and nurses in this catastrophe firmly established the hospital in the hearts of the people. The following year the hospital reported that it had cared for 418 patients during the year and that there had been an average of two operations and five X-rays per week. The total cost of operating the hospital, $65,000, had been met. That measure of self-support could not always be maintained, but the hospital has proved to be a very valuable ministry.

Meantime, the church had re-established itself in the community and was having good attendance and steady increases in membership. Mr. May had become a loved and respected member of the community. In all respects, this venture at Cordova has justified itself.

In 1952 agitation began for a new hospital building, and in 1955 it was built by the community. A large part of the cost was met by the territorial government. The cost to the Home Mission Society was a loan of $42,000. This is to be repaid through the local hospital organization, with the interest covered by a contingent mortgage, the contingency being that the Society shall continue to have the contract for the management of the hospital.

In 1954 the Society, in cooperation with the Woman's Society and the Cordova church, expanded its ministry in Cordova to include a Christian Center. This met with an immediate response in a large enrollment in activities and in community support.

By 1955 Anchorage was rapidly becoming the chief center in Alaska, and the other denominations were pressing the Home Mission Society to start a church in the center of that city. This was being earnestly considered. For a time the Society had a missionary in Fairbanks, attempting a church extension program there. However, the failure of the housing area to grow and the lack of another site not already pre-empted by another denomination, caused the work to be discontinued. Alaska is a land of opportunity, and in all probability the Society's work there will be greatly expanded.

Administration of the Department

In 1932, Dr. Frank A. Smith was secretary of the Department of Missions in the United States. In 1936, that department was divided into the Department of Cities and the Department of Town and Country. Dr. Smith was continued as secretary of both departments until his retirement, August 31, 1936. July 25, 1936, Rev. John W. Thomas came as field representative in the Department of Cities, and the Executive Secretary was asked to give general oversight to the department until the new worker could become familiar with the field. Mr. Thomas later took over the entire responsibility for the department and served very effectively until February 28, 1945, when he resigned to go to the faculty of Crozer Theological Seminary. Rev. Lincoln B. Wadsworth was called to the department on July 1, 1945, and served until 1953. At that time church extension had become so important a factor in Home Mission work that it was decided to withdraw that work from the Department of Cities and set up a separate department. At about the same time, Mr. Atkinson resigned as secretary of the Department of Edifice Funds and Building Counsel. It was decided that Dr. Wadsworth should be put in charge of these two departments, and Rev. Paul O. Madsen, pastor of the First Baptist Church of Boulder, Colo., was called to be the secretary of the Department of Cities.

In 1955, integration with the Woman's Society was established by action of the annual meetings of the two Societies at Atlantic City, N. J. By this action there was added to the Department of Cities all of the work the Woman's Society was doing in that field. The work of the General Society in Alaska was withdrawn from that department and transferred to the new Department of Alaska, Indian Work, and Schools in the United States. Mr. Madsen was continued as secretary of the integrated Department of Cities, while Miss Dorothy O. Bucklin, of the staff of the Woman's Society, was placed in charge of the new department.

VII

Mission to Rural and Village America

IN 1932 THE HOME MISSION SOCIETY was still feeling its way in town and country work. From 1919 to 1922, Dr. Rolvix Harlan had been secretary of Social Service and Rural Community Work. His service to the rural area was chiefly in the field of research. From 1929 to 1933, Rev. Edwin E. Sundt had been a field worker. He began an educational campaign among the rural churches on behalf of a program more closely related to the total community. His work was done under the direction of the Department of Missions in the United States. As has been explained, in 1935 that department was divided; one part became the Department of Town and Country and the other the Department of Cities.

Rural Life Sunday was first observed in Baptist churches in 1931, and in that same year financial assistance was first provided for rural pastors attending summer schools.

The year 1932 witnessed the first presentation of "The Rosa O. Hall Honor Certificate for Distinguished Service in Town and Country Fields." From three to five rural pastors, with their wives, are honored each year at the meetings of the American Baptist Convention, and a record of their meritorious service is recited to the Convention delegates. By choosing the recipients each year from the area in which the Convention is being held, pastors from every section of the Convention have an opportunity to be eligible for this recognition. Rosa O. Hall lived for many years to see the happiness which these awards brought. She was a Connecticut woman, a central figure in her home community. She served for twenty-one years on the Board of Managers of the Connecticut Baptist State Convention. Her death occurred on October 7, 1953.

Rev. Ellsworth M. Smith was the field representative of the Department of Town and Country from October 1, 1936 to August 31, 1938. He largely continued the work Mr. Sundt had been doing.

On September 1, 1938, Dr. Mark Rich succeeded Mr. Smith as field representative. He became secretary of the department on June 15, 1942. Because Dr. Rich had his doctorate from Cornell University in rural sociology and had written his dissertation on work done in a rural pastorate on a federated field, he brought to the work an unusual measure of technical training and practical experience. He remained with the Society until August 31, 1952, rendering constructive service of far-reaching importance. His influence was felt throughout his own denomination and in interdenominational rural church circles as well.

During Mr. Sundt's leadership a plan had been launched for appointing State Commissions of Town and Country Work. At one time as many as twenty such commissions were reported. They rendered valuable service, and in 1956 they were still a regular part of the approach of state conventions to rural fields. The difficulty which faced these commissions was that they had no staff person to work with them, except when someone already overburdened with other tasks was assigned this added responsibility. Consequently they were constantly frustrated by the fact that they had no effective way of carrying out the excellent ideas which they developed. There was a clear need for staff persons who could give to this task their entire time.

One of the early moves of the department under Dr. Rich's leadership was to meet this need by securing the appointment of directors of town and country work on the staffs of the state conventions, with the understanding that the Society would share in their salaries and expenses. These directors gave their time to the development of the town and country churches in their state. They aided these churches in securing pastors, and by conferences with groups of churches or with single churches encouraged them to carry out a more effective program. They led in state-wide movements for specific objectives in rural church life, and in general they kept the needs of the town and country churches before the other churches of the state. At one time there were twenty-two such directors. Later the number declined. Chiefly because of limited funds and the pressure of other needs, the tendency grew to assign this responsibility to a staff member who had other responsibilities and so could devote only a portion of his time to this demanding work. At this writing, the number of full-time Town and Country directors is again on the increase.

It soon became evident that these directors needed an opportunity to share experiences and to discuss their plans. For this purpose, they held in 1944 a three-day conference. Such a conference became an annual feature of the town and country program. The participants soon began to develop a yearly program which all would promote within their states. Each year the program emphasized two or three specific needs and outlined plans for meeting them. These conferences afforded an excellent opportunity for cooperative planning by the national and state departments of Town and Country. At first they were held just preceding the sessions of the Northern Baptist Convention at some convenient nearby place.

Out of these conferences grew a Town and Country Fellowship which included directors, pastors, and lay persons interested in the town and country church movement. The membership has never been as large as it should be, but it has been another effective means of spreading information and of encouraging rural churches to undertake new features in their local programs.

One method widely used has been the Lord's Acre plan. Under this plan, a farmer dedicates a field to the Lord's use, usually with a formal dedication ceremony. He plants it, cultivates it, and on selling the harvested crop, donates the proceeds to the church. The plan has many variations. Sometimes a woman dedicates the eggs which her hens lay on Sundays; sometimes a field is given and the whole community joins in planting, cultivating, and harvesting it. Often a boys' or girls' club carries out a project. In some cases the money is used for the local expenses of the church; in others, for missions. The plan seems to meet with the greatest response from the people when the money raised is used for some special cause outside of the regular church budget.

Advocates of the Lord's Acre plan do not consider it primarily as a way to raise money. They regard it rather as a means of establishing in the minds of the people a closer connection between their daily work and their service to God. Churches that have used the plan seem to find the spiritual results quite as valuable as the money raised. This plan has been widely promoted by the state directors of Town and Country.

One of the difficulties on the rural field is the too great frequency of the vicious cycle faced by the small church: low salary, poorly trained minister, diminishing church membership. The directors of Town and Country were certain that the small membership of the country churches usually was not inherent in the situation, but was due most often to the lack of training, and consequent lack of vision, on the part of the pastors. After many long discussions of what could be done about this, in 1945 two conferences for rural ministers were held at the American Baptist Assembly, Green Lake, Wis., which the denomination had acquired the year before. Each lasted a month. It was not easy for these pastors to leave their fields for four weeks to attend such a conference. Therefore, the living was put on a cooperative basis so as to make it as inexpensive as possible. Scholarships were provided, help was given to defray travel costs for those who came longer distances, and there was opportunity for the men to earn part of their expenses by working on the grounds at Green Lake for a certain number of hours each day. Arrangements also were made to supply the pulpits while the pastors were away, and the churches continued to pay their salaries so that their families were provided for. By these means satisfactory groups were brought together.

These conferences met with so good a response that they were continued, grew in number to four each year, and developed into schools. An expert in some field of rural life serves on each faculty, competent Bible teachers conduct classes, and there are seminars on the program of the rural church. The developing of curriculum, the securing of faculty, the enrolling of students, and the management of the schools while they are in session demand most of the time of one person. At first Rev. C. R. McBride was stationed at Green Lake for this purpose. Later, Rev. H. C. Loughhead took his place. Then Rev. Robert T. Frerichs went to Green Lake to give his whole time to the Rural Church Center, the schools, and some rural developments in nearby states. By 1950 pastors from every state in the Convention except Delaware had attended, as had also quite a few from Puerto Rico, Nicaragua, and Alaska. By 1955 thirty-one Baptist schools had been held, besides five interdenominational schools; and more than seven hundred pastors had received training. One of the nation's most competent educators has declared that these schools are the denomination's most creative enterprises in the entire field of ministerial training.

During these years a well-equipped Rural Church Center has been developed at Green Lake. The major expense has been met by the Home Mission Society, but The Board of Education and Publication has shared in the planning and expense. The administration of the Center has been in the hands of the Home Mission Society. An unusually comprehensive rural church library has been assembled for the use of the schools and for the lending of books by mail. A group of buildings has been set aside and furnished to provide housing for the staff throughout the entire year, and classrooms, library, office, chapel, handcraft shop, and other facilities. Some rural paintings of special merit have been assembled. Besides the schools at Green Lake, extension institutes are held in various parts of the country. Often the extension institutes include choir clinics to help volunteer musical leaders.

For some time the need had been felt for a National Planning Conference. The hope was to bring together a substantial number of people to discuss what the denomination could do to be more helpful to the town and country churches. At the suggestion of the Home Mission Society, the Associated Home Mission Agencies took up the project and from July 28 to August 3, 1948, the first such conference was held at Green Lake. There were 130 persons in attendance, among them a representative group of rural pastors and lay persons. Out of this conference came a worth-while program of advance in rural church work. The findings, published in a series of pamphlets, have been widely used by leaders and churches.

As a result of this planning conference, the Associated Home Mission Agencies set up a Commission on Rural Advance. The resolution establishing this commission stated its purpose as being "for interagency cooperation in developing policies and carrying out the program for rural church advance, for voluntary coordination of the activities of the agencies working directly in rural fields, and to advise the agencies of rural needs and rural religious conditions." The Commission consisted of representatives of the two Home Mission Societies, The Board of Education and Publication, the Council of State Secretaries, the Council of City Secretaries, the Directors of Town and Country, the pastors, the laymen, the seminaries and colleges, the National Committee on Woman's Work (later the National Council of American Baptist Women), the National Council of American Baptist Men, the Baptist Youth Fellowship, and the Council on Christian Social Progress. The commission was given this comprehensive representation in order to bring to bear on the rural task all of the resources of the denomination. It had the right to add to its membership representatives from any other denominational agency that in its judgment might have a contribution to make to its effectiveness.

The commission planned to meet annually for two days to study thoroughly the needs, to build programs, and to meet special situations as they might arise. It has made an important contribution to the coordination of efforts on the rural field, thereby making the work of all the agencies more effective.

Another outcome of the conference of 1948 was the Baptist Rural Convocation held at Green Lake in 1951. This was a more popular gathering and had about five hundred in attendance. It featured general addresses and seminars. Out of it came a Standard for the Rural Church and a series of six study leaflets on *The Mission of the Church*. These documents became the standard handbook for rural church work for some time. This Convocation proved so successful that it was determined to hold others at regular intervals. One was held in 1954 and at the time of this writing quadrennial conferences are being planned, beginning in 1959. There had been for some time an inter-denominational Rural Convocation in which Baptists had always participated. The desire of several denominations to hold their own convocations led to a plan by which the interdenominational meeting would be omitted once every four years, and the denominational convocations would be held in that year. This arrangement has become a regular part of the rural church program in the American Baptist Convention.

A basic problem of the small church is to provide a sufficient salary to support a well-trained minister. This has been recognized from the beginning, and one of the tasks of the Home Mission Society and of every state convention through the years has been to make grants-in-aid, however named, to assist in the support of such pastors. For a number of years there had been great dissatisfaction with this method, for it did not seem to be accomplishing its purpose. One reason may have been that the amount appropriated tended to remain the same, and under changed conditions might be entirely inadequate. After much study, the Minimum Salary Plan was devised. This plan called for each state to establish a minimum salary to be paid to all pastors in churches which met certain standards of training, planning, and program. The money was to be provided by all the churches of the state, each being asked to contribute a certain per cent of the amount it paid its own pastor, or a certain per cent of its local expense budget, thereby creating a fund from which the salaries of the qualifying pastors could be supplemented so as to bring them up to the minimum standard which had been set.

A full discussion of the problems involved finally led the National Planning Conference of 1948 to recommend that the plan be put into effect experimentally in three or four states. This was done, and within three years the plan was adopted by six states: Ohio, New York, Massachusetts, Washington, Pennsylvania, and West Virginia. There were some surprising results. A number of churches, when approached about the matter, said that if the amount set by the state convention was considered the minimum salary, they could pay it themselves, and they at once raised their pastor's salary accordingly. A great many churches could not qualify because their program did not meet the requirements or because the pastor had not taken sufficient training. Gradually the minimum salary was raised until a balance was struck between the money available and the number of churches qualifying. In 1956 the minimum ranged in different states from $2,800 to $3,400. This cooperation has proved to be the most effective means so far found for enabling the churches to secure the trained leadership they need. The Ministers and Missionaries Benefit Board has been giving leadership in this field, and so also has the Central States Project.

Colporter Work

There were always, in the parts of America that were being settled, large areas in which the population was too sparse to have meeting houses and regular church services. In some sections the natural resources were such that they could support only a few settlers. Yet, in the aggregate there were many

people there who needed a religious ministry. In response to
this need, itinerant missionaries were sent into those areas to
go from house to house, bringing the Christian message into the
homes, leading family worship, gathering little groups for
worship and Bible study wherever that was possible, and talking
with such individuals as they might encounter. These colporters
carried with them Bibles and other religious literature which
they sold to the people, as well as tracts for free distribution.
In the early days they were pioneer evangelists. They organized
Sunday schools and established churches. They helped the young
churches to put up buildings and to call pastors. More recently
they have carried on a more permanent type of ministry in
sparsely settled areas. Even today the problem of adequately
churching these areas challenges our denomination and others to
intensive study and creative planning.

These missionaries used such means of transportation as
the times afforded. The first of them walked. Often a colporter
bore a yoke across his shoulders by means of which he carried
his burden of Bibles and other religious literature. Some rode
horses and stowed their literature in well-loaded saddle bags.
Later they used horses and buggies or light spring wagons. Still
later, automobiles became the standard means of transportation.
There also were gospel boats that visited remote sections of the
seacoast. In 1956 one such boat, *The Evangel,* was in use in
the waters around Kodiak Island, Alaska.

Another variant was the chapel car. Each of these railroad
cars contained an apartment in which the missionary lived and
also a chapel in which meetings could be held. The chapel
would accommodate from ninety to one hundred and twenty-five
persons and was equipped with a handsome brass lectern, an
organ, and pews with hymnbook racks. Seven such cars were in
use at one time or another. In the days of railroad building they
were very popular. The railroads welcomed their aid in establishing new communities along their lines and provided free
transportation. Later, the railroads charged for transportation and

for laying the spur on which the car would remain for the duration of its visit to a community. At the same time that these charges were becoming heavier, the need for this type of service was decreasing and other methods were being found more effective. In 1946, Chapel Car Grace was withdrawn from service and placed on the grounds at Green Lake as a part of the group of buildings known as the Rural Church Center. There it stands as a memorial to Christian service in a day that has gone, and as a mute testimony to the inventive genius of the missionary societies in adapting their methods to the needs of the times. Chapel Car Immanuel has come to rest on the assembly grounds in South Dakota. Other cars became the basis for church buildings. All of them are now honorably retired from service.

A more recent substitute for the colporter's horse and buggy was the auto-trailer chapel, with living quarters for the missionary and space to hold small gatherings. It could be taken into a community where there was no church and used for the initial work. In 1944 there were seven such car-trailers in service.

The colporter ministry was begun by The American Baptist Publication Society in 1840. Later The American Baptist Home Mission Society also began appointing colporters. At one time there were over two hundred of them. For many years the work of these missionaries of the two Societies was so similar that administrative difficulties arose. Efforts to adjust them met with little success until 1918. At that time the two Societies reached agreements which placed Christian education entirely with The American Baptist Publication Society and (by implication) the founding of churches with The American Baptist Home Mission Society. The administration of the colporter work was to be in the hands of one Society, but it was to be conducted in fullest conference and cooperation with the other Society. In 1918 the administration of this work was placed with the Home Mission Society. In 1922 it was transferred to the Publication Society under the direction of its Bible and field secretary, Rev. Samuel G. Neil, who later was succeeded by Dr. John C. Killian.

Changing conditions, however, made it increasingly evident that colporter work would have a decreasing interest to the Publication Society and would be a more natural activity of the Home Mission Society. Informal discussions took place from time to time, and in 1942, when Dr. Killian retired, there was a general reassignment of the work. Colporters in Latin America were transferred to the Latin-America Department of the Home Mission Society. Colporters among bilingual people were transferred to the Department of Cities of the Home Mission Society, which administered all other phases of the Home Mission Society's bilingual work. In both cases, upon the retirement of those already under appointment, the work was integrated into the general field program. The work was continued, but under a different name. Colporters supported wholly by one Society went to that Society for administration. Those that remained with the Publication Society became known as Christian education workers, rather than as colporters. There remained twelve colporters and three chapel-car missionaries who were jointly supported. These were assigned to the Home Mission Society in the Department of Town and Country.

This arrangement continued until 1949 when the Publication Society's share in colporter and chapel-car service was transferred entirely to the Home Mission Society. Thus was brought to a conclusion an issue that had been before the denomination for more than fifty years. Democracy works slowly, but in the end the problem was solved and everyone was well satisfied with the result.

Colporter work, although considerably reduced, is still meeting a specific need. Recently the Annual Report of the Society stated: "These colporters work out from a center for fifty to a hundred miles in all directions. In many instances they are the only missionaries in the area." In Moab, Utah, a town of twelve hundred people, which is 55 to 60 per cent Mormon, Rev. Floyd L. Butler was pastor of the only non-Mormon church. He had in his congregation Catholics, Baptists, Methodists, Presbyterians,

Disciples, Congregationalists, Episcopalians, and cultists. He traveled among the other small communities of the county, held services as he could, and visited the ranches in the open country. He reported a campaign of home visitation evangelism, led by one of the directors of evangelism of the Home Mission Society, as a result of which fourteen were baptized and eleven united with the church by letter or experience. All but four of these were adults. On May 1, 1954, that field became self-supporting. In 1956 an ordained woman, Rev. Jeannie Sherman, in South Dakota, was ministering to an area of 4,000 square miles, in much of which she was the only Christian worker. Rev. Clifford W. Jervis, in the Devil's Tower Larger Parish, centering at Hulett, Wyo., was covering one-third of the county, and counties in the west are as large as some states in the east!

Dr. Mark Rich had felt for some time that the burden of administration prevented him from doing the creative work in the field of the rural church that needed to be done. Accordingly, on March 17, 1948, the department was divided. The Indian work, the colporter work, and the aiding of rural churches were placed in a department entitled the Department of Rural and Indian Missions. The general work with rural churches was retained in the Department of Town and Country. Dr. Rich handled both departments until a secretary could be found for the new one. Later in the same year, the Board called Rev. Joseph H. Heartberg, pastor of the First Baptist Church of Webster City, Iowa, as secretary of the Department of Rural and Indian Missions. This set Dr. Rich free to give his entire time to the more general program of the rural church, including the development and management of the increasingly important Rural Church Center at Green Lake.

This arrangement continued until August 31, 1952, when Dr. Rich resigned to join the faculty of the Columbia Bible College in Columbia, Mo. The two departments were then reunited, and Mr. Heartberg was placed in entire charge. To assist him, two field workers were appointed: Rev. Richard

Furman, to devote himself entirely to the work with Indians, and Rev. Clayton A. Pepper, to give his whole time to the rural churches. Rev. Robert Frerichs continued as director of the Rural Church Center. Thus Mr. Heartberg had an adequate organization for handling this large work.

On November 15, 1955 an experiment in helping pastors who had received only a limited training was begun in five states: Minnesota, North Dakota, South Dakota, Nebraska, and Iowa. It is called the Central States Project. Use will be made of all the techniques found valuable, such as: in-service training, pre-service training, recruitment, minimum salary plans, larger parishes and other methods of grouping churches, placement procedures, and the use of auxiliary (lay) ministers.

A General Central States Project Council directs the program. It is made up of representatives of The Board of Education and Publication, The American Baptist Home Mission Society, The Ministers and Missionaries Benefit Board, the Commission on the Ministry, the Ministers' Council, the National Council of American Baptist Men, the five State Conventions, Sioux Falls College, Northern Baptist Theological Seminary, and Central Baptist Theological Seminary. Administratively it is related to The Board of Education and Publication. The budget is provided by The Board of Education and Publication, The American Baptist Home Mission Society, The Ministers and Missionaries Benefit Board, and the five State Conventions. Rev. Otto Nallinger, formerly the executive secretary of the South Dakota Baptist Convention, was called as director.

Thus the Department of Town and Country administers quite a large group of missionaries, but its more important task is to bring broader vision and better methods to all of the churches in the town and country area. Strengthening the ministry, enriching the program, increasing funds both for salaries and for service, and securing a clearer understanding of the needs of the field and a better adjustment of the means of meeting them— all are included in its objectives.

Integration of the work of the two Home Mission Societies affected the work of this department in two ways: certain missionaries of the Woman's Society who were working in the rural field were transferred to this department, and the Indian work was taken from this department and placed in the new department of Alaska, Indian Work, and Schools in the United States. Mr. Heartberg was continued as secretary.

VIII

Ministry to the Original Americans

THE STORY OF THE TREATMENT of the Indian Americans by the Caucasian Americans is largely one of injustice. The brightest chapter in the story has to do with the attempts of Christians to share their faith with their Indian brethren. From the beginning, Baptists have been active in this effort and have made a large contribution to the total result. The period covered by this book has been one of steady advance in this work.

The American Baptist Home Mission Society works among the Indians in six states: Oklahoma, Arizona, California, Nevada, Montana, and New York. Besides the evangelistic efforts and church leadership of the missionaries, the Society maintains Bacone College at Bacone, Okla., and Murrow Children's Home on the campus of Bacone College. Three Christian Centers have been established in recent years to minister to the Indians in Reno, Nev.; Clovis, Calif., and Anadarko, Okla.

The work of the Society with the Indians has been extended at several points. After World War II a large tract of fertile irrigated land at Poston, Ariz., was opened by the government to settlement by Navajo and Hopi Indians from the northern part of the state. The families to occupy this land were carefully selected on the basis of their probable success in developing good farms. The land was sold to them on an easy long-term payment plan, and money was loaned to them to buy the materials for houses, which had to be built according to approved plans. When the first group of families was selected, it was found that thirteen of the first fifteen families came from the mission of the two Home Mission Societies at Keams Canyon and First and Second

Mesa. These Indians wanted one of their missionaries to go to the new location with them. Since there was no religious work at Poston, the Home Mission Society agreed to send Rev. Arthur F. Loveridge to this field. He arrived there November 15, 1948. This land had been used during World War II as a relocation center for interned Japanese-Americans, and the temporary shelters provided for them were still on the grounds. One of these was assigned to the missionary as a dwelling and two were made available for use by the church. In these very inadequate quarters the work began, and in June, 1949, a Baptist Community Church was organized.

In 1951 the Woman's American Baptist Home Mission Society sent Miss Lolita Stickler and Miss Mabel Olsen to assist in this work. In 1954 the Home Mission Society provided funds to build a parsonage for Mr. Loveridge and his family. Land had been assigned for a church and in 1955 the building was started. For this purpose the Society loaned the money, which the church will repay. Additional funds are still to be raised. The church has become interracial, through having received Mexicans and Negroes into its membership. The congregation had grown to 104, with a Sunday school of 152.

This situation was unusual. The Indians were a selected group, chosen for their probable success in farming. They had good irrigated land, with better prospects financially than any other Indians with whom American Baptists had worked. This meant that the church could go farther in self-support than most Indian churches have gone. It had unusually strong lay leadership also and therefore could be expected to develop an effective program. This church has fully justified the Society's expectations.

In 1932 the Arizona Baptist Convention was supporting work among the Indians at Clarkdale, Middle Verde, and Camp Verde. In 1935, when the financial situation of the Arizona Convention became very difficult, the Home Mission Society agreed to take over this Indian work. Rev. William J. Gordon was the missionary at that time. Upon his retirement he was succeeded by Rev. Perry L. Jackson, who moved there from the Saddle Mountain field in Oklahoma.

This work has steadily advanced. In 1956 there were three churches with 198 members. A new church building, a very beautiful structure faced with stone, has been erected at Middle Verde. All of the construction work was done by the missionary and the Indians, and most of the money was given by them and their friends. The other churches have made major improvements.

For many years the Woman's American Baptist Home Mission Society had supported missionaries at the Carson Indian school at Stewart, Nev., as well as in some of the Indian communities of that state. The American Baptist Home Mission Society had maintained a work at Reno and some outlying points. After careful consideration these Societies decided in 1939 that this field should be organized after the larger parish plan, so that all of the activities could be coordinated and thereby carried on more effectively. The missionary at Reno had resigned, and Rev. George W. Smart was appointed by the Home Mission Society to go to Stewart and share in that work. The Society built a residence for him there. At the same time, the Woman's Society enlarged the chapel and provided an apartment in it for their two missionaries. For a time the work of both Societies in the entire area was directed from this center.

The situation of the Indians in Reno was distressing. They were living in dire poverty and the moral conditions were extremely bad. There was not always a missionary in residence, and the lack of a missionary contributed to the delinquency and the people's slow response. It was thought that the Christian Center idea which had been so successful in the crowded areas of the cities might be adapted to this situation. In 1952 the Society built a small Christian Center and repaired and enlarged the chapel. Rev. Harold D. Shock was appointed missionary in charge. The work was carried on in the face of great difficulty. In 1955 Mr. Shock resigned to go to the foreign field under appointment by the American Baptist Foreign Mission Society. At that time further improvements were made on the property, and Rev. Hubert C. Matthews, Jr., was appointed to succeed him. The response to his efforts encouraged the hope that even more impressive results might be expected.

The promise of this Center, as well as of one conducted by the Woman's Society at Clovis, Calif., suggested their use at other points. Anadarko, Okla., was the seat of the government agency, and many Indians came there on business with the agency, to trade, and for other purposes. They had no place to gather in any social way except in the saloons. The missionaries believed that a Christian Center would be of real help. Conference was held with leaders in the city who were interested in the situation and the Society finally decided to establish a Center there. The people of the city took a great interest in the project. They provided the lot and some funds for the building, and the Society provided the remainder. This Center was dedicated in July, 1953, under the leadership of Rev. Charles R. Osborn, a missionary of the Society. It has developed in a gratifying way. It is managed by a Board of Directors, one-third of whom come from the Home Mission Society, one-third from the Indian churches in Oklahoma, and one-third from the community. This is a strong board and gives excellent leadership. The Center serves the other minority groups of the city as well as the Indians. There is a broad program of interest groups and crafts, as well as of Christian teaching and worship.

The properties of the Indian churches were greatly improved during these years. New churches were built at Red Stone and Rainy Mountain, Okla. (the latter replacing one that had burned), and at Poston and Middle Verde, Ariz. The church at Keams Canyon, Ariz., was completely rebuilt. Parsonages were erected at First Mesa, Keams Canyon, and Poston. The church at Crow Agency, Mont., was remodeled and a social hall added to it. Major improvements had been made at a number of other places.

Two problems that remained unsolved were closely related: self-support and Indian leadership. A number of Indians had secured college and seminary education. Although this number was not large, it probably was as large in proportion to the total Indian constituency as the number that had come out of the Caucasian churches. These graduates, however, had not stayed in the Indian work. Two fully trained Indian ministers were serving as pastors of Caucasian churches. Another was called to a place of leadership in the Indian work of the Southern Baptists. Rev. Wilkin Willis stayed in the work for several years, but finally became pastor of a Caucasian church. Rev. David Owl, missionary on the Cattaraugus Reservation in New York, was the only one who had consistently stayed with American Baptist Indian Missions. Rev. Barry E. Shongo, a Seneca Indian from New York and a product of Mr. Owl's work, went to Geary, Okla., in 1953, as pastor of a church there. He received his support from the Home Mission Society.

Self-support was related to this situation. When a man had gained a college and seminary training, he could not be expected to live as did so many of his fellow Indians. On the other hand, the Indians were neither willing nor able to provide the kind of salaries which the missionaries needed. Consequently, the support of the missionaries remained, with two or three exceptions, entirely with the Society. In those cases in which the Indians provided some help, the Society had to carry the larger portion of the expense. Some denominations had sought to solve this problem by using pastors who had received much less training, and who were willing to live more nearly at the level of the people whom they served. This arrangement had not seemed wise to the Board of Managers of the Home Mission Society.

A partial solution had been found where churches were closely grouped. Rev. J. Lester Raney, missionary at Anadarko, Okla., had been placed in charge of several churches. At the same time, lay leaders who were paid only an allowance for travel had been enlisted to assist him. Mr. Raney trained these men and directed their activities. This plan had worked out with reasonable satisfaction, but was feasible only where the churches were close enough together to be served in this way. The securing of adequately trained Indian pastors for Indian churches, properly supported by those churches, remained an unsolved problem.

On the Cattaraugus Reservation in New York an unusual piece of cooperative work was being done. Rev. David Owl went to that field first as missionary to the Baptist church. Later, when the Presbyterian missionary retired, the Presbyterian Board suggested the possibility of Mr. Owl's taking care of both churches. Thereafter he represented the two denominations. The other three churches (Methodist, Disciples, and Episcopal) cooperated closely; and some of the time Mr. Owl, as the only ordained missionary living on the field, gave friendly assistance to all. He was supported jointly by the Home Mission Society and the New York State Convention. The supreme testimony to his standing among the Indians was shown when the "longhouse people," the old pagan group, asked him to conduct a funeral for them.

Bacone College

In the early days of the Society's work among the Indians in Oklahoma, Dr. Almon C. Bacone (at the time under no appointment) felt the need of a Christian school and started one in Tahlequah under the name of The Indian Normal and Theological School. December 13, 1880, the Home Mission Board appointed Dr. Bacone as the principal. In 1881 he secured from the Creek tribal council a grant of 160 acres of land near Muskogee. He then obtained funds from certain friends of the Indians, among them being Mr. John D. Rockefeller, Sr., which made possible the erection of Rockefeller Hall to house the school. In May, 1885, the school was removed to its new location and became Indian University. At that time it had four teachers, a matron, and seventy students.

Indian University later became Bacone College, renamed in honor of its founder. A purchase of additional land enlarged the campus to three hundred acres. The number of buildings on the campus has steadily increased. The decade of the 1930's was one of considerable building activity. The General Education Board gave substantial support, the Society contributed generously, and friends of the college provided the remainder of the necessary funds. Dr. B. D. Weeks, president of the college at that time, raised a considerable amount. The new buildings erected were the Art Lodge, a dormitory, a building for Industrial Arts, the Home Demonstration Building, and the Chapel. Later a gymnasium was added.

Dr. Weeks continued as president until May 31, 1941. He was succeeded, May 1, 1943, by Rev. Earl Riley, a graduate of the college, and of Redlands University and the Eastern Baptist Theological Seminary. He held also the degree of Master of Arts in Education from the University of Pennsylvania. Between the resignation of Dr. Weeks and the inauguration of President Riley, Dean Edwin Dolan administered the school the first year, and Dean Marc Jack Smith the second. Mr. Riley was a member of the Creek tribe, though with but a small percentage of Indian blood. He served until December 31, 1947.

During Mr. Riley's administration an Advisory Board was organized to consult with the president and with the Board of Managers of The American Baptist Home Mission Society. It was elected by that Board, and was composed of nine representatives from Oklahoma, nine from the American Baptist Convention, and nine from the Board of Managers of The American Baptist Home Mission Society. This Board met twice a year to review the entire program, to make recommendations to the president concerning the policies and program of the college, and also to the Board of Managers of The American Baptist Home Mission Society concerning the general administration.

Following the administration of Mr. Riley, Dr. C. S. Detweiler was acting president. For many years he had been secretary of the Department of Latin America in the Home Mission Society and was nearing the time of retirement.

Rev. Wilbur Larson had been associated with him with a view to succeeding him. This made it possible for Dr. Detweiler to go to Bacone College as acting president, where he rendered a greatly needed service.

In the summer of 1948 Rev. Francis W. Thompson became president and served until September 30, 1955. Mr. Thompson had the degree of Bachelor of Arts from Redlands University and the degree of Bachelor of Divinity from Newton Theological Institution. While president he received the honorary degree of Doctor of Divinity from Redlands University. He had taught for a time at Bacone College. During his administration much was done to improve the school and also to spread a knowledge of it among the churches of the American Baptist Convention. In this he was greatly aided by the Bacone singers who became widely known and greatly loved.

From 1932 to 1957 there had been a steady improvement in the work done by the college. Rising costs were making it increasingly difficult to maintain the standards of the school, but the efforts put forth met with gratifying success. The academic level of the faculty had varied, but on the whole had risen. Indian art had been encouraged in a remarkable way under the leadership of Professor Walter Richard West. Professor West had done graduate work at Redlands University and had the degree of Master of Fine Arts from the University of Oklahoma. He had painted, among other subjects, some remarkable Indian interpretations of biblical events, and the students had the benefit of his unusual talents. Weaving, printing, and other industrial arts were taught. The farm belonging to the college was used to train the students in agriculture, so that those who went back to their farms would be able to cultivate them to better advantage. An outstanding graduate in this field was Tully Morrison, who operated a large ranch and raised blooded cattle.

In 1954 the Board of Managers of the Home Mission Society decided that in view of the celebration in 1956 of the seventy-fifth anniversary of the college, there should be a financial campaign for the rehabilitation of old buildings and the erection of some new ones, for endowment, and for the enlargement of current operations. The firm of Ketchum, Inc., was employed as financial counselors and Rev. Clifford G. Hansen, Public Relations Secretary for the Home Mission Society, gave a great deal of time to this campaign. Although the goal was not fully reached, the finances of the school gained a new stability.

Bacone College is an essential part of the program for the evangelization of the Indians. It is the only junior college in America entirely for Indians. It is accredited by the Oklahoma State Board of Education. It possesses a beautiful campus and does a grade of work of which the denomination can be proud. In 1955 it faced the rising tide of sentiment against segregated schools, and its future is uncertain. The free admission of white students would probably mean that the Indians would be crowded out by sheer force of numbers. This had happened in the early history of the school when both were admitted. It then had been found necessary to exclude the white students (aside from exceptional cases) to continue the services needed by the Indians. If the school should become simply another college which all who wish may enter, and with no specific missionary objective, it would cease to be an institution which the Home Mission Society should support. Many problems are involved and the solution is not clear. At the time of this writing, the college continues to render to the Indians a service that no other is providing. It had, in 1955, an enrollment of 176, representing fifty-five tribes from twenty-three states, Mexico, and Central America. On October 2, 1956, Mr. Roger Getz was inaugurated as president of the college.

The Murrow Children's Home

A home for homeless Indian children, started by J. S. Murrow, a missionary to the Indians, was moved in 1910 from Unchuka, Okla., to the campus of Bacone College, where better provision could be made for it, and where the management of the home and the college could be combined. In 1919 two large buildings, the best of their type in that day, were erected to house the children, and they were still in use in 1956. For several years, however, it had been recognized that the buildings were outmoded and that the cottage plan should be introduced. At the same time the college found itself crowded.

In view of this condition, when the campaign was launched by the Society in 1954 to raise funds for the college in connection with its approaching seventy-fifth anniversary, a campaign was also conducted to provide cottages to house the children. The latter campaign was directed by Dr. Gordon Palmer, long a member of the Board of Managers of The American Baptist Home Mission Society, and a good friend of all home mission enterprises. He was carrying on a widespread radio ministry and used that means to secure funds for the home. The campaign was successfully completed and three cottages are under construction. When the children move into the cottages, the vacated buildings will be remodeled and made into dormitories for Bacone College, thereby providing housing for a considerable number of additional students.[1]

Relocation of Indians

After World War II there was an increasing movement of Indians to the cities. The Bureau of Indian Affairs reported that during 1955, thirty-five hundred Indians moved from the reservations to places of greater employment opportunities. This was the largest number to go in any one year. The Bureau maintained relocation personnel in sixteen agencies to train Indians interested in making such a move. The missionaries also had their part in preparing the Indians for the new situations which they were entering.

Although these Indians moved to many different cities, the largest groups settled in Chicago, Denver, Los Angeles, and

[1] The Murrow children moved into the new cottages in October, 1956. An impressive dedication service was held.

Oakland. The Indian Bureau maintained a staff in those cities to aid the Indians in finding places to live and opportunities for work. There was a definite effort to have the Indians scatter throughout the city rather than to settle in colonies. Although this was wise for the Indians, it made more difficult the task of the Christian forces that sought to minister to them. A few churches had been quick to recognize their responsibilities to these new neighbors, but others showed no interest, or possibly were unaware of their presence. The Denver Christian Center reported in 1956 an Indian Fellowship meeting in its building with an attendance of from fifty to one hundred persons. The Christian Friendliness missionaries and volunteers did an outstanding work in establishing connection between the Indians and the churches.

The majority of the Indians, however, remained on the reservations. At the end of 1955 the Bureau of Indian Affairs reported about 250,000 Indians on the reservations. The missionaries continued their ministry in both situations and endeavored to adapt their methods to the changing conditions.

Another trend in 1956 was the inclination of the government to reduce its control over Indian affairs. There was no unanimity of opinion among the Indians themselves as to the desirability of this change. All agreed that they should have a voice in the disposal of tribal lands and that they should be prepared for the management of their own affairs. The missionary now found a new opportunity to be of service to his people. He needed to help them understand the regulations under which they lived, and at the same time he must prepare them in all possible ways to accept the larger opportunities of the new day.

When the two Societies became integrated, the work with the Indians was transferred from the Department of Town and Country to a new Department of Alaska, Indian Work, and Schools in the United States. Miss Dorothy O. Bucklin, who had directed the Indian work of the Woman's Society, was made secretary of the new Department.

IX

Ministry to Latin America

PART 1: MEXICO, CUBA, AND PUERTO RICO

THERE IS NO UNANIMITY OF OPINION among the denominations as to whether work in the part of Latin America which lies north of the Panama Canal is home missions or foreign missions. Some place it all with the one and some all with the other; some divide it between the two. Because the motto of The American Baptist Home Mission Society is "North America for Christ" and because all of the work of American Baptists in Latin America is north of the Panama Canal, American Baptists have placed all of this work with the two Home Mission Societies. The American Baptist Home Mission Society has work in three islands of the West Indies—Cuba, Haiti, and Puerto Rico; in Mexico; and in two countries of Central America —El Salvador and Nicaragua. The Woman's American Baptist Home Mission Society shares in the work in all of these fields except Haiti.

General Lines of Progress

The decade, 1930 to 1940, was a trying one in Latin America, as it was everywhere. The economy of the people was so linked with that of the United States that the depression here, combined with conditions there, created a difficult situation. Furthermore, the declining income of the Society forced a reduction in its support of the work. Throughout this period it was the policy of the Society to make a lower percentage of reduction in Latin America than in the States, because here the State

115

Conventions also could provide aid, whereas in Latin America there was no source of help except the two Home Mission Societies. It is a tribute to the broad vision of all of the secretaries that they readily agreed that this decision was wise. In spite of this policy, however, the reductions were grievous and were a source of great hardship to the workers in Latin America. The salaries of missionaries were reduced twice. The salaries of nationals declined in some cases to one-half of what they had been. Much to the credit of these workers, they continued their work faithfully throughout this period of trial. It was a great relief to everyone, therefore, when in 1941-42 it became possible to increase slightly the budget allotment to Latin America. The amount provided (with only minor setbacks) increased steadily, if slowly, until in 1951-52 it exceeded $175,000.

During this twenty-five year period the work has steadily expanded. Evangelism has gone forward, for the people in those countries are evangelists to an extent unknown in the United States. Baptist work in Latin America is a laymen's movement. Every well-established church has its outstations conducted largely by laymen. One pastor was reported in 1944 as having two "town churches" and sixteen preaching points. One of the churches reported that eighteen of its officers were regularly going to outstations and holding services; another reported that it had helped in starting twenty-five chapels. The church in Port-au-Prince, Haiti, had about fifty outstations served by more than one hundred laymen. These congregations may have been outstanding in the number of places at which they were working, but their methods were not at all exceptional. All the churches expected to have some outstations, many of which in time would become regularly organized churches. This has been the secret of growth on the mission fields, and it has produced remarkable results in Latin America.

This evangelizing spirit has developed also into a missionary spirit. Each country has its own organization for carrying on missionary work within its borders. The oldest are those in

Mexico and Puerto Rico, both dating from 1903. The Mexican Baptist Convention supports workers, mostly in the Indian villages of the more remote areas. In Puerto Rico the churches make their contribution directly to the budget of the mission. The amount spent in Puerto Rico for pastoral support (exclusive of school expenses and the salaries of missionaries) in 1955 was $9,300, of which the Puerto Rican churches gave $1,860. In Cuba the Convention was organized very early in the history of the mission, and in 1955 it supported about eighteen workers, most of them at new points and in rural areas. The Cuban churches in 1954-55 contributed $14,705 for missions. The local organizations in Nicaragua, El Salvador, and Haiti are much younger, for those fields were entered more recently, but they too have given a good account of themselves.

Not only did the people contribute to the missionary work of their own conventions, but from time to time they sent offerings for the general work of the Home Mission Societies and the American Baptist Convention, and even for relief work in Europe. A soul-stirring example of this occurred in 1948 when the Haitian churches, out of their own great poverty, sent an offering to the World Relief Committee of the Northern Baptist Convention. Thus a strong sense of missionary responsibility was developed among these very young churches.

Another marked development on these fields was the extent to which nationals have taken places of leadership. In the beginning, all of the work necessarily was done by the missionaries. But they immediately began to train their converts for leadership, and by 1956 all of the pastors and one of the six general missionaries were nationals, and another, Dr. Oscar Rodriguez, general missionary in Cuba, and his wife were from Puerto Rico. With the exception of two missionaries from the United States (one an appointee of The American Baptist Home Mission Society and the other an appointee of the Woman's American Baptist Home Mission Society), Colegios Internacionales in El Cristo, Cuba, was staffed entirely by nationals, and the theological seminary was conducted in large part by nationals. Puerto Rico had sent a missionary to Nicaragua. In Mexico all the workers were nationals except three doctors and two women missionaries.

Many of these nationals have had a commendable degree of training. Dr. Parajon, pastor of the First Baptist Church of Managua, Nicaragua, had done postgraduate work at Berkeley Baptist Divinity School and had received from that school the honorary degree of Doctor of Divinity. Dr. Donato Ramirez-Ruiz, general missionary in Mexico, held the degree of Bachelor of Divinity from Colgate Rochester Divinity School; he had done postgraduate work in the University of Mexico and at Central Baptist Seminary, and had the honorary degree of Doctor of Divinity from William Jewell College, his Alma Mater. Dr. Oscar Rodriguez, general missionary in Cuba, had done postgraduate work in Columbia University and Union Theological Seminary, and had the degree of Doctor of Philosophy from the former institution. Rev. Luis Fidel Mercado, pastor at Caguas, Puerto Rico, had the degree of Bachelor of Divinity from Eastern Baptist Theological Seminary and the degree of Master of Arts from the University of Pennsylvania. Rev. Alejandro Trevino Ojedo, pastor of the First Baptist Church in Mexico City and a professor in the seminary there, had the honorary degree of Doctor of Divinity from the Berkeley Baptist Divinity School. He is a thorough scholar, as much at home in Greek as in his native Spanish.

The training of pastors was one of the first concerns of the early missionaries. At first this had to be done by placing them in the work and then helping them in so far as conditions permitted. The writer met Rev. Joaquin Antunez, one of the first pastors appointed in Cuba. When asked how he became a minister, he related that he had been a captain in the Cuban army, and had been converted in a street meeting. He began to help as an interpreter, then to give his own testimony and to exhort his hearers to come to Christ. After a time he was sent to a rural area to evangelize the people and organize a church. Asked how he was trained, he replied: "Dr. Routledge, who was the general missionary at that time, would lend me a book. After I had read it I would spend a day with him discussing it and the problems on my field. Then he would lend me another book." It was another case of "Mark Hopkins on the end of a log and a student on the other end." At least five of the churches in Cuba in 1955 had been organized by Pastor Antunez, and three of them had come to be numbered among the strongest churches in the Cuban Convention.

Such methods belonged to the pioneer days, and later other methods had to be developed. Institutes for the pastors were held by the secretary of the Department for Latin America from the beginning, and have been of great value. In 1956, visiting the pastors was still a regular part of the secretary's duty. Occasionally students were sent to the States, but this method of training was expensive and frequently proved unsatisfactory as a basic education for the ministry. Educational theory and practice in the States were too far removed from the conditions under which these young pastors would work. Only postgraduate work, and that by mature men, could be done to advantage in the States. Some workers from Haiti were sent to Calabar College, the British Baptist college in Jamaica. The results were good, but the expense prevented sending very many. Difference in languages also was a major difficulty.

In 1932 Puerto Rico was the only one of these countries that had a theological seminary. Some training for the ministry was given in a theological department in the Colegios Internacionales at El Cristo, Cuba, but this was not adequate. By 1949 seminaries had been established in Cuba, Haiti, Mexico, and Nicaragua. The one in Nicaragua also cared for the needs of El Salvador. Thus, formal training was provided for ministers on all of the fields.

A less formal mode of developing leaders has been the sending of them to conferences, such as the Madras Conference;

the World Sunday School Conventions in Mexico City and in Toronto; and the schools for rural pastors at the Rural Church Center at Green Lake, Wis. Some pastors from these fields have been effective as deputation speakers in the States and have gained from their travels a broadened outlook.

It has been the policy of the Society from the beginning to transfer leadership to nationals as soon as possible. The steady improvement in training made such transfer feasible in a comparatively short time. Probably no mission conducted by American Baptists has made more rapid progress in this respect than Latin America.

Churches are not fully established until they are self-directing, self-propagating, and self-supporting. Of these essentials, self-support is the most concrete and most easily measured. In this matter also the churches in Latin America have made remarkable progress. In 1932 there were very few self-supporting churches in these countries. This was true even in Mexico where the Society had worked the longest. Since that time there has been marked progress. In 1956 there were many strong, self-supporting churches. The Convention or Home Mission Society of each country has done excellent work in organizing new churches.

This twenty-five-year period has also been one of marked progress in securing adequate housing and equipment, and this in spite of the high costs. First Church, Santiago de Cuba; First Church, Port-au-Prince, Haiti; Santurce Church in Puerto Rico; First Church, Mexico City; First Church, Puebla, Mexico; First Church, Santa Ana, El Salvador; First Church, Managua, Nicaragua—all have erected new buildings within this period.

At the same time, many smaller congregations, just as significant in their communities as these larger ones are in theirs, also were building. The Home Mission Society has aided with some grants of money, but more largely with loans without interest. Thus the work of God in these countries is today much better housed and better equipped.

Good church buildings have a significance beyond the fact that they enable the church to do better work. They are silent witnesses in the community. A church, like other institutions, is considered unstable and transitory until it has its own house. The character of the building bespeaks the strength and serious-ness of purpose of the people who worship in it. A substantial building will greatly aid a church in establishing its standing in the community.

The Protestant denominations working in Latin America carry on their cooperative work through the Committee on Cooperation in Latin America; and in the West Indies, through the West Indies Committee of the Division of Home Missions of the National Council of the Churches of Christ in the U.S.A. The West Indies Committee confines its interest to those islands and operates as a volunteer committee.

The Committee on Cooperation in Latin America was organ-ized in 1916 and at first operated as an independent organization. Later, it was related to the Foreign Missions Conference and then, through the Division of Foreign Missions, to the National Council. It has maintained a headquarters in New York city and has a field staff which has produced literature and audio-visual aids for the Latin-American fields. The literature has been printed in Mexico City and Buenos Aires. It also has promoted evangelism and has carried on an effective radio program. At the time of this writing, the Committee was engaged in producing a complete church school curriculum in Spanish, for previously no satisfactory curriculum for general use had been available.

The Home Mission Society has cooperated with this com-mittee from the beginning and has furnished a fair share of its support. It has been active also in the West Indies Committee from its inception.

Ministry in Mexico

Baptist work in Mexico began in 1864, when Rev. James Hickey, an Irish Baptist minister, went there as a colporter of the American Bible Society. Preaching in Monterrey, he soon made three converts. Two were Mexicans; the third was Thomas Westrup, a mechanic from the States. These three were baptized January 30, 1864, and with Mr. and Mrs. Hickey organized a church and made Mr. Westrup pastor. This is the oldest Protestant church in Mexico or in any of the Spanish-speaking countries in which American Baptists work.

The Home Mission Society heard of this work, made a careful study of it, and decided that it offered Baptists an opening in Mexico. The Society established connection with the work in 1870. From that small beginning, the number of churches had increased, by 1956, to thirty-three. These thirty-three churches maintained 117 outstations and had 5,298 members. There also were two schools and a theological seminary; one of the best hospitals and nurses' training schools in Mexico; and a rural clinic in an extremely needy area in southern Mexico, directed by Dr. Ota G. Walters, a highly competent physician.

The hospital purchased its first property in Puebla in 1915. During the present period it has been in charge of Dr. F. L. Meadows, a skilled physician and surgeon and an utterly devoted missionary. Under his leadership the hospital has come to be recognized as one of the outstanding medical centers in Mexico. The training school for nurses also has a very high standing, and the graduates are so much in demand that it has been difficult for the hospital to maintain an adequate staff for its own work. In 1956 the only foreign worker in the hospital besides Dr. Meadows was Dr. Everett B. Myer, who went there in 1953. The rest of the personnel were Mexican. All of the doctors have taken postgraduate training in the States and visit the States from time to time for refresher courses.

The two schools mentioned above, one at Puebla and the other at Monterrey, were established by the Woman's American Baptist Home Mission Society. The Mexican law required them to be under local direction, but the Woman's Society continued to contribute to the cost of operation.

For many years the laws of Mexico were such that there could be no theological seminary. During that time some men were sent to the Spanish-American Baptist Seminary in Los Angeles, but the expense was high and the results were not wholly satisfactory. Finally, in 1947 it became possible to organize a seminary. Under the Mexican law religious teaching is not allowed anywhere but in a church. Accordingly, the seminary acquired a property which provided living quarters for the president and one of the professors, as well as for the student body. During the first few years the classes were held in First Baptist Church, Mexico City; but in 1955 a chapel was built and dedicated for church services, and thereafter the classes were held there. The course was of a nature to fit the students for work in their own country, and regular appointments in the churches within reach gave them practical experience.

The seminary was organized under the leadership of Rev. Orlando Tibbetts, who at first was president as well as general missionary. Later, when Dr. Donato R. Ramirez became general missionary, Mr. Tibbetts gave his full time to the school. In 1953 Mr. Tibbetts returned to the States, and Dr. Ramirez became president of the seminary, in addition to being general missionary. Already this seminary has made a real contribution to the life of the churches. In 1955 fourteen graduates were in the pastorate and eleven students were enrolled.

During the 1950's the First Church of Mexico City began erecting what probably will be the largest and best equipped Baptist church building in any of these fields. The congregation had outgrown their property long before, even though they had enlarged it. On January 1, 1949, they began replacing the old church and a building on an adjacent lot with a new structure, tearing down one part and carrying on their work as well as they could in the remainder, while they put up the new building on the land thus vacated. When this became usable they moved into it, tore down what was left of the old building and built the rest of the new. At the time of writing, this undertaking had not been completed. This construction was due very largely to the initiative and ability of the church, the aid of the Home Mission Society being definitely a minor part.

The Development in Cuba

Missionary work was begun in Cuba within two weeks of the signing of the peace treaty with Spain. In January, 1899, Rev. H. R. Moseley came from Mexico to direct it. At that time there was a group of Evangelical Christians in Havana, but none, so far as the record shows, in eastern Cuba. The masses of the people were not even aware that there was any church other than the Roman Catholic. They were immediately interested, however, and soon in Santiago a little group of believers was organized into a church. Before long other groups sprang up in various places. From the beginning the people have been warmly evangelistic. The believers have witnessed constantly, and by their Christian living they have made their testimony effective. The churches which were formed have regularly sent out their members to other communities to witness to the people. Often individuals went on their own initiative and at their own expense on extensive evangelistic tours.

In 1943 the Cuban Baptist Convention organized a simultaneous evangelistic campaign in which the pastors and people widely participated. As a result, over eight hundred professions of faith were reported. The churches were aroused to a new sense of responsibility for the unreached and became more active in their efforts to win them for Christ.

In 1953 Dr. Rodriguez reported another campaign which had some unique features and accomplished a great deal of good:

"The Board of Evangelism, in cooperation with our Baptist Seminary, has undertaken a new venture of community evangelism through the rural areas. After studying the plans submitted by Rev. Pedro Abella, head of the Department of Evangelism of the seminary, a rural area was chosen to serve as the field of operation for this project. A carefully chosen group of specialists joined the seminary students and spent a whole week at Realengo Diez y Ocho, one of the most promising rural areas in our Cuban mission. A medical doctor, a lawyer, an agronomist, a dentist, an economist, a school teacher, a social worker, and a nurse—all of them Christians—joined three seminary professors and the students to carry out the plan. Starting at eight in the morning and ending with the evangelistic meeting in the evening, the group engaged in a program which made itself felt in all phases of community life. Each specialist did his part in making Christianity a working reality for a community of which Realengo Diez y Ocho is a type. It was an object lesson in the workings of the gospel in a community opened to its influence. The people were face to face with a reality which they had never before experienced. It was the church at work in putting forth the content of the gospel of Christ. The sick were ministered to, and the homes were touched through the practical presentation of Christian homemaking, including order, cleanliness, and discipline. It was a revelation to the many who came in touch with this plan. The farmers heard of practical methods for improving their plantations and their stock; wives were given instructions as to self-care and the raising of children; steps were taken to organize a producer's and consumer's cooperative.

"This has grown into a movement in that community which has brought together farmers who were never interested in the church. The president of the cooperative, now in its early stages, is a Roman Catholic who is beginning to show understanding of what the gospel is and what it takes to be a living witness of the teachings of Christ. Other rural areas are in our plans for similar visits. We believe that this new approach to rural evangelism is one of the great needs of a country like Cuba with its 60 per cent rural population. Before we can hope to carry this program forward we must get some needed equipment, such as a jeep with trailer, a portable power plant, a movie projector, a public speaking system, and such other essential items as will make possible the various aspects of the project."[1]

There also has been an excellent growth in self-government and self-direction. Very early in the history of the mission, the Cuban Convention set up a committee to supervise the assignment of funds received from the Home Mission Society for the support of pastors. This committee undertook to decrease the subsidies from the Society and to increase correspondingly the share carried by the churches themselves. This was done with

[1] The American Baptist Home Mission Society. Annual Report for 1954. p. 84.

a view to using the released funds for new work in Cuba. This plan was developed successfully despite the limited financial means of the people. The pastors and lay persons of the churches have acquired an initiative and ability for self-direction that could have been produced only by throwing such responsibility on them.

The Cuban Baptist Convention has become a significant institution. Organized early in the history of the mission, it has grown through the years until in 1955 it was supporting eighteen missionaries and was responsible for most of the advance work in Cuba. One of its missionaries gave his full time to ministering to the Haitians who worked on the sugar plantations. Others were pastors at new points where the churches were just getting started.

The Haitians referred to above had been brought to Cuba specifically to do the heavy work on the sugar plantations. There were many thousands of them, just how many is not certain. There were Evangelicals among them, who came from the American Baptist mission in Haiti. These began to gather for prayer and Bible study and soon there were informally organized church groups. A time came when they had converts whom they wanted baptized. They also wanted the Lord's Supper administered, but there were no ordained ministers among them. Although they were French speaking, while the Cubans were Spanish speaking, they turned to nearby Cuban Baptist ministers for aid. Language barriers were surmounted as best they could be, and the Cuban pastors gladly helped. This association grew, and finally the Cuban Baptist Convention sent one of its workers to give his full time to this work.

This ministry has had gratifying results. In 1940 a Haitian Baptist Convention was organized in the Province of Camaguey. In 1952 Dr. Rodriguez, the general missionary in Cuba, reported forty-three Haitian churches. Many of the Haitians who went back to their homeland started churches in communities where there had been none. Thus the history of the Home Mission

Society among foreign language groups in the United States has been duplicated in Cuba.

The system of Baptist schools in Cuba centers in Colegios Internacionales, at El Cristo, which was established early in the history of the mission and filled the chief place in training for leadership. It was well equipped, with the best set of buildings of any of the schools which the Home Mission Society operated in Latin America. Unfortunately, by 1955, the buildings were becoming old and much in need of expensive repairs. The enrollment of the school, which was about 250, was divided between the primary school and the secondary school. Dr. Routledge, throughout his administration as president of the school was also the general missionary; and so also was Dr. Larson later. When Dr. Rodriguez was sent as general missionary, Rev. T. H. Shupbach was appointed president. In 1954 he returned to the States, and Rev. J. Mario Casanella succeeded him.

This school has steadily fulfilled its purpose in producing trained leadership for the churches and for the nation. The high place which it holds in the minds of the leaders of the republic was demonstrated at the celebration of the fiftieth anniversary of the opening of the work in Cuba. On that occasion, the people raised a fund to bring Dr. Routledge from London, Ontario, Canada, where he had made his home since his retirement in June 1940. At the principal celebration there were present not only the leaders of the Cuban Baptist Convention, but also several high officials of the state. Among them were the Under Secretary of the Department of the Interior, the personal representative of the Governor of the Province, and the Provincial Superintendent of Schools. The Governor expressed his regret at not being able to be present in person, and a few days later he gave a reception in honor of Dr. Routledge at the Governor's palace. The unanimous expressions of appreciation of Dr. Routledge and for the school gave a clear indication of the standing of the school in the estimation of the public. This was further certified when Dr. Routledge was decorated with the Order of

Carlos Manuel de Cespedes, the highest honor the Cuban Government awards to civilians.

The work in Cuba has been distinguished by the large number of self-supporting day schools conducted by the churches.
Classes were held in the church building, and usually the pastor
and his wife both taught. In the larger schools, additional teachers were employed. The people were very willing to pay the
reasonable fees charged for attendance. In 1955 the primary
and elementary schools reported an enrollment of 1,885 and
the secondary schools an enrollment of 576. There were 143
teachers in all.

The need for these schools in the churches arose from a
number of factors: Public education was not developed to the
extent it should be. The Roman Catholic Church dominated the
public schools, and Protestants were under a handicap. It was
claimed that the discipline and the moral standards in the public
schools were low. The people, therefore, desired that the churches
should conduct schools. These schools were attended, however,
not only by the children connected with the churches, but also
by many who had no connection with them. As long as these
other students were ready to receive the religious instruction given
and conduct themselves in a suitable manner, they were welcome. These schools greatly strengthened the work of Colegios
Internacionales. They served as feeders to it and also extended
training where it could not reach.

Such a school did not prove to be a distraction in the life
of the church; instead, it added to the prestige of the church
in the community, and it produced for the church a better trained
leadership. It raised the educational level of the community,
and thus became a bulwark against fanatical hostility. There
seldom was serious persecution where there was an effective
school. As to the effect directly on the church, it was reported
that when the day school was opened in Palma Soriano, the
Sunday school attendance jumped from fifty to two hundred and
fifty.

In Cuba, as everywhere, the training of the ministry is crucial in the work of the churches. Apparently the first effort in Cuba at formal training for the ministry was made when Colegios Internacionales established a theological department in which men studied for the ministry and women for missionary work. In 1939 sixteen young people were fitting themselves for Christian service. However, there was still need for an institution giving its entire attention to theological education.

In 1944 Dr. Ralph Felton, a widely known specialist in rural church work, visited Cuba to study the situation there. He recommended that an interdenominational seminary should be located in some rural area and devote itself particularly to training men for the rural ministry. His recommendation grew out of the fact that much of Cuba is rural and that the rural areas were sorely neglected. This recommendation was received by the Cuban Evangelicals with much interest, but it was never carried out.

In 1947, however, an interdenominational seminary was opened at Matanzas by the Presbyterians and the Methodists. It was hoped that the Baptists would share in that effort, and for a time the attempt was made. Both The American Baptist Home Mission Society and the Cuban Baptist Convention voted to cooperate in this movement and two students were sent there. This arrangement proved unsatisfactory, for the school was outside Northern Baptist territory. When the work was opened in Cuba, it was agreed that the Home Mission Board of the Southern Baptist Convention should occupy the western part of the island and The American Baptist Home Mission Society should occupy the two eastern provinces of Oriente and Camaguey. The fact that Matanzas was in Southern Baptist territory meant that the students did not have opportunity for serving small churches while in the seminary unless the Southern Baptists appointed them, and in that case they naturally were influenced to remain in the Southern Baptist work. There was further agitation, therefore, for the opening of a seminary which would strengthen American Baptist work.

On October 10, 1949, the Cuban Baptist Convention on its own initiative and without the formal cooperation of the Home Mission Society, opened a theological seminary in the First Baptist Church of Santiago. The building was well adapted to such use and served satisfactorily as a temporary home for the school. It opened with eight regular students and twenty-two students in the extension department. Although planned on the basis of a four-year course of study, it was unique in that one class covered the entire course before a new class was admitted. This enabled the faculty, all of whom were pastors of churches, to give more attention to each class than could otherwise be done. The location in Santiago had several advantages: it made possible additional study in the university; pastors could more readily be enlisted to give a part of their time to teaching in the seminary; and numerous opportunities for work were available to the students. From the beginning this school has been a success. By 1955, nine students had graduated and become pastors, and twelve more were in training.

It was soon felt that the school must have a home of its own. In 1950 a property was found which could be purchased at a price that could be afforded. It was located in an outlying section of the city which could easily be reached by bus. Some buildings were on it, others have since been built, and many improvements have been made. The Home Mission Society made a loan for the purchase of the property and contributed $1,000 a year toward the operating expense. The Woman's Society provided a missionary who served as the house mother. Otherwise, the seminary has been supported entirely by the Cuban Baptists.

Thus, the Cuban Baptist Convention has a well-articulated educational system, the most complete of any in the Latin-America mission. The local schools are entirely self-supporting; the school at El Cristo completes the student's preparation for the university; and the theological seminary trains the pastoral leadership for the churches.

While carrying on very effectively as a denomination, the Cuban Baptists have always been active in cooperative work. In 1941 a Council of Churches was organized. It was led by a pastor who gave part of his time as secretary. It had a small budget to which the Baptists, along with the other denominations, contributed. The Council held one of its annual meetings at Colegios Internacionales. One year, Dr. Rodriguez was the president. The Baptists always send a large delegation to the annual meeting.

Baptists not only have cooperated but also have furnished their full quota of leadership for the numerous international conferences. They were well represented at the youth conference in Havana in 1946, which brought together one hundred delegates from eighteen Latin-American countries, and had seven thousand in attendance at one of the public meetings. Three Baptists were on the Cuban delegation to the Curriculum Building Conference at Cienfuegos, Cuba. There also were Cuban Baptists in the delegation to the World Sunday School Conventions held in Mexico City and in Toronto.

In Cuba, as elsewhere, this quarter of a century has been a period of extensive property improvement. The greatest building enterprise was that of the First Baptist Church, Santiago. In 1932 an earthquake had so damaged the building that it was unfit for use. Although temporary repairs had been made and the services had been continued as well as could be under the circumstances, something more had to be done, and the congregation alone was quite unequal to the task. Since the property had a strategic location in the center of the city and was on a corner that was valuable for business, it was thought best to erect a large building, fully equipped for the manifold ministry which this church carried on, but with stores on the ground floor, the rent from which would provide a good income. Between January, 1936, and April, 1937, the Society provided $105,000 from its permanent funds, part of the amount as a grant and part to be repaid through the rental of the stores.

At that time this was the largest Baptist church building in Latin America, and the congregation proved worthy of it, holding a place of leadership in the entire Cuban mission. The erection of this building gave Baptists a place of dignity in the city.

Many other churches have erected new buildings or have enlarged or improved their old buildings during this time. Usually this was done with the help of the Home Mission Society. Sometimes a grant was made for such an enterprise, but more commonly a loan was made from the edifice funds, to be repaid within a few years and usually bearing no interest.

In March, 1949, the Cuban Baptist Convention celebrated the fiftieth anniversary of the opening of the work on the island. When, in 1899, the first missionary arrived, there were no known Evangelicals in the eastern part of the island, but a remarkable change had been wrought in the fifty years. In 1949 there were 78 Cuban churches with 4,081 members, and 37 Haitian churches with about 900 members. There were 430 Sunday schools with a total enrollment of 12,933 and an average attendance of 9,618. The churches carried on work in 235 preaching stations and 146 organized missions. In that year they contributed $55,771 for church support and $10,000 for missions. How great are the results of faith and dedicated service in the hands of God!

A delegation from the States visited Cuba to share in celebrating the anniversary. The members of the delegation were royally entertained, and they spent several days visiting the churches. When the Convention held its sessions in the First Baptist Church, Santiago, the members of the team shared in the program. How effectively the work had been done was clearly demonstrated by the efficient way in which the Convention carried on its business.

Maturing Work in Puerto Rico

The year 1932 was a time of great difficulty for the work in Puerto Rico. There had been a severe hurricane in 1928 and the effects of it had not yet been overcome. The churches were handicapped and many of the members were suffering greatly. The two Home Mission Societies had raised $90,000 for relief, but this sum had not sufficed to restore the damaged church property, to say nothing of also helping the people. Aid from the Federal Government was inadequate for the need.

The work was not to go forward without further testing. The Pentecostals had come to Puerto Rico, and they pursued a policy of disrupting existing Christian bodies rather than evangelizing the unreached. For a time the Baptist churches were disturbed. Two of the pastors became infected with the new doctrine, and one of them led his church to secede from the mission and go over to the new group. This incident, however, proved the strength of the Baptists. The Puerto Rican Baptist Convention took the matter in hand, forced the withdrawal of the other disaffected pastor, and cleared the other churches of such disturbing influences. In a short time the church that had withdrawn from the mission dismissed its pastor and returned to the Convention. This trouble left the Baptists stronger, more closely knit, and more sure of their ground than they had ever been before.

Barranquitas Academy encountered new competition about this time. The Roman Catholic Church, which had never paid any attention to the rural areas in any of the Latin-American countries until the Evangelicals came and undertook work there, began to enter these fields. When it was seen that Barranquitas Academy was raising up trained leadership in the central part of the island, the Roman Catholics built a high school nearby. Because they were able to put much larger resources behind it than the Society could put behind Barranquitas Academy, the Baptists feared, for a time, that the usefulness of their school might be affected. However, their fear proved groundless. Only a few years later the Academy was reporting the largest enrollment it had ever had and was turning away students for lack of room.

Political agitation has always been rife in Puerto Rico, and about this time two pastors resigned from their churches to become leaders in political parties. It was uncertain for a time whether others would follow, but soon the matter righted itself, and the pastors were left with a surer sense of their mission than ever before. Thus the beginnings of the period being surveyed were troubled indeed. As it turned out, however, the trouble was only a backdrop for a period of marked advance.

In 1937 there occurred in Rio Piedras an event which, though seemingly unimportant, had results of far-reaching significance. When a new *barrio*[1] was organized in Latin America, it was customary to set aside a plot of ground in a strategic location near the center for a church which, it was taken for granted, would be Roman Catholic. A new *barrio* was being discussed in Rio Piedras with the usual assumption about the church, when a member of the city council unexpectedly asked, "Why does this have to be a Roman Catholic church? Might it not be a good thing to give this lot to some Evangelical group?" This revolutionary idea was discussed frankly, and in the end it was decided to offer the lot to an Evangelical group, if such a group could find the resources for a suitable building. The Baptists accepted the opportunity, the money was raised, and today in that *barrio* a Baptist church stands on the site where it had always been assumed that a Roman Catholic church would be built. The securing of such a location for an Evangelical church was important, but far more so was the fact that the tradition that the central church must be Roman Catholic had been broken.

The period was one of constant demand for buildings. Many of the new churches being organized had been former outstations with simple meeting houses. As they grew, a pressing need arose for larger quarters better equipped for the work. The churches already established had constant need for new housing, sometimes because of damage done to them by termites, but more frequently

---

[1] "Ward" or "borough" would be the nearest American equivalent.

because the old building could no longer accommodate the growing work. Sometimes this meant a new building, sometimes a major enlargement of the building in use. A considerable number of buildings and parsonages have been built or bought, and many have been remodeled. Although the Society has taken part in all of this growth by grants and loans, almost always without interest, the people themselves have carried the major responsibility and have raised the greater part of the money. Always on such projects there has been a large contribution of labor, and sometimes of material as well.

Another matter which showed the greatly improved standing of the Evangelical group occurred in the political field. The Roman Catholic Church, without consultation with other religious groups, secured an order for released time religious instruction in the public schools. The Evangelicals were much opposed to this plan because they lacked the strength to use the opportunity which it offered. Only the Roman Catholic Church would benefit by it. A campaign for the repeal of the order was carried on by radio, newspapers, magazines, sermons, posters, leaflets, and personal canvass—all with the backing of many community organizations that saw the peril. The opposition was successful in securing the repeal of the order.

After this, the Roman Catholic Church conducted a campaign to elect only their own people to the Insular legislature, so that they could control all legislation. Again the Evangelicals accepted the challenge and won the victory. These events were important and showed the strength and high rating the Evangelicals had attained. On the other hand, it did not mean that all political alignments were tending to become church issues; it simply meant that on special issues the Evangelicals were able to make themselves heard, and that in a just cause they could win the contest. Neither did it mean that the Evangelicals were coming into a position where they could dominate politics for selfish ends. They were merely demanding that equal rights be extended to all.

The Protestant missionary effort in Puerto Rico has been characterized by a strong interdenominational program. From the first there was a comity agreement by which the territory was allocated and competition largely avoided. Since then, cooperation has gone on to a positive, constructive program. The churches, through the Evangelical Council of Puerto Rico, have supported an Evangelical pastor at the University. He has worked with the students, of whom in 1955 about one thousand were Evangelicals. An Evangelical pastor has been maintained to serve the island penitentiary, the tuberculosis sanitarium, the leper colony, and the psychiatric hospital. An Evangelical paper, *Puerto Rico Evangelico,* is published and Evangelical literature is produced. When any public issue of religious significance arises, the Evangelicals unite to meet it. The fiftieth anniversary of the opening of work in the island was observed in a celebration in which all denominations joined. This united Evangelical approach has done much to further the cause of Christ in Puerto Rico.

Barranquitas Academy has made marked advancement during this period. Started in 1926 without a budget, it was conducted by the resident missionary and a pastor on a farm loaned by an interested farmer. Little by little it grew, but for a long time it was housed in the flimsiest of buildings and forced to operate on a very limited budget.

In the World Mission Crusade a reinforced concrete building, containing administration offices, an assembly hall, and classrooms, was made possible by a gift from Mrs. A. M. Conaway and Mr. and Mrs. A. O. Birch, friends of the work in Latin America who had provided the first building for the seminary. This donation completely revolutionized the work and the school went forward rapidly. However, one good building naturally called for another, and plans were drawn for a building having a central unit and two wings. One wing was to house the boys and the other the girls. The central unit was to house the supervising faculty and contain the dining hall and kitchen for the entire school. No funds were available for such a building, but the Board proposed that if the Puerto Rican Convention would raise $10,000 toward the cost of the central portion and the boys' wing, the Society would secure the balance. This was the first time that the Puerto Rican Convention had ever faced a proposal of such magnitude, but after serious consideration, it pledged the amount suggested. They fully met the conditions and erected the building during the school year of 1952-53. Thus, for the first time in its history the school had permanent housing for the administrative offices and for classrooms, proper quarters for the boys, and dining facilities for the entire school. Funds were badly needed, however, for the other wing to accommodate the girls.

The school had also advanced in the range of its work. From 1946 to 1950 Mr. Stanley Miller was principal of the school. He was on loan from the Mennonites, and was an experienced farmer as well as an excellent schoolman. During his administration, the Heifers for Relief program brought the school a registered Holstein-Friesian bull and eight heifers. Unfortunately some of the calves proved to have Bangs Disease and had to be killed. From the ones left and some which were bought, the school raised an excellent herd. A bull calf out of this herd was sent to Rev. Justino Caraballo, pastor at Cedros, and the upbreeding of the cattle in that area was started.

Mr. Miller also began importing Rhode Island Reds. The chickens on the Island were small and had a poor laying record. At first the farmers did not believe that the heavy, pure-blooded birds could be raised successfully in that climate, but Mr. Miller demonstrated that they could. Gradually the people began to buy the baby chicks which Mr. Miller imported, and soon these chickens could be seen generally in the area around the school and to a lesser degree in other parts of the Island. These steps greatly increased the production of both meat and eggs. Unfortunately, when Mr. Miller left the school, it became impossible to continue this program.

In 1944 the Woman's Society opened in a building adjoining the campus of Barranquitas Academy, a training school for women workers. It was similar to one that had been carried on in Rio Piedras from 1922 to 1931. Although that school had done a good work, the depression had forced it to close. Upon its reopening in 1944, it was under the direction of Miss Ruth Maldonado, a Puerto Rican, who had graduated from the Baptist Missionary Training School in Chicago. The work was integrated with the curriculum of the Academy so that the girls could take the courses given there; while Miss Maldonado and another missionary, Miss Laura Fish, taught the specialized subjects needed for their preparation for Christian work. Later, when it was decided that the work could be done more effectively by sending selected young women for training in the United States, the school was again closed. During its period of service, however, it trained a number of young women for work in the churches. A number of the graduates married pastors and made use of their training in assisting their husbands.

The enrollment of the Academy in 1955 was something over a hundred, of whom about sixty were boarding students. After Mr. Miller left to go back to his work with the Mennonites, Mr. Leonard D. Wilson was appointed principal. Mr. Wilson filled that position very ably until 1953 when he returned to the States to complete his preparation at Berkeley Baptist Divinity School. During 1954 Rev. Luis Mercado administered the school; he was followed the next year by Rev. Angel Luis Gutierrez.

The training for the ministry took a different course in Puerto Rico from that on any of the other Latin-American fields. Early in the history of the mission, the Presbyterian Seminary, also serving the Methodists, and the Baptist Seminary, attended by Baptists, Congregationalists, and Disciples, combined to form the Evangelical Seminary in Rio Piedras, supported by all five of these denominations. Each provided one of the professors and a share of the financial support. From the point of view of high-grade training, this school was the best in any of the Latin-

American countries in which the Society works. The fact, however, that it would receive only men who had considerable preparation gave rise to a serious problem. Some men who needed training and who could be used very effectively in various phases of the work could not meet the entrance requirements. The result was that a number of men had to be used who had received very little specialized training, and the educational gap between the trained men and the untrained men became unusually wide. Of course, this problem eventually would solve itself, but until then it would be the source of a certain amount of agitation for another school to train men who had received somewhat less academic preparation.

During this period the missionary outreach grew greatly. By 1955 the number of outstations had increased from about one hundred to nearly three hundred. They were supported by the local groups that organized them and were operated by the pastor and his laymen. Churches sometimes had as many as twenty outstations, with probably twice as many laymen engaged in this work. This made a constant demand for buildings, both for the newly organized missions and for those that had outgrown their quarters.

There also was a steady development in self-support. After the great hurricane of 1928, many churches that had been self-supporting were compelled to appeal for aid. Since that time, however, there has been a steady advance, so that in 1956 Puerto Rico was the outstanding field in the matter of self-support. In this respect, the Baptist churches were in the lead among the Evangelicals there.

Perhaps the advance that is most significant in the transition from a mission field to an indigenous church, self-supporting, self-directing, and self-propagating, is the rise of nationals to places of leadership. In this matter also, Puerto Rico has made remarkable progress. Every church has a national as its pastor. The principal of Barranquitas Academy had always been a missionary from the States except for a brief period when Rev. Angel

Mergal was principal, but in 1956 the principal was a Puerto Rican. The general missionary, Rev. Aaron F. Webber, was the only appointee from the States regularly in the work there at that time, though the Rev. Robert Dixon was on a temporary assignment at the seminary. When Mr. Webber was on furlough the work was carried on by Rev. Felix Castro Rodriguez, pastor of the church in Carolina.

This rise of leadership is most significant. Of course it had not come about by chance, but has been the result of a policy carefully pursued by the missionaries and the Board. Rev. H. P. McCormick, the first missionary, had introduced the idea of placing a member of the church in charge as pastor as soon as possible after it was organized. Dr. Detweiler, one of the early missionaries on the island, later general missionary, and still later secretary of the Department of Latin America, placed leadership in the hands of local people just as far as this was possible. This policy has been consistently followed on all Latin-American fields and has resulted in an enviable record in the percentage of the workers that are nationals. It has also stimulated self-support, for self-support develops more rapidly when leadership is in the hands of the people themselves.

An important occasion in the life of this mission was the celebration in 1949 of the fiftieth anniversary of its founding. It was observed by all denominations, all of whom sent delegations from the States. The Baptists observed the occasion in a special session of their Convention. The session was a high point in every respect. It was at this session that they voted to raise the $10,000 for the dormitory for Barranquitas Academy. The interdenominational celebration consisted of two great public meetings. At the first on Saturday night, held in front of the Capitol, the speakers stood on the portico. The crowd filled the spacious grounds, the avenue in front (the police had directed all traffic away from this area), and the park across the avenue. The police estimated that about eight thousand persons were present.

On Sunday, the meeting began at 9:00 A.M. in the ball park at San Juan, and it ran continuously until nearly 3:00 P.M. Delegations with banners and bands came from all over the island. The grandstand and bleachers were filled and the crowd spilled over on to the diamond. One paper estimated the attendance at thirty thousand; another paper, not to be outdone, placed it at fifty thousand. No one knows the exact figure, but certainly there were many thousands present. It was a great occasion in the life of the churches and an impressive demonstration of the strength attained by the Evangelical movement in fifty years.

This period in the history of the Puerto Rican mission, therefore, was one of steady advance and progressive outreach. At its close, both the churches and Barranquitas Academy were better housed; local leadership had been greatly strengthened; the status of the Evangelicals on the island had steadily risen. They faced the future with confidence and devotion.

X

Ministry to Latin America *(continued)*

PART 2: EL SALVADOR, NICARAGUA, AND HAITI

THE THREE MISSIONS WHOSE STORIES were told in the last chapter were all founded before 1900. Since that date, The American Baptist Home Mission Society has entered three additional fields: El Salvador, Nicaragua, and Haiti. In this chapter their stories will be told. Each of these fields has its distinctive characteristics, problems, and achievements.

Ministry in El Salvador

The work of the Home Mission Society in El Salvador began in 1911. The year before, Dr. L. C. Barnes, field secretary of the Society, had been sent by the Board of Managers to El Salvador to consider whether a mission should be opened in that country and, if so, where. There had been Christian work in that country and the neighboring countries for many years, first by the British Baptists in Honduras, then by the British and the American Bible Societies and by the Central American Mission in several countries, and finally by the Moravians in territory which in 1955 belonged to Nicaragua. The Society had received requests from the Moravians and also from individual Evangelical Christians to open work in Central America. Thus Dr. Barnes found that seed had been sown and some of it had borne fruit. However, none of the groups working there was organizing churches or bringing the congregations of believers together in

142

any kind of fellowship. He believed, therefore, that the time was ripe for a regular denominational agency to open a mission.

On Dr. Barnes' recommendation, the Board in 1912 appointed its first missionary, Rev. William Keech, who had been sent there by the British Bible Society. They also appointed Rev. Percy T. Chapman, a member of the LaSalle Avenue Baptist Church of Chicago. Mr. Chapman supported himself. He was located at Santa Ana, where he had won a group of believers, organized a church, and put up a building. He also worked out from that center into other parts of the country and exerted a widespread influence.

In 1924 Rev. John G. Todd was named general missionary, and he continued to serve until his retirement in 1950. In 1934 the Society appointed Rev. Thomas F. F. Dixon to assist Mr. Todd. He lived in Santa Ana, and gave leadership to the churches in that area. In 1950 when Mr. Todd retired, Mr. Dixon became the general missionary, and Rev. Jason E. Cedarholm was appointed to assist him. Mr. Dixon moved to San Salvador and Mr. Cedarholm went to Santa Ana.

In 1955 there were two outstanding churches in El Salvador. One was in San Salvador, the capital city. It had become a strong church with good leadership. In 1956, the building was found to be in poor condition and there was need for a new one. At that time the church was finding it hard to decide whether to build on its present location in the center of the city or to seek a new location in a residential area. This church was entirely self-supporting and maintained, in addition to a pastor, an assistant pastor and one missionary who worked in the outlying areas. Their Sunday school was large and carried on an excellent work.

The other outstanding church was in Santa Ana. This was the church that had been founded by Mr. Chapman in the early days of the mission. Although housed in a very unsatisfactory building, it had made a steady and encouraging growth. For a long time the members had been collecting money for a new building. On February 5, 1946, Dr. Detweiler and the Executive Secretary, while making a trip through Central America, met with the building committee of the church, and together a plan was worked out by which the church was to collect a certain amount of money (a much larger sum than they first thought they could raise), and the Society would help with certain grants and loans. Through this arrangement the church was able to build a very attractive, commodious sanctuary with a reinforced concrete frame. The church then, for the first time, had an adequate place in which to worship. No sooner was the church built than the people began at once to raise money for an educational plant. In the meantime, their school used an old building.

In San Salvador the Woman's Society conducted an elementary day school with Miss Evalena McCutcheon as principal. It was an excellent school and trained many of the children of prominent families in the city.

The Woman's Society maintained a school in Santa Ana also, with primary and secondary classes for both boys and girls, and a boarding department for girls. Miss Ruth Carr was principal, and she was assisted by Miss Estoy Reddin and Mrs. Grace Hatler. This school and the one in San Salvador have been the only two which Baptists have maintained in El Salvador. Their excellent work has contributed much to the friendly attitude of the people toward the mission.

Aside from these two churches and two schools, the work is largely in the villages and rural areas. Unfortunately, it is led to too large an extent by pastors of limited training. In fact, in 1955, in the twenty-three churches and seventy-nine out-stations, there were only eight ordained pastors and fifteen unordained ministers. The churches, however, have made steady progress, and many of these unordained workers have achieved results of a high order. Their genuine Christian character, their love for people, and their love for God make their witness effective in spite of their limited schooling. They are gathered for training institutes at least once a year, and the missionaries give them as much help as possible. For a time a theological seminary was conducted in El Salvador. Then it was moved to Nicaragua where it was hoped that it could serve both countries, but El Salvador has not found this arrangement satisfactory.

There is comparatively little religious persecution in El Salvador. The Roman Catholic Church is unfriendly, and occasionally stones are thrown at the chapels; but in general the attitude of the people is such that no serious trouble has arisen. Social pressures are exerted by families and friends, and sometimes there are business disadvantages, but in those countries Christians strong enough in their faith to be received into the churches are not greatly bothered by such things.

There was one serious outbreak of violence during this period. In 1934 the churches had organized the El Salvador Baptist Convention. In 1951, when this convention held its annual meeting in Guatajiagua, a remote rural village, the priest there stirred up some of his parishioners; church bells were rung, and several attacks with stones were made on the church in which the people were meeting. Rev. Jason Cedarholm slipped through the crowd that had gathered and went for the police, while Rev. Thomas Dixon stayed with the people, encouraging them, and making certain that they did not commit any hasty acts that would arouse further hostility and prejudice their cause. As soon as the authorities learned what was taking place, the police came, order was restored, and the convention continued its sessions. This is the only case of serious violence against the Baptists that has occurred in El Salvador during these twenty-five years. Five years later this church became fully self-supporting.

Self-support and the leadership of nationals are being developed. In the fiscal year 1954-55 the Salvadoran churches contributed $993.38 for missions, $12,635.99 for local church support, and $9,288.64 for other purposes. All of the pastors and all of the teachers in the two schools except four single women were nationals.

From 1950 to 1955 the churches dedicated five new chapels and three more were nearing completion. Thus, in 1955 El Salvador had twenty-three churches with seventy-nine missions and outstations. The churches had 1,616 members and had baptized 135 during the year. Thirty-eight Sunday schools had an average attendance of 1,580, and eleven vacation schools had an attendance of 329. The church properties, including parsonages, were valued at $126,720. The school properties of the Woman's Society were valued at $300,000.

Era of Progress in Nicaragua

The work in Nicaragua began in 1916 when the Board of Managers of the Home Mission Society recorded its purpose to enter this, the largest of the Central American republics. There had been much providential preparation through the work of Bible Society colporters, traveling evangelists, and independent missionaries. Furthermore, the Panama Congress in 1916 had requested the Board to enter Nicaragua as well as El Salvador. Rev. George H. Brewer, who was the first superintendent of the work there, organized a church in Managua and established two other missions. Rev. William Keech led the work for a few months; then in October, 1918, Rev. D. A. Wilson, who had been the general missionary in Cuba, came to Nicaragua and served there until his death, February 24, 1923. Rev. Charles S. Scott served as general missionary from 1927 to 1937. Rev. Robert W. Dixon followed Mr. Scott and served until 1954, when ill health made it necessary for him to limit his activities to the presidency of the theological seminary. In 1954, Rev. Leonard D. Wilson, who had formerly served as principal of Barranquitas Academy in Puerto Rico, became general missionary.

In 1932 the church organized by Mr. Brewer in Managua, although still small, had begun to grow. That year it reported a Sunday school of 350. There was a total of eight churches in the country with a membership of 697, and they maintained thirty-eight outstations. Four primary schools were conducted, each with a small attendance. The Evelyn Briggs Cranska Memorial Hospital, established by the Woman's Society, had been dedicated and recognized by the government in 1930. The country was just working its way out of the ruins left by the earthquake of March, 1931, in which the Societies suffered a property loss of some $90,000. It was also affected by the financial stringency then gripping the whole western world. The Christians, in general, were the poorest people in the country. Such is the background against which the progress of these twenty-five years must be seen.

During this period the number of churches and their membership increased steadily. Here, as in other Latin-American countries, the advance has been made largely through the missions started by the churches. The Nicaraguan Convention sent its workers into the most promising of these missions to organize them as churches. Although this process was guided and encouraged by the missionaries, the initial drive came from the Nicaraguan Christians themselves.

Two events in the growth of the churches during these twenty-five years deserve recounting. First was the conversion of Dr. Jose Maria Ruiz, the best educated Roman Catholic priest in Nicaragua. Dr. Arturo Parajon, pastor of the thriving First Baptist Church in Managua, made a practice of going into the country districts by bus, visiting outstations, looking for new openings for missions, and calling on persons whom he was seeking to win to Christ. On one such trip a Roman Catholic priest sat down beside him on the bus to talk with him. Their conversation led to a long series of conferences and the lending of many books. Finally this priest, Dr. Ruiz, declared his faith in Christ and asked to be baptized and received into the Baptist Church.

Dr. Parajon made it perfectly clear to Dr. Ruiz that he could not be given any immediate appointment if he became a Baptist. There were two reasons for this. One was that the mission did not want to lay him open to the charge by the Roman

Catholics that he had changed his religion for mercenary reasons. The other was that while he was highly educated for the priesthood, he did not have the special training needed by a Baptist minister. In fact, he needed much instruction as an evangelical Christian. Clearly recognizing this fact, he openly declared his faith. He began tutoring, writing, and doing similar things for which he was prepared. At first he eked out a very precarious living, but slowly he established himself on a surer footing. During the whole time of his testing he never wavered, but by his words and life gave a clear testimony that led many to Christ. After some years, when his education in Baptist doctrines was considered sufficient, he was made a professor in the theological seminary in Managua, where he became a tower of strength. He was a dynamic speaker, and was in demand for evangelistic meetings not only in Nicaragua but also in neighboring countries.

The second event, of which this first was a prelude, occurred in 1948 in the town of Diriomo. The people in their religious processions in the streets had engaged in some practices that the Roman Catholic bishop regarded as sacrilegious. When he went to remonstrate with them, the crowd became incensed, and one of the marchers threw something which struck him. This so angered the bishop that he laid the town under an interdict. This meant that there could be no religious service of any kind in the town. No one could be married, no one buried, no one baptized, no masses said, none of the sacraments administered. It is difficult for American Protestants to realize what a terrible weapon the interdict is in a town where there is no church but the Roman Catholic, and where the people accept without question that Church's power to determine the soul's final fate.

It so happened, however, that Dr. Ruiz, mentioned above, had been a priest in Diriomo and was greatly loved and trusted. Some of the people sent for him to come and counsel with them. As a result, a number of people became believers, were baptized, and formed a Baptist church. This development so frightened the bishop that he lifted the interdict. However, his action came too late. A Baptist church was established with a solid group of believers, and the people had learned that there was an appeal from an interdict. A deep impression was made on the thinking of the whole town. This church grew to such an extent that six years after it was organized, it was strong enough to entertain the Nicaraguan Baptist Convention. The following year it became self-supporting, and in 1955 it was one of the five self-supporting churches in that country.

These churches go to great lengths to entertain the Convention and to do other things for the cause of Christ. In 1941 the Convention, then three years old, met with the church in El Salto. Since the building was entirely too small to hold the crowds that would come, the members tore out the walls and built booths of cornstalks and palm leaves on all four sides of the building. They also built a wall to shut off the street so that the traffic would not disturb the meetings.

This account would not be complete without the story of First Church, Managua. Started by Mr. Brewer in 1918, it was still a small group in 1932. Its growth began that year and has continued steadily. The church property had been destroyed by the earthquake in March, 1931, and the congregation was meeting in the assembly hall of the Colegio Bautista. It was hoped that this would be necessary for only a short time, but the hall was still their meeting place in 1955. Rev. Arturo Parajon came as pastor in 1922. He was a Nicaraguan, educated for the Baptist ministry through the mission in Mexico, a brilliant man who was a trained musician as well as a minister. After a number of years as pastor of the Managua church, he spent a year in graduate study at Berkeley Baptist Divinity School. That school gave him the honorary degree of Doctor of Divinity. Mrs. Parajon was a cultured lady, also an accomplished musician, and gave him great assistance in the work.

Under the leadership of these earnest Christians, the church by 1955 had become strong and aggressive, maintaining twelve missions. Ever since their building had been destroyed, they had dreamed of a new one, but they had made little progress toward that end. For some time they had been slowly accumulating a building fund, but in 1951 they set a goal of raising 1,000 cordobas ($140) every Sunday for their building fund in addition to their regular offerings for their church and for missions. This goal was reached and later that year the construction of their building was begun. The Home Mission Society provided a grant of $23,000 and a loan of $10,000 without interest. They were going ahead only as they had the money to meet the cost. At one time when funds were exhausted and it looked as though construction would have to stop, the young people of the church undertook to raise 25,000 cordobas (about $3,500). They were led by four boys, the son of the pastor, the son of another pastor, and the sons of the two missionaries, Mr. Wyse and Dr. Pixley. They were successful in their project, and construction continued. At the time of this writing, the building is nearly completed. Plans have been made to hold the dedication service on March 3, 1957. It will be by far the largest and most desirable Evangelical church building in Nicaragua, and one of the best in the entire Latin-American mission.

This achievement is made the more significant by the fact that while they were raising the money for their own church, they aided several of their missions to build chapels.

With this victory must be recorded a great loss. In 1951 Mrs. Parajon was called to her reward, and in 1954 Dr. Parajon followed her. They will long be remembered by the Christians in Nicaragua. Their monument is in the life of the churches of that country.

The Nicaragua Baptist Convention has played an active part in the progress of the work in that country. It was organized in 1936 and in the first year supported a missionary on a field where there was no other leadership. Each year for several years one more worker was added to the list of missionaries supported by the Convention. In 1955 the Convention was supporting five pastors without aid from the Home Mission Society. It was giving visible evidence of the passion of the people to reach their own nation for Christ.

There were two schools in the educational system of the Society in Nicaragua. One was the Colegio Bautista in Managua, the other the theological seminary. In the beginning of the mission the Woman's Society started a school with a boarding department for girls. Afterwards the General Society started one for boys. Soon the two were combined. The General Society became responsible for the school and dormitory for boys, the Woman's Society for the dormitory for girls. They furnished two teachers, who also had the responsibility of supervising the dormitory for girls.

The buildings of both the school and the girls' dormitory were destroyed in the earthquake of March, 1931, but both Societies were able to rebuild. The Colegio Bautista plant was rebuilt to accommodate about four hundred students, of whom from fifty to sixty could be boarding boys. In 1937 the enrollment was five hundred; by 1951 it had reached eight hundred. Large numbers were being turned away for lack of room. Many of the government officials and wealthier families sent their children there so far as they could be received. The school has steadily followed the policy of enrolling first the students returning from the previous year, then the children of Evangelicals who desired to come, and finally others as far as there was room for them.

Colegio Bautista prepares students for the University of Nicaragua. Under the Nicaraguan system of education the examinations for all schools preparing students for the University are given by the Department of Education of the Nicaraguan government. Passing this examination entitles one to receive the degree of Bachelor of Arts and to enter the University. One indication of the high grade of work done by Colegio Bautista is the fact that in 1955 all of the students presented for this examination won their degrees. It was the only school in the country of which that was true. Largely on account of the influence of this school and of the hospital, the entire mission has enjoyed the confidence of the general public and of the official groups. It has met with very little formal opposition.

The graduates of this school have furnished leadership in their own country and far beyond. Rudolfo Mejia, an attorney and head of the loan department of the Bank of Nicaragua, is a deacon in the First Baptist Church, the treasurer of its building fund, and a past president of the Nicaragua Baptist Convention. Amos Britton, a scholarship student and a distinguished athlete, pursued his medical studies in Columbia University and in Europe, and is a distinguished physician and surgeon in Bogota, Colombia. Esteban Rodriguez, a prominent Baptist layman in El Salvador, is assistant principal in Colegio Bautista in Santa Ana. Alfredo Silva is a physician and surgeon with the United Fruit Co. in Costa Rica. Gustavo Wilson, on the faculty of Colegio Bautista, is an outstanding Christian leader, choir director and youth counselor; he represented the Boy Scouts of Nicaragua at the Jamboree in Canada in 1955. Adolfo Robleto, pastor of the First Baptist Church of Managua, is described as "author, poet, and traveler." Two of the graduates are pastors in Nicaragua, another is a pastor in El Salvador, and yet another is a pastor in Panama. At least ten of the graduates are on the faculty of the school.

The theological seminary has a much more modest history. It was started in El Salvador, but later was removed to Nicaragua with the thought that it would serve both countries. In Nicaragua it opened June, 1941, in Masaya, where the mission had bought a farm on which were some small buildings that could be used until funds could be secured for better ones. It was believed that the farm would furnish much of the food for the seminary, and that the students could do much of the farm work as a regular part of their education. About a dozen pupils gathered for the opening of the school; later there were usually from twelve to sixteen enrolled. Dr. Ruiz was the only full-time teacher. Mr. Dixon, who administered the seminary and did some teaching, also administered the general work of the mission. Some of the better-trained pastors taught, as they could give the time.

The plan was excellent except that the distance of Masaya from Managua was a great handicap in securing the help of the best pastors who were in or near that city, and in enrolling students, the majority of whom came from that area. Mr. Dixon, as general missionary, necessarily had his headquarters in Managua. In view of these difficulties it was decided that a location must be sought there. In 1951 ground was purchased just outside of the city and the seminary was moved. The farm at Masaya was sold.

The story of the seminary in Managua is a troubled one. Although most of the better trained pastors in Nicaragua and El Salvador are graduates of this school, their training was carried on under much stress. In 1955 the students were housed and boarded in Colegio Bautista, and the classes were held in a room in the new Baptist church. A local committee elected by the Nicaragua Baptist Convention served as an advisory board in cooperation with the missionaries. In the absence of Mr. Dixon, who had been sent to Puerto Rico on a temporary assignment, Dr. Ruiz was carrying on the school with the assistance of local pastors. The American Baptist Home Mission Society provided for Dr. Ruiz' salary and other local expenses. The Nicaragua Convention was paying Colegio Bautista for the board and room of the students. This was not regarded as a permanent solution of housing for the school, but plans for the future were indefinite. The El Salvador churches were not happy over their relation to the school, and that problem was still unsolved. In spite of these difficulties, however, the seminary has filled a vital need in the development of these two missions.

The third very important institution in the Nicaraguan mission is the Evelyn Briggs Cranska Memorial Hospital, conducted by the Woman's Society. It was dedicated and recognized by the government February 28, 1930, and has done an outstanding work from the beginning. Dr. John S. Pixley, the physician in charge, has shown constructive leadership. The nurses' training school, in 1956, was under the leadership of Miss Dorothy Lincoln, a missionary of the Woman's Society. The hospital has been enlarged several times, and in 1955 another building was erected, completing a very adequate plant.

The year 1953 was one of building in the Nicaragua mission. The First Church in Managua, the Colegio Bautista, and the Evelyn Briggs Cranska Memorial Hospital were all making additions. The church has proceeded with its building as it has obtained funds. The chapel was completed in 1954, and construction was going forward on the rest of the building. In 1955 the hospital completed its construction. The school had completed an excellent building for the high school department, with administration offices, classrooms, an auditorium that would accommodate the student body, a library, and an apartment for the president of the school and his family. This released space in another building, making it possible to enlarge the dormitory. This was in charge of Robert D. Brenner.

In 1955 the Nicaragua mission reported eighteen churches and forty-eight outstations. The churches reported 1,851 members and 157 baptisms. Thirty-nine Sunday schools had an average attendance of 2,283. Twenty vacation schools were conducted. There were eight ordained ministers and fourteen unordained. The churches contributed a total of $10,180. The church properties, including parsonages, were valued at $150,000 and the school properties at $500,000. The hospital property was valued at nearly $357,000.

Evangelistic Growth in Haiti

The mission in Haiti, a Negro Republic, is the youngest of the missions conducted by The American Baptist Home Mission Society in Latin America. It is also the only one which is not Spanish-speaking. The people use two languages. French, the official language, is used by the educated people; Creole is spoken by the masses, especially in the rural areas. It is a native language, probably a development of ancient African tongues mixed with French and with variations introduced by the creative genius of the people. Life there is more primitive than in any of the other five countries. Poverty, illiteracy, and illegitimacy are common. Because of these conditions, or in spite of them, the Haitians have responded to the gospel far more readily than the people of any other country in which The American Baptist Home Mission Society works.

There has been Baptist work in Haiti for more than a hundred years. It had come from three different sources. Different groups in America had sent missionaries there. The Baptist Missionary Society of Massachusetts sent a worker there in 1823 with the idea of establishing a permanent work, if the results justified it. Apparently they did not. Other agencies sent missionaries and had some converts, but they likewise established no organized work. At the same time, the Baptists of Great Britain sent missionaries to Haiti and carried on a work there for a time. Finally they turned it over to the Baptists of Jamaica. The Jamaica Baptists eventually were forced to give it up.

Thus, when The American Baptist Home Mission Society in 1923 sent Rev. A. Groves Wood to Haiti, there was an appreciable body of Evangelical Christians, and some small groups of believers. However, they were unorganized, without leadership, and weak. Mr. Wood's first task was to establish relations with the persons working there, find groups of believers that he could assist, and lead them into a full and active church life.

By 1932 the mission, under Mr. Wood's leadership, had come to have fourteen cooperating churches; besides, there were a number of independent churches which at that time were not cooperating. The cooperating churches had 1,550 members and conducted sixty-five outstations. There were ten schools conducted by local churches with no outside help. While these schools were limited as to grades, they were valuable in view of the great amount of illiteracy in the area.

The twenty-five-year period since that time has witnessed phenomenal growth. The people have responded as they have on no other field, and the missionaries have carried on such careful training of the converts that there is a high level of Christian living. Converts cannot be baptized until they have had careful instruction in the teachings of the Bible and have demonstrated in daily living the reality of their conversion. This work has been done so thoroughly that when Rev. C. Stanford Kelly, who had succeeded Mr. Wood as general missionary, was asked what percentage of those baptized dropped out of active Christian life, he replied: "Certainly not more than five per cent, probably not more than two per cent." Compared with the experience of the churches in the American Baptist Convention, this is an amazing record.

When asked to what he attributed the phenomenal growth of the churches in Haiti, Mr. Kelly replied: "As far as there is a human explanation, it is simply the fact that every Christian considers it his responsibility to win his neighbors to Christ." Every member is an evangelist. The pastor shepherds the flock, trains the workers, and instructs and baptizes the converts. Not only do they win their neighbors, but also they often go out into other communities and give their testimony there until they have gathered together a group of believers who become another outstation of the church from which the original witness came. Only recently has a Haitian Baptist Convention been organized, but the churches were carrying on a very effective extension program long before its organization.

The growth resulting from this passion to witness for Christ is shown by the following figures: In 1930 the churches connected with the mission had a membership of 1,267; in 1935 they had nearly doubled their membership, having 2,155 members. Four years later they had again doubled their membership and reported 4,400 members. In another four years (1943) they reported 9,704 members. In 1950 they had 16,040 members. In 1951 several churches which had not been cooperating came into relationship with the mission and the membership became 21,099. In 1955 the membership was 26,077. To appreciate fully the significance of this growth, it must be remembered how carefully the converts are trained and tested before they are baptized, and how nearly all of them remain loyal to their first profession. Because of that careful testing, there is a large number of "believers" who have professed their faith in Christ but have not been baptized. Some of them wait a long time for baptism; some of them are never baptized. There is no record of the number of "believers," but it is estimated that they outnumber the members.

Where growth is so rapid, church buildings are a problem. New groups are constantly demanding meeting places, and established churches are constantly outgrowing their quarters. The people are poor beyond understanding in the States, and money for buildings represents real sacrifice. The people, by their own labor, can gather much of the material. Stone, laid with lime mortar, is commonly used. The people gather the stone, and often they burn their own lime. But the roof must be of corrugated iron, which is imported, and therefore is costly. The same is true of all hardware. At that point the Society helps with grants and with loans without interest. During the twenty-five years under consideration the Haitians have built twenty-two churches and seven parsonages.

The people will go to great lengths to build. In 1935 the church at Hinche erected a church building with stone walls measuring forty by sixty feet. The Home Mission Society loaned the church $300, a friend in England gave $250, and the rest was provided by the people themselves, largely in labor and materials. An English friend gave them a very large window, the oak frame of which had to be made in Cap Haitien. It was shipped to the end of the railroad, forty miles from Hinche. Fourteen men volunteered to carry it that last forty miles!

The church at Port-au-Prince, the capital of the nation, is the largest in membership, and has one of the most beautiful buildings of any kind in Haiti. It has had an interesting history. Probably the first time the gospel was preached in Port-au-Prince was when that town was visited by Rev. Thomas Paul of Boston, the missionary sent out in 1823 by the Baptist Missionary Society of Massachusetts. Mr. Paul, however, went on to Cap Haitien and apparently did the rest of his work in that area. In 1846, a Rev. W. L. Judd[1] of Meredith, New York, was appointed by the American Baptist Free Mission Society, a strongly antislavery group, as a missionary to Haiti. He settled in Port-au-Prince and spent his entire ministry there. He organized the First Baptist Church, and was highly regarded by the government officials. In 1869 a political upheaval forced him to flee to Santo Domingo, where he soon died of fever. The church remained pastorless and was led by a committee of members until 1890.

One of Mr. Judd's converts, a Mr. Hippolite, in 1875 sent his son, Lucius, to be educated in the United States. After graduating from Colgate University and Newton Theological Institution, the young man went to France for three years' further study. After a year in Jamaica, he became pastor of the church at Port-au-Prince, and remained in that position until 1928. Dr. C. L. White in *A Century of Faith*, says: "The pastor had a small patrimony which supplied his modest needs." In other words, the church gave him little or no support. When Rev. Lucius Hippolite closed his pastorate, the church had about fifty members and a building that would seat possibly two hundred persons. It was a churchly building, but very old and in need of repair. It had been seriously damaged during a political disturbance of an earlier time.

In 1929 Rev. Ruben Marc went to Haiti under the appointment of The American Baptist Home Mission Society. He was the son of Rev. Eli Marc, a Frenchman, who while a student at Newton Theological Institution in Newton Centre, Mass., had heard of the spiritual destitution of Haiti and had gone there in

---

[1] Mr. Judd was of the same family as the late Orrin R. Judd and his son, Orrin G. Judd, both active and honored persons in the affairs of the American Baptist Convention.

1894. He opened a store at Trou to support himself and began a remarkable missionary work. He organized churches in nearby areas, trained laymen to go to them as pastors, and established both day schools and night schools in which both children and adults could receive an elementary education. Ruben Marc, Eli Marc's son, was a graduate of the University of Haiti, and had taken the usual course and one year of postgraduate work at Newton Theological Institution.

Ruben Marc became pastor at Port-au-Prince in 1929, and with his coming a period of amazing growth began. He preached both in the city and in the surrounding towns and villages. He established some fifty outstations, and trained laymen to lead them. Usually in such an outstation, laymen conducted a Sunday school and a preaching service each Sunday afternoon and a prayer meeting one evening in the week. Once a month the people who attended these outstations came in to the church in Port-au-Prince for the communion service. All of those baptized were members of the church in Port-au-Prince. In a very short time the old building would not hold the people, but there was no other place for them to go. Worshipers stood in the aisles, in the entrance of the church, and outside the windows which were low enough so that they could see the preacher in the pulpit. Later a public address system was set up for the benefit of the congregation outside, which often was much larger than the one in the building.

The people began raising funds for a new building. Out of their dire poverty they gave $17,000. Friends in the States gave $2,500. The Home Mission Society made a grant of $5,000. Friends in Haiti gave $1,000. At the last they borrowed from the Home Mission Society $6,000 without interest. (Much of the cost of the building was contributed in labor and material and is not included in these figures.) They bought a large and valuable site on a main avenue, near the President's Palace, and across the street from the large park in which the government buildings are located. On this site they built a church seating twelve hundred, one of the most beautiful buildings in Haiti, which, with donated labor and material, is valued at $50,000. It was dedicated March 6, 1949. The deputation that went to Cuba and Puerto Rico for the fiftieth anniversary of the opening of the work there also went to Haiti for the twenty-fifth anniversary of that mission and attended the dedication service. The Executive Secretary of The American Baptist Home Mission Society had the privilege of preaching the dedication sermon. The building can seat twelve hundred, but there were about two thousand present. Many high government officials showed their friendly interest by their attendance. The President of the Republic had expected to attend, but was prevented by a government emergency. Many of the American community were there. All this was in a country where only a few years before, it would have been political suicide for a government official to attend a Protestant service. In 1955 this church found it necessary to have two morning services, so large was the attendance.

The educational program in Haiti has not been developed as much as it should have been. Rev. Eli Marc, in the early days of the mission, had established some elementary schools in the churches, and these schools had done a pioneer work. This system has been continued to a considerable extent, and has been useful in the back country where illiteracy is so high, and where the government school system has been making such slow progress. These schools were intended to be self-supporting, but in later years they have received a small amount of aid from the mission. In 1953 there were forty-one such schools. They employed seventy-five teachers, enrolled about twenty-eight hundred pupils, and were subsidized to the extent of $3,000.

Beyond this there have been several attempts at schools of a higher grade, but the only one that has worked out satisfactorily is the school for girls in Cap Haitien, conducted by Miss Edith Robinson, the daughter of a Haitian attorney at one time prominent in government affairs. She went to the church at Cap Haitien as a child, gave her heart to Christ, and dedicated her life to Christian service. She came to the States to study, and after graduating from the Baptist Missionary Training School in Chicago, returned to Cap Haitien and eventually found a way to establish a school for girls. This became a good school of secondary grade. In 1955 there were over two hundred students and the school had a high standing in the community and with the educational authorities of the Republic. It was subsidized by the Society to the extent of $1,200, although Miss Robinson was not under formal appointment by the Society. There was great need for a similar school for boys, but no way had been found to establish one.

The one school officially established by the Society and conducted by a missionary from the States was the theological seminary at Limbe. Rev. Harold K. Heneise was appointed in 1947 to open this school for the training of pastors. A property on which were several buildings was secured that spring in Limbe. One of the buildings was used as a home for the missionaries, and the other small buildings were used for dormitories, kitchen and dining room, classrooms, and administration. The seminary was opened that fall and experienced the usual difficulties of a school just starting in a country where nothing like it had ever been done before, and where the people were almost totally unprepared for it. However, it has steadily progressed. The first graduate of the seminary in 1951 became the pastor at Belladere where he has been doing a good work. Since then, the seminary has graduated many other students, all of whom are serving in pastorates in that country.

A seminary serves many purposes on a mission besides its formal work. The pastors are regularly brought there for "in-service" training. Thus the level of the ministry is constantly being raised. Workers in the churches, particularly in Sunday schools, also are brought there for institutes. Teachers and students go out into the surrounding villages on week-end evangelistic tours. They have led many to Christ and have established new outstations, some of which eventually will become churches. Because there was no satisfactory evangelical Sunday school literature in French, Mr. and Mrs. Heneise and their helpers undertook to produce some materials which were adapted to their situation. In this way, this consecrated couple extended their influence into the total life of the republic.

The medical program in Haiti was still in an elementary stage. Although the need was great, so far it had been possible only to make a beginning. There were few hospitals and few doctors in Haiti, and as is usually the case, these were concentrated in the large centers, leaving the smaller towns and the open country with little in the way of medical help. Of course the native witch doctor, an inevitable accompaniment of their Voodoo religion, was everywhere, victimizing the people through their ignorance, and often doing the patient actual harm. The situation at Limbe, where the theological seminary was established, was typical of conditions throughout the country. Limbe, a town of some 5,000 inhabitants, was surrounded by villages and thickly settled open country. The population of the area was as high as 15,000 to 18,000. The nearest hospital or resident physician was in Cap Haitien, some twenty-two miles away. (Distances in Haiti must be considered in the light of the fact that there are no paved roads, streams must be forded, and in the wet seasons both roads and fords are completely impassable.) Certain diseases, such as malaria, yaws, syphilis, and dysentery, were endemic. The children especially suffered greatly from the lack of medical care, as well as from the lack of knowledge of child health on the part of the mothers.

The mothers began coming to Mrs. Heneise, then a young woman whose first child had not yet arrived, begging her to do something for their sick babies and for their own diseases. Mrs. Heneise says: "Mrs. Yeghoyan, who works with us here at the seminary, and I went to visit a clinic some distance away, where we might learn to give injections. We bought some of the literature, studied up on it, and learned what remedies were necessary for the most prevalent tropical diseases. We learned what we were permitted to do officially, what kind of medicines we could administer without a certificate."

When these two missionary women had taken this limited training, they set up a clinic under a large tree, and the people flocked to them by the hundreds. They found themselves doing things which in this country only a fully trained doctor would be allowed to do. In this way thousands of lives were saved, and many other thousands had their lives transformed by the treatment received. At the same time, they found healing for their souls through the work of the missionaries and their Haitian helpers.

While this was going on, the Society was seeking funds and a suitable person to continue and extend this work. In 1953 Miss Millicent Engel, R.N., was appointed. She was assigned to the clinic at Limbe, and immediately found herself overwhelmed with patients. In the latter half of 1956 she was able to visit and build up two other clinics in neighboring centers.

The people, feeling the need for a structure in which to house the work of the clinic, gathered the stones and other necessary materials and erected a building without any help from the Society. Thus, the medical program has been begun. It must go on to full development.

Such was the progress in evangelizing this important Caribbean republic. The people were responding as on no other field. The Roman Catholic Church was hostile, as in all countries where it is dominant, and there has been some persecution. In 1942, however, when the priests attempted to arouse the people to stone evangelical churches and in some cases to kill the converts, the public press took up the cause and defended the rights of the Evangelicals. This persecution was soon halted. Progress has been made with the full support of the people in general, and there is a bright future for the church in Haiti.

XI

A Developing Evangelism

When Dr. Benjamin T. Livingston resigned from the position of secretary of the Department of Evangelism in November, 1930, Dr. C. S. Detweiler, secretary for Latin America, was asked to carry the work of both departments. This action was due in part to the serious decline in the budget and in part to the lack of an Executive Secretary to discover and recommend a suitable person for the position. But in 1934 the decision was made to rebuild the staff in spite of declining finances, and the first officer sought, following the election of the Executive Secretary, was a secretary of evangelism. In 1936, Dr. Walter E. Woodbury was called to that position; he took office September 1 of that year, and continued in the work until his retirement in 1956. Thus his term of service, for all practical purposes, covered the entire period which is being considered in this book.

All of the workers of the Home Mission Society have been evangelists, and their purpose and methods from the beginning have been those of the evangelist. They have been pioneers, for almost always they have had to win their people to Christ before they could do anything else. The purpose of a separately organized Department of Evangelism has been to stimulate the spirit of evangelism in the churches and to train workers in the use of those methods that produce the largest results in our time. The department has sought also to cultivate the spiritual life and to recover members grown negligent.

The need for such a department is emphasized by the very conditions that have made its work so hard. The intellectual

164

atmosphere has been hostile to spiritual achievement. A materialistic science and secularism have made Christian work difficult; at the same time, they have forced a review both of the methods of Christian work and of the content of the Christian message. The demands of Christian living have become much less simple and less easily stated. Furthermore, the need for a wider application of the Christian spirit has tended to center attention on development, turning it away from the basic issue of personal commitment. It has put the emphasis on the development of the congregation, rather than on the winning of those outside the church. It also has turned people against certain ill-advised types of evangelism, and in doing so has often brought an unfortunate and unjust hostility to all evangelistic effort.

At the same time, changes in population were having a marked effect. The tremendous immigration from Roman Catholic countries in the earlier years, the rapid growth of the cities, and the steady extension of the areas of deterioration in the larger cities—all were combining to make the work of the churches in those sections more difficult. The newcomers did not respond to the traditional program of the Protestant church. Many were bitterly hostile to religion as they had known it in their homeland. Others are indifferent to everything but the material side of life. In the rural areas the increasing use of machinery was rapidly reducing the number of workers needed on the farms and so reducing the population in the area surrounding many country churches. Furthermore, the advent of the automobile, making it possible for people to go farther to worship, created a tendency toward larger, but fewer, churches. As a result of all this, many churches either combined with others to meet the situation better, or passed out of existence entirely.

Then, too, the tendency to division, so characteristic of Protestant churches in general and of Baptist churches in particular, continued throughout this period. The German and the Swedish groups withdrew from the Northern Baptist Convention, each forming a Convention of its own. This did not reduce the results of the earlier work, but it did reduce the number of churches affiliated with that Convention. The withdrawal of the so-called "Regular Baptists" and the so-called "Conservative Baptists," though not actually taking many churches out of the Convention, did much damage by centering attention on controversy, rather than on winning the world for Christ.

It is probably true also that the decline in reality was less than the statistics indicated. An earlier generous inclusiveness gave way to realism, and an effort was made by the churches to submit reports which were more accurate. This reduced the number of members, but not the actual strength of the churches.

Whatever the reasons, two facts remained: The number of churches in the Convention was smaller in 1956 than it was in 1932; although the membership had increased somewhat, it had not at all kept pace with the growth of population. These facts emphasized the need to develop among church members a greater sense of responsibility for those outside of the church and to discover more effective means of reaching them. It is in the light of this situation that the work of the department must be appraised, for it is to this need that it has directed its attention and efforts.

In spite of the adverse conditions, the period was one of real advance in evangelism. New methods were introduced, the staff committed entirely to evangelistic work was greatly enlarged, and there were highly gratifying results. There was more active cooperation with other denominations through the Department of Evangelism of the Federal Council of the Churches of Christ in America, later the National Council of the Churches of Christ in the U.S.A. The department gave to the churches of the denomination a more aggressive leadership in evangelistic effort than ever before.

Evangelistic Conferences

The Department of Evangelism has given serious attention to bringing together pastors and lay persons for conference and prayer about this basic task of the church. As early as 1918 it set up in Atlantic City an Evangelistic Conference for two days prior to the meetings of the Northern Baptist Convention. This was found so helpful that it became an annual event which was attended by large numbers of pastors and laymen, as well as by those directly involved in the program of evangelism. However, when Dr. Woodbury came to the Society in 1936, he found that the number of pre-convention meetings had increased so greatly that it was difficult to secure a satisfactory attendance. Accordingly, when in 1944 the American Baptist Assembly grounds at Green Lake became available, the Department of Evangelism united with the National Ministers' Council to hold a conference there for a week during August. What response there might be, especially in view of the wartime restrictions on travel, was unpredictable. It turned out, however, that about two hundred persons, largely pastors, attended. They came from every state in the Convention except Delaware and Wyoming.

The response, both in attendance and in appreciation of the program, was such that this conference became an annual event. In some years the attendance has risen above five hundred. The staff workers in evangelism were brought there at the same time to plan their year's work. Thus it was a source of inspiration for the public and likewise a workshop for those officially involved.

When the Evangelistic Conference was moved from the convention city to Green Lake, a mission to the convention city took its place. The Baptist churches of the city, usually with churches of other denominations participating, set up meetings in parks, in shops, on the street, anywhere that a group could be gathered. These meetings were addressed by outstanding ministers who were in attendance at the convention, and always they met with an appreciative response. In Chicago in 1952 the committee reported forty-two pulpits filled, eighty radio messages and television programs, fifteen preachers in the Pacific Garden Mission, Chicago United Mission, and the Chicago Victory Center, and one speaker at the Chapel of North Central College, Naperville, Ill. In Atlantic City in 1955 speakers were provided for fifty-five meetings on the beach and boardwalk, in jails, and before luncheon clubs.

Council on World Evangelism

The Northern Baptist Convention, meeting in Rochester in 1934, established the Council on World Evangelization as an agency in which the Home and Foreign Mission Societies could unite to study the problems of and lay plans for the evangelization of the world. The Council had its first meeting in Chicago in December, 1934, and elected the Executive Secretary of the Home Mission Society as its chairman, and Dr. Charles H. Sears, Executive Secretary of the City Societies of New York and Brooklyn, as its secretary. It soon became obvious that while the representatives of the Foreign Societies gave their full support to the movement, its effectiveness would be chiefly on the home field. The result was that the Secretary of Evangelism of the Home Mission Society became the actual administrative officer, and the main work of the Council lay with that department.

The Council held conferences and issued statements from time to time to the churches. Probably its greatest achievement lay in the extent to which it made evangelism central in the thinking of all the agencies of the denomination. One of the more concrete things that grew out of the work of this Council was a plan known as Printed Page Evangelism. This method had been used effectively by the Presbyterian Church in the U.S.A., and that body was glad to have other groups adapt it to their needs. Under this plan, four or five evangelistic tracts were specially prepared, one to be used each Sunday in January. The pastor would preach a sermon on the theme of the leaflet; then the members would visit their neighbors and use the leaflets in presenting the claims of Christ. The first year, the tracts were offered free in any quantity which the churches would use. The demand for them quite astonished the Council, which soon found itself with a deficit several times as large as its annual allotment of fifteen hundred dollars. That first issue of four leaflets finally ran to more than a million copies. The plan has been continued through the years, but the churches now are invited to contribute the cost of the leaflets, though orders are filled whether the churches pay for them or not. The budget of the Council was soon integrated into that of the Department of Evangelism of the Home Mission Society, which became responsible for any deficits that might occur. In 1956 these January leaflets were in such demand that about five hundred thousand were required, the largest number issued in any single year since the first.

When the Northern Baptist Convention met in Boston in 1951, it decided that the work of the Council could be handled more effectively by the Department of Evangelism of the Home Mission Society. The Convention, accordingly, voted to disband the Council and referred its work to that department.

Preaching Missions

In 1935 the morale of pastors and churches was at low ebb because of what they had suffered through the depression, and all state conventions and city societies were hard pressed financially. Because the smaller conventions in some of the middle western and Rocky mountain states were in an especially critical situation, it was suggested that state-wide conferences for the pastors would help. The difficulty lay in the fact that the states did not have the money to finance such conferences, nor did the pastors have the money to attend them. In the states where the special Clinton Fund could be used, the Society offered to pay the total cost of the program and the travel expenses of the pastors who attended, if the state convention would arrange with the church where the conference was held to entertain the pastors for the two nights they would be there. This offer was gladly accepted, and for several years the Department of Evangelism provided the speakers and paid the travel expenses for these conferences. Practically all the pastors attended, for they felt that this was the first assistance that had been within their reach for a long time. A time came when the state conventions and the pastors themselves wished to take over these meetings, and the Society withdrew, feeling that the special need it had sought to meet had passed. However, from 1934 to 1937 the Society had financed and led twenty-seven such preaching missions in eleven states.

About this time the whole movement of retreats for pastors and for laymen was intensified. The department was called upon to help in setting them up and in providing the programs. The secretary and the area directors gave considerable time to them. These retreats have grown steadily in importance, and in 1956 they were held in nearly every state. They served a great purpose in deepening the spiritual life and in increasing the effective service of both ministers and laymen.

An Aggressive Field Program

When Dr. Woodbury came to the Society, the appointees in this department consisted of nine state directors of evangelism, jointly supported by certain states and the Society, and two others, also jointly supported, one with the Danish Conference and one with the Norwegian Conference. This system had several weaknesses, chief of which was the fact that the limited funds did not permit the appointment of workers for all the states. Usually, since the states that needed assistance the most were not able to pay their part of the joint support, they were without help, while the Society's aid went to those states better able to supply their own staff. There was great need for some system which would make trained workers available for all.

To accomplish this, the Society decided to appoint seven area directors who would be supported and directed entirely by the Home Mission Society, each with certain states assigned to his care. In this way the entire territory of the convention was covered, even though the area of each director was unduly large. Joint appointments with the Danish and Norwegian Conferences and with some state conventions were continued. These men always worked in cooperation with the state conventions and city societies, making appointments in any state or city only after conference with the responsible secretary. This method has been followed throughout the period and has proved to be more satisfactory than any other that has been suggested. When the important conference on planning for evangelism was held in Chicago in 1944, this plan was specifically approved. Although it has not always been possible to maintain so many as seven area directors, the grouping of states which was set up at that time has generally been followed.

The directors held conferences with pastors when requested, and aided in any type of evangelism that was desired by the churches. It has been the aim, in conducting campaigns, to have them include all the Baptist churches of the area and where possible the churches of other denominations as well. The method which they have usually found most successful, and therefore have used most, is home visitation evangelism. This method was used to some extent by Dr. Livingston when he was secretary of the department, but through the years it has been developed and improved until it has reached a degree of effectiveness never before attained. Under it more persons are brought into the church than by any other plan. Fully as important, it leaves the church with a group of trained laymen and a method by which they can continue the work permanently. The work of the director is primarily in training the pastor and a group of his strong laymen. After that, the work can go forward without outside leadership.

The extent and success of this home visitation program may be judged from the secretary's report in 1951. It stated that the secretary and the seven area directors that year had aided 204 churches in 90 communities, had trained 5,122 laymen, who in turn had visited 17,929 persons and had secured 2,026 "first decisions" for Christ and 1,466 additional members by letter or by the renewal of membership.

An interesting adaptation to rural areas was demonstrated in Bradford County, Pa., a strictly rural district. There a county-wide campaign was held, each church doing its own visiting, but all doing it simultaneously. Their program included a survey of every community in the county, a self-study of the evangelistic potential of every church, a rally in one of the churches attended by over two hundred persons, and a home visitation campaign in every local church. As a result, these nine rural churches reported fifty-two baptisms and seventy-two reclaimed.

From time to time the theological seminaries have sought the leadership of the secretary of the department to train their students in this method. In November, 1946, Andover Newton Theological School invited Dr. Woodbury to lead a campaign in Newton Centre and the surrounding area. Nearly two hundred laymen were enlisted, with a student teamed with each layman. The students were excused from classes so that they might attend all of the training conferences. Thus they were prepared to use this method in the churches of which they would become pastors. This clinical training has also been used by Colgate Rochester Divinity School, Berkeley Baptist Divinity School, and Central Baptist Theological Seminary.

Winning the Children for Christ

In 1944 there arose a remarkably creative idea for drawing children into the church school, winning them to Christ, and bringing them into the church. Nothing in recent years has been so effective in this particular field. The Child Evangelism movement, an undenominational movement which had some undesirable features, was attracting much attention. Both Dr. Luther Wesley Smith, Executive Secretary of The American Baptist Publication Society, and the Executive Secretary of The American Baptist Home Mission Society felt that there was something sound in the idea, and that it could be cleared of its defects and be put to good use within the denomination. After long study they agreed upon a movement to be called Winning the Children for

Christ. It was supported by the two Societies equally. The administration was placed with The American Baptist Publication Society, for it would work through the church school. The planning was a joint process.

The plan finally adopted was to invite the children of a neighborhood who did not attend any church or church school to one of the homes in their neighborhood for a story hour, to be held one afternoon a week, after school, for five weeks. A trained storyteller with build-up picture sets would tell them Bible stories, and give each child one of the build-up pictures to take home, so that he could tell the story to his family and friends. Often other groups heard the story. In some cases it was told to a school group.

After the interest of the children was aroused, they were invited to attend the church school, and the majority of them did so. In order that the church school might use this opportunity to the best advantage, there was also a program to prepare the officers and teachers of the school to receive the children and fully integrate them in the church school. Large numbers of these children have since accepted Christ and come into the church.

This plan was worked out under the leadership of Miss Pearl Rosser, then Director of Children's Work for The American Baptist Publication Society. Miss Lois Blankenship was called to direct the program. Under her leadership five young women were put in the field. Each would go to a city where careful preparation had been made. They would discover hostesses who would invite the children to their homes; they would enlist and train storytellers to lead the story hours; they also would train the church school workers to care for the children who came to the church school. In this way the workers in the church were trained in a program which they could continue to use. At a time when the birth rate was as high as it was from 1940 to 1955, and when the number of children in the population consequently was increasing steadily, any method that could reach the children was basic to the growth of the church.

From the inauguration of this plan in May, 1944, to April 30, 1955, the reports show that 43,709 children attended 4,271 Bible Story Hours. Of this number, at least 21,861 have been enrolled in church schools. In 1947, Rev. Pieter Smit, pastor of the First Baptist Church of Marshaltown, Iowa, recounted a visit of one of these workers to his church as follows: "Fifteen neighborhood Bible Story Hours had an enrollment of 146, with an average attendance of 120. Seventy-five enrolled in the Sunday school, and the Sunday school attendance jumped from eighty to one hundred ten. Contact had been established with seventy new homes. One hundred and twenty children came to the Saturday night party. Some Catholic and some Negro children were in the group. A Junior Church has been established for children up to the junior high school age, with an attendance of fifty to eighty, many of them from unchurched homes." This gives a picture of what has happened in many places and what can happen almost anywhere.

When Miss Rosser went to the International Council of Religious Education, now the Division of Christian Education of the National Council of the Churches of Christ in the U.S.A., Miss Blankenship took her place, and Miss Margaret L. Crain, one of the field workers, became head of the program of Winning the Children for Christ.

The Chicago Conference

A peculiarly significant evangelistic conference was held in Chicago, March 7-8, 1944. The concern in the denomination over the lack of effective evangelism had impelled the department to call this conference to study the situation and discover what could be done about it. About seventy delegates, carefully selected for the contributions they could make to such a study, were present. Among them were pastors, laymen, and city, state, and national secretaries. There were few speeches, but much conferring, with a great deal of time spent in prayer. On the second evening a great public meeting was held in the Methodist

Temple in the Loop. This meeting was addressed by Dr. Daniel A. Poling, at that time pastor of the Baptist Temple in Philadelphia.

Out of the conference came a number of recommendations. Among them was the approval of the Winning the Children for Christ program. It was recommended that this program be enlarged, and this was done. Approval was given to the plan for Area Directors of Evangelism with which the Society had been experimenting, and it was recommended that four more area directors be appointed. The Society responded by appointing Rev. Paul Smith, Rev. Ray Dugger, Rev. Samuel Fehl, and Rev. W. J. McCullough.

Perhaps the greatest value of the conference lay in the encouragement it gave to the evangelistic movement and the challenge it placed before the churches. There was a wide response to the call issued by the conference and a general feeling that it had stimulated all of the churches.

New Friends for Christ

In 1945 Dr. Oliver deWolf Cummings was Executive Secretary of the Baptist Youth Fellowship. He and his cabinet felt strongly the need for a staff person who could give his full time to a program through which the young people would be led to seek out their friends and win them to Christ. Conferences were held with the Home Mission Society, and a plan was worked out whereby that Society would place on its staff a person to do this work; this person, however, was to work under the direct administration of the Baptist Youth Fellowship. The program was to be developed and the individual chosen in conference between the two organizations. This proved to be another creative and effective move on the part of the Society. Rev. Forrest B. Fordham, a young minister of Philadelphia, then in his first pastorate, was selected for this work. The essential feature of this program was the week-end Discipleship Convocation, to be held by the young people of a local church or of a group of churches in one area under Mr. Fordham's leadership. To this convocation were invited the young people in the congregation or outside of it who had never confessed Christ. The endeavor was to bring them into the fellowship of the youth group, and to secure definite decisions for Christ. This program, called New Friends for Christ, has been widely used with excellent results. In the year 1945-46, for example, New Jersey reported an increase in the enrollment in the Baptist Youth Fellowships of about twelve hundred, chiefly as a result of this program. In this effort, as in the Winning the Children to Christ, the close association with The American Baptist Publication Society was a happy one.

Crusade for Christ Through Evangelism

In 1945-46 the Northern Baptist Convention set up as its program the Christian Life Crusade. About two hundred one-day meetings were held across the territory of the convention. Each meeting brought together the leaders of the churches in that area and directed attention to six phases of the life of the local church: Christian Ministry to Service Personnel, Missions, Evangelism, Christian Education, Christian Social Progress, and Stewardship. Leaders in each of these fields came to Green Lake to prepare themselves to conduct the conferences in the two hundred meetings. Each agency financed and furnished training leadership for its own work. The Home Mission Society was deeply involved, for it was solely responsible for two of these items and shared with the other three national missionary societies in a third. The plan was carried through with great success and the conferences proved to be very helpful in the life of the churches.

As a result of this Christian Life Crusade, a group of pastors came together at the time of the Northern Baptist Convention in 1946 in Grand Rapids, Mich., and after careful discussion made a formal presentation to the Home Mission Society and the Northern Baptist Convention. They asked them to set aside another full year for similar meetings devoted entirely to evangelism. As a result of this recommendation the Convention set up a Five Year Plan under the general title, Crusade for Christ. One year would be given to each of the following lines of work: Evangelism, Christian Education, Stewardship, Christian Social Progress, and Missions. This plan was launched by the General Council in 1946 and approved by the Convention in Atlantic City in May, 1947. It was understood that this was to be the program of the Northern Baptist Convention, but that the Home Mission Society was responsible for making the Evangelistic Crusade effective.

A committee which represented all phases of the denomination's life was set up to lead the Crusade for Christ Through Evangelism. Dr. Sidney W. Powell, pastor of Tremont Temple in Boston, a member of the Board of Managers of The American Baptist Home Mission Society and chairman of its Committee on Evangelism, was made chairman, and gave a great deal of time and thought to the Crusade. This committee met quickly and made the basic arrangements. For staff, they chose the Executive Secretary of the Home Mission Society as executive director of the Crusade and the secretary of evangelism as associate director. Rev. R. Dean Goodwin, secretary for Public Relations of the Home Mission Society, was made associate director responsible for publicity. Dr. Evan J. Shearman, of the staff of the Council on Finance and Promotion was made associate director responsible for personnel. He graciously accepted several additional assignments.

Before this plan had developed far, Dr. Luther Wesley Smith, Executive Secretary of The Board of Education and Publication came to the Executive Secretary of the Home Mission Society with the proposal that the second year, which had been assigned to the Publication Society for Christian Education, should emphasize evangelism through the church school, and that the two Societies together should set up a two-year program of evangelism. This proposal was adopted, and Dr. Richard Hoiland, then the Executive Director of the Division of Education for Home, Church, and Community of The Board of Education and

Publication, was made associate director of the Crusade with major responsibility in connection with the church schools.

The committee decided that four handbooks should be prepared: *The Biblical Basis for Evangelism, Evangelizing Our Constituency, Evangelizing the Unchurched,* and *Christian Growth and Development.* A conference, after the pattern of the Christian Life Crusade, was to be held in Green Lake to train one hundred and twenty pastors (thirty in the use of each of the four handbooks) who would go to two hundred state and city conferences for the training of representatives from the local churches. Each local church was urged to give one night a week for four successive weeks to training its congregation in these four lines of evangelistic endeavor, and to adopt a month by month program for the year. An Eight O'clock Fellowship of Prayer was set up, and thousands covenanted to join in prayer at eight o'clock each morning.

The executive secretaries and the directors of evangelism of the state conventions and city societies also were brought to Green Lake to consider the part they could take in promoting this plan. They were vitally interested in it and gave themselves wholeheartedly to the work. The plan proved very successful. The great majority of the churches joined in it, each using the methods that seemed best adapted to its own constituency; and a lasting impact was made on the life of the churches and of the denomination.

For the second year of the Crusade, the committee decided to center the program entirely upon the local church and to appeal to every congregation to enter into some specific evangelistic endeavor. The plan suggested was the Ten Day Cooperative Crusade. It was hoped that all the churches of an association or other area would unite in evangelistic services at one time. The program called also for a campaign of New Friends for Christ among the young people from Friday night through Sunday night of that period. The church would have meetings from Sunday to Sunday combining a preaching ministry with home visitation. Each church would invite some neighboring pastor to be its "Crusader," to preach, and to help in the visitation. There would be a leader for the Crusade with whom the pastor and his crusaders would meet at breakfast each morning for conference and prayer.

This two-year program was the most intensive evangelistic effort Northern Baptists had ever undertaken. The majority of its churches entered into the Ten Day Cooperative Crusades with great enthusiasm. No effort was made to tabulate the results, but there was a steadily rising stream of baptisms for several years, and at no time up to 1955 did the churches drop to so low a number of baptisms as had been reported in several preceding years. The churches possessed a larger number of persons trained for personal witnessing than ever before, and there was in the churches a concern for people far greater than previously.

There were many adjuncts to this Crusade. The radio was widely used. Dr. Sidney Powell, chairman of the committee, made two sets of recordings that were widely used on the radio. A movie trailer, introducing the Ten Day Cooperative Crusades, was made professionally, and it was shown in the best moving picture theaters everywhere. Posters were displayed in almost every church in the Convention. Although there is no record of the output of literature, it was enormous and put to good use. Dr. Edwin T. Dahlberg's handbook, *The Biblical Basis for Evangelism,* was translated into Spanish for use in Latin America. Many of the plans that were recommended were adopted for use on foreign mission fields. Altogether, it was a very fruitful program. It is interesting to note that this program, with some adaptations, was adopted by the Methodists and the Lutherans, and was widely and successfully employed by them.

A Quaker Contribution to Baptist Church Life

Baptist ministers had for some time been deeply impressed by the books of Dr. Elton Trueblood, a Quaker, who was professor of philosophy at Earlham College in Richmond, Ind.

When they expressed a desire for a better acquaintance with him, the Home Mission Society undertook to make this possible. After considerable negotiations, it was arranged that he should come to Green Lake for the Minister's Conference and the Conference on Evangelism in the summer of 1949. His services were secured also for a series of conferences with ministers to be held from coast to coast during March and April, 1950.

Twenty conferences were conducted from Boston to Portland, Ore. Each lasted through a full morning and afternoon with a lunch. The entire expense was borne by the Home Mission Society. Dr. Trueblood presented the situation in the church as he saw it, and the ministers had full opportunity to discuss his proposals for improvement. These meetings proved to be most stimulating, not the least of the benefits being the opportunity to become acquainted with this outstanding leader in Christian thought.

Out of this series of meetings came the Yokefellows Group. Dr. Trueblood had said in several of the conferences that the Christian Church had overlooked the use of the yoke as a Christian symbol. He suggested the possibility of enlisting people to wear a yoke as a symbol of their complete commitment to Christian living. After much discussion, it was decided that the Home Mission Society should take the lead in promoting this idea. A small yoke pin was designed and produced in an inexpensive form. The idea spread rapidly, for Dr. Trueblood gave it considerable publicity. Soon the movement spread to other denominations. Finally, because of the interest of a large group of laymen, there was formed under Dr. Trueblood's leadership, a Yokefellows Group which made definite commitments and held retreats from time to time. The minimum discipline agreed to by the members of this fellowship may be seen in the following sevenfold commitment:

1. To pray every day, preferably at the beginning of the day.
2. To study every day a portion of the Holy Scriptures.
3. To join, at least once a week, in the public worship of God.

4. To give a definite portion of my income to the promotion of the Christian cause.

5. To give a portion of my time to the ministry in common life.

6. To use my daily work as a holy vocation.

7. To develop my mental powers by careful reading and study.

This movement now has largely passed out of the hands of the Home Mission Society, but it is significant that the Society was the first to give the idea tangible embodiment.

Literature

One of the regular activities of the Department of Evangelism was the production and distribution of evangelistic literature. Some of it consisted of technical instructions in the methods of evangelism; some was designed to stir the souls of Christians to their responsibility in this task. Tracts were provided for the man outside of the church. Posters were produced, or were taken over from other sources, and made available to the churches. Valuable handbooks were prepared. Turnover charts and recordings were produced for use in training workers in evangelism. There is no complete record of the literature distributed, but in the year ending April 30, 1955, the Department of Evangelism produced eighty-three different leaflets, twenty different cards, and ten different booklets. The total number of copies ran to nearly two million. One of the booklets that year went into its thirteenth printing, making a total of 225,000 copies that had been used by the churches.

The Wider Fellowship

This department has always worked in close cooperation with the Department of Evangelism of the Federal Council of the Churches of Christ in America, and later with the Department of Evangelism of the National Council of the Churches of Christ in the U.S.A. The Secretary of Evangelism gave much of his time to the meetings of this department and also to field work under its direction. The Society has shared in the various

National Preaching Missions and in other general interdenominational programs. Much time was spent in cooperative planning. All were free to adopt any of the plans, and to adapt them to their own denominational needs. For example, Baptists received the plan of Printed Page Evangelism from the Presbyterians and contributed the Ten Day Cooperative Crusade to the Methodists and the Lutherans.

Conclusion

Through these means, the Home Mission Society has contributed to the life of the entire Convention and all of its churches. Much of the work has been done in places of special need and with people outside of the church. Some phases of the work, however, have been with the churches themselves; and in these activities the Society serves the Convention as a whole. Through the Department of Evangelism the entire denomination has been led to a new appraisal of its evangelistic task and a more aggressive approach to it. Probably no agency and no individual has made a larger contribution to the evangelistic life of the denomination than this department and Dr. Woodbury, who was its secretary.[1]

[1] On November 1, 1956, Dr. Jitsuo Morikawa became Secretary of Evangelism for the American Baptist Home Mission Boards, and has announced a statesmanlike program to be pursued. Concerning Dr. Morikawa, see chapter VI.

XII

Building New Churches

BEFORE THE MIDDLE OF THE LAST CENTURY it was clearly recognized that if new churches were to be established on the frontier, the Society must have money with which to aid them in securing buildings. One missionary wrote to the Board of Managers, "Better one missionary with some funds for buildings than ten without." In view of this need, the Society in 1853 established the Church Edifice Fund, and that year collected for it $5,678. Dr. Coe Hayne states in an article in *Missions* that the first edifice loan was made to the First Baptist Church of St. Paul, Minn., November 28, 1849. Presumably the money came out of the Society's general treasury, for the Church Edifice Fund had not yet been established. Dr. C. L. White, in *A Century of Faith*, states that the first loan from the Church Edifice Fund was made to a church in the state of New York. By 1866 this fund had grown to $72,000. Since loans in those days were small, frequently only $100 or $200, a great many churches could be aided. Other edifice funds were started at different dates for various purposes, but all served one common cause: buildings for the churches.

The growth and usefulness of these funds down to 1932 is well recorded by Dr. White in the book mentioned above. In 1932 three men were giving their full time to this work. Dr. George E. Merrill, a licensed architect, was secretary of the Bureau of Architecture, and gave his entire time to helping the churches plan their buildings. A charge was made for his services, for it was intended that the bureau should be self-supporting. During the depression, however, that goal could not be achieved.

183

Dr. Merrill died in November, 1933, and was not replaced. It was decided that the Society should no longer provide architectural advice, but that the Department of Edifice Funds should counsel with the churches concerning their needs, and that the churches should employ such architectural services as they thought best. Apparently at that time the requests for loans were presented to the Board of Managers by the Finance Committee, upon the recommendation of the Secretary of Edifice Funds. Dr. John S. Stump had retired as Secretary of the Department of Edifice Funds in 1930 and Dr. C. M. Dinsmore, previously the Executive Secretary of the Indiana Baptist State Convention, had succeeded him.

In 1932, Dr. Charles E. Tingley also was a secretary in this department. At first he worked at raising the revolving fund for church building that had been undertaken in 1928. The plan was that each state that wished to do so should raise its own fund. Dr. Tingley was to help, and the Society was to receive 20 per cent of the amount raised. Dr. Tingley was to solicit money also from individuals in states not in the campaign. The Society's share was put into the edifice loan funds. The amount was small, for the campaign was not very successful. When it closed, Dr. Tingley became the office secretary, while Dr. Dinsmore, the other secretary, worked mainly on the field. Dr. Tingley died in 1932, and he was not replaced. At that time, the Bureau of Architecture having been discontinued, the department became the Department of Edifice Funds and Building Counsel with Dr. Dinsmore as its sole secretary. Apparently it was at this time that the requests for loans began to be brought to the Board of Managers by the committee of this department, rather than by the Finance Committee.

In 1932, the beginning of the period under consideration, practically no new church buildings were being erected, due to the general financial situation. The great concern of the churches at that time was to pay their debts and not lose such buildings as they had. During the 1920's, optimism had run high, and many churches had gone heavily into debt for large buildings. In 1934 the secretary of the department reported to the Board of Managers that two thousand Baptist churches were carrying debts totaling $26,000,000, that many of them were not able to meet their obligations, and therefore were in danger of losing their buildings. In this situation the department gave itself almost entirely to saving these churches.

Rev. T. D. King was brought to the department on February 1, 1937. He had shown unusual ability in helping churches raise money to pay their obligations, and he was secured to assist those churches that were not able to meet their obligations to the Home Mission Society. During this period he aided many churches, and as a result they felt deeply grateful both to him and to the Society.

When the need for this work had slackened somewhat, Mr. King began to work with churches that were raising money to pay other debts or to recondition their buildings. In this phase of the work up to 1955, he had aided sixty-two churches and had led them in raising approximately $3,500,000.

It is worthy of note that during the entire depression period only four churches failed to return to the Society the full principal of their loans. This loss totaled only $4,541. However, a substantial amount of interest was never paid. Not more than one or two Caucasian churches lost their buildings during this very distressing period; many of them were saved through assistance from the Society. Usually the amount provided by the Society was comparatively small, but it was lent at a crucial time when the church, with its best efforts, could not quite meet the situation.

After 1950 there was a great demand for leadership in fund raising. Accordingly, in 1956, Rev. Wesley Dixon and Rev. Harold J. Litsey were added as field staff members to engage in this work.

On March 20, 1939, the Society celebrated the eighty-fifth anniversary of the establishment of the Church Edifice Fund by a public meeting held in Emmanuel Baptist Church in Brooklyn, N. Y. A historical pageant, recounting the circumstances that attended the establishment of the fund, was presented. The cast was made up entirely of board, staff members, and office employees. It was stated at that time that the edifice funds had aided in the erection of churches in every state in the Union, five provinces of Canada, six countries of Latin America, Alaska, and the Canal Zone. More than $5,000,000 had been invested in buildings, and the face value of the loans at that time amounted to over $1,000,000.

From 1932 to 1954 the edifice funds grew from $750,000 to $2,000,000. However, when the resurgence of church building began in 1945, the Society was still unable to cope with the situation. The great rise in the cost of building required that the loans be in much larger amounts. Besides, the rapid growth of population and the extensive movement of people into new areas produced a demand for more new churches than ever before. This led to the campaign for Churches for New Frontiers (see Chapter V). By 1956 that effort had brought to the Society $2,278,773 with which to aid new churches, but the legitimate needs presented amounted to more than twice that amount. In the face of this situation the Society did the best it could, but many appeals could not be answered. The magnitude of this task is indicated by the fact that in the meeting of September 21, 1955, the Board of Managers granted requests for thirty-seven loans amounting to $360,553. It was reported at that time that from May to September, 1955, the money paid out on church edifice loans, including church extension loans, amounted to nearly a half million dollars.

Such an increase in construction also demanded an increased amount of building counsel. It was important to the Society, as a lending agency, that the plans for the new buildings should be as wisely drawn as possible. This was even more important to the success of the churches. Most members of the building committees did not have the knowledge and experience necessary to plan a building to the best advantage, either from the point of view of utility or from the point of view of economical construction. Furthermore, many professional architects, while competent in their own field, had only very general ideas of what is called for by the program of a Baptist church.

In this situation the Department of Edifice Funds and Building Counsel has rendered invaluable service to churches about to build or to remodel their buildings. This department, in conjunction with the Department of Church Extension, maintained two field men: Rev. Edward E. Chipman, in the western states, and Rev. Edward Catlos, in the Middle West, and as far east as West Virginia and Pennsylvania. The secretary and these two field men were able to visit the churches and to counsel with them in regard to their needs, style of architecture, building programs, plans for financing, and all kindred matters. The churches were encouraged to employ architects of their own choice. However, the Society secured the services of a competent consultant, widely experienced in erecting Baptist church buildings. When a congregation and its architect desired it, this architect, with the secretary of the department, reviewed plans and made suggestions as to their better adjustment to the proposed uses.

Dr. Dinsmore served the department until he retired in 1942. Rev. C. Harry Atkinson was called from the pastorate of Brunswick Street Baptist Church, Fredericton, New Brunswick, Canada, to succeed him. He began his work September 1, 1941. Thus he had some time in the office with Dr. Dinsmore in which to become familiar with the work. He led the department faithfully until 1953, when he resigned to become secretary of the Bureau of Church Building of the National Council of the Churches of Christ in the U.S.A. The Society, through Dr. Dinsmore, had helped to set up this bureau when it was connected with the Home Missions Council and had shared generously in its support. In fact, in the early days of its existence, the Society's support had been crucial to its continuance. Mr. Atkinson succeeded Dr. Dinsmore as the Society's representative on the bureau.

When Dr. Conover, the secretary of the bureau, died, Mr. Atkinson was called to succeed him.

Dr. Lincoln B. Wadsworth, then secretary of the Department of Cities, was transferred to this department. At the same time, the new Department of Church Extension was set up and Dr. Wadsworth was made secretary of both. In this way he became responsible for administering the Society's share in the greatest church building program in the history of the American Baptist Convention.

XIII

Philanthropic Institutions
and Services

PHILANTHROPY HAS ALWAYS BEEN one of the expressions of the Christian religion. In fact, the good Samaritan is at the heart of the church's practical theology. As early as 1869 American Baptists began to establish Homes for the Aged. Their first Children's Home was established in 1874, and their first Hospital in 1893. These institutions were always local in their range of service and appeal for support. Most frequently they were sponsored by independent corporations electing Boards of Trustees. Sometimes the Board of Trustees was self-perpetuating. In a few cases the institutions were controlled wholly or partly by the state convention. Three were supported, wholly or in part, by the Home Mission Societies.[1] In no case was there a formal connection with the Northern Baptist Convention.

Very early these institutions began to feel the need of fellowship, conference, and cooperative planning. The history of the development from this sense of need to the organization of the Department of Homes and Hospitals of the Home Mission Society has been told by Rev. Osgoode H. McDonald, Secretary of the Department, as follows:

"It was at the Washington Convention in 1926 that the late Dr. Charles H. Sears of New York proposed the establishment by the Northern Baptist Convention of a Board of Homes and Hospitals. This proposal was taken under advisement by the Executive Committee with the result that, at the Detroit Convention of 1928, it was agreed that a Commission

---

[1] These were the Murrow Indian Orphans' Home, Bacone, Okla.; the Chung Mei Home for Chinese Boys, El Cerrito, Calif.; and the Kodiak Children's Home, Kodiak, Alaska, which included a cottage at Ouzinkie.

on Homes and Hospitals be appointed. Finally, at the Cleveland Convention of 1930, a committee consisting of seven members was announced. This Committee on Homes and Hospitals, with Dr. George Earl, of St. Paul, Minn., as chairman since 1932, continued as one of the committees of the Convention until May, 1954.

"At the Colorado Springs Convention of 1935 the Committee on Homes and Hospitals proposed a meeting of representatives of Homes and Hospitals. This was held in Chicago in December of that year. The result was the organization of the Association of Baptist Homes and Hospitals in the interest of 'all Baptist institutions in the territory of the Northern Baptist Convention.' Dr. George Earl was elected president, an office to which he has been repeatedly re-elected. At the Atlantic City Convention in 1940 this Association was granted the status of an Associated Organization of the Northern Baptist Convention.

"As this Association met, year by year, at the time of the annual Convention meeting, there was an ever-increasing consciousness of the need of a closer working relationship between our Baptist institutions, one with another, and all with the Convention. So, at the Buffalo Convention of 1951, a special committee was appointed by the Association to study this problem. After three years of study and negotiation the new Department of Homes and Hospitals of The American Baptist Home Mission Society came into being."

The Department of Homes and Hospitals was established at the Minneapolis Convention, May, 1954, and Rev. Osgoode H. McDonald was called as secretary of the Department. Dr. McDonald, a graduate of McMaster University and of the Divinity School of the University of Chicago, came to this work from the pastorate of Immanuel Baptist Church, Rochester, N. Y. He had been chairman of the special committee of the Association of Baptist Homes and Hospitals, and was in close touch with the desires of the institutions. As chairman of that committee, he had participated in all of the negotiations relating to setting up the department. Thus he was peculiarly qualified for the position.

The purpose of the department has been very well stated by Dr. McDonald as follows:

"The purpose of this Department is not 'administrative supervision or financial subsidy of existing institutions,' but, rather, the promotion of 'an effort to relate the work of our institutions to our denominational enterprise, to raise the standards of operation, to acquaint our denominational constituency with the work of our various philanthropies, and to promote the training of institutional personnel.' This Department replaces the Convention's Committee on Homes and Hospitals. However, the Association of Baptist Homes and Hospitals continues. It appoints a most useful Advisory Committee, made up of people directly related to the work of the institutions. Indeed, it is hoped that this Association, with its inclusive membership of Convention related and other Baptist institutions, may now become more active than ever. Its Advisory Committee will be particularly helpful to the new Department."

It will be noted from the above quotation that the secretary of the department serves with two committees. Administratively he works with the committee of the Department of Homes and Hospitals of the Board of Managers of the Home Mission Society. All appropriations of funds are made by the Board of Managers on recommendation of that committee. In all matters pertaining to the policies and plans of the institutions he has also the advice of the Advisory Committee appointed by the Association of Homes and Hospitals. This committee is made up entirely of people who are involved in the work of the institutions. They are familiar, therefore, with the problems of the institutions and are professionally competent to advise in regard to policies and technical matters. It may be noted that this idea of an advisory committee composed of technically qualified persons who are not members of the Board of Managers has been followed in several other cases, notably in Juvenile Protection, Christian Centers, and certain phases of the Christian Ministry to Service Personnel. The plan has proved its usefulness in each case.

At the time of the establishment of the department in May, 1954, there were thirty-three Homes for the Aged, fifteen Homes for Children, and five Hospitals. It is a surprising fact that at that time the total of the operating budgets of these institutions exceeded and continues to exceed the Unified Budget of the American Baptist Convention.

The years 1954-1956 saw unusual activity in the enlarging of existing institutions and in the establishing of new institutions.

Building expenditures exceeded $9,000,000. By 1956 there were fourteen Children's Homes, forty Homes for the Aged, and seven Hospitals. The marked increase in the number of Homes for the Aged was a natural response to the increase in the percentage of the population over seventy years of age, and to the growing public concern for their welfare. It was made possible by the greatly increased financial strength of the people in those prosperous times, and by legislation providing new sources of self-support for the aged.

In the very brief time that the department had been in existence, several notable things had been accomplished. Of course, the secretary's first undertaking had been to visit all of the institutions and familiarize himself with their situations. This was a large and time-consuming undertaking, but it was necessary and it proved profitable. Not only did he visit each to become acquainted, but he often was called in for conference about special problems. In many cases, these problems made necessary additional visits. No new institution was established without conference with him as to the wisdom of the move and the best procedures to be followed.

A breakfast for all interested in these institutions had been held for many years at each session of the American Baptist Convention. This procedure has been continued and has taken on new enthusiasm since the department has given the institutions a formal relationship to the Convention. At this breakfast, the business of the Association has been conducted and reports have been made on matters of special interest. Sometimes speakers have addressed the group.

The first National Conference on Homes and Hospitals was held at the American Baptist Assembly at Green Lake, Wis., July 16-23, 1955. This proved an auspicious beginning of what it is anticipated will become an annual event. Eighty persons, representing twenty-eight institutions, were present. It was a technical conference, rather than one calling for wide attendance from the churches. A competent faculty offered a general course on the principles underlying such work and specific courses in the particular problems of each of the three types of institutions. The usual devotional periods, vespers, and Bible study completed the program. All who attended considered it a worth-while conference. Dates were set for another conference the following year.

The establishment of this department was the first move the American Baptist Convention had made to establish relations with these independent philanthropic institutions. It will be of great benefit to the institutions in providing an effective means for cooperative study of their problems and opportunities, and for cooperative planning. Since Baptist churches are not united through an ecclesiastical organization, but are drawn together by a common interest in a cooperative missionary enterprise, this united approach to the work of homes and hospitals is a forward step in binding all of the churches together in Christian service.

Another quite different but closely related task has lately been assigned to the department. It concerns the chaplains serving hospitals, homes, and correctional institutions. Some were employed by state or federal bodies; others were employed by city or state Councils of Churches. They were American Baptist ministers, but their work had no relation to the American Baptist Convention, and the denomination had nothing to do with their appointment. Because of these facts, they had no status as ministers in the denomination and were not eligible for membership in the pension fund set up by the Ministers and Missionaries Benefit Board. Nevertheless, it was evident that their work was important, and that the denomination should take an official interest in it. In 1956 there were twenty-four American Baptist ministers giving full time to such work and over one hundred giving part time. Most of these men had taken special clinical training for the work and wished to make it a life vocation.

At the Convention in Atlantic City in 1955 these chaplains were officially recognized and related to the Department of

Homes and Hospitals. Arrangements were made for them to be accredited after endorsement by the same committee that endorses military chaplains. The secretary of the department was made an ex-officio member of that committee. These institutional chaplains could then, if they so desired, become members of the pension fund of the Ministers and Missionaries Benefit Board. Thus these workers were finally given a recognized status and the same protection against sickness and old age as is provided for other Baptist ministers.

At the same time there was organized an Institutional Chaplains' Fellowship. This group will meet at the time of the American Baptist Convention, will share in the program of the conference at Green Lake, and will be called together at such other times as may be desirable. It will serve, through a committee, as an advisory group to the department and its secretary.

This recognition of the chaplains serving in public institutions met a long-felt need. The denomination previously had had no voice in choosing the ministers who represented them in this ministry. Under this new arrangement, it gained the same relationship to these chaplains that it had established with the chaplains in military service. Hitherto these men had felt cut off from the denomination; now they had a definite, official relation to the American Baptist Convention and to all of its ongoing work. The denomination had assumed a responsibility for their welfare that too long had been neglected.

With the integration of the two Home Mission Societies, the Department of Homes and Hospitals will be continued along the same lines that it has followed since it was established by the General Society.

XIV

Administering Emergency Aid

GREAT MISFORTUNES COME TO CHURCHES as well as to individuals, and frequently they produce crises. When such a trial comes and help is needed, the church commonly turns for aid to the state convention or city society with which it is related. These organizations are always ready to give all the help that lies within their power. Sometimes, however, when fire, flood, hurricane, or drouth has affected a large section of a state or several adjacent states, the assistance needed is beyond the resources of the state convention or the city society. Sharing the burden at such times is a regular part of the work of The American Baptist Home Mission Society. There have been several such emergencies in the period under consideration, and the Society has helped to meet them.

The Great Drouth

The first of these situations was the great drouth in the Middle West in the 1930's. The plight of the farmers had been serious even during the 1920's. World markets had declined greatly. This meant unsold surpluses and falling prices. The farmers were heavily in debt for new machinery and for farms bought at greatly inflated prices and largely on credit. The prices of the things the farmers had to buy had not declined in proportion to the prices of the things they had to sell. The depression further reduced the farmer's market by cutting the food budget of America roughly in half. As a consequence of these adverse conditions many farm owners lost their land and were compelled to become tenants or farm laborers.

195

Into this situation came the great drouth of the 1930's. In some places, the farmers for seven years did not harvest a crop that paid the cost of planting. Consequently, in several states the churches were in dire straits and sent desperate appeals to the Home Mission Society. These appeals came just at the time when, on account of the depression, the income of the Society had declined greatly, and the Board of Managers was retrenching in every possible way. The outlook, therefore, was especially dark for all concerned.

Providentially in 1934 the income from a substantial trust fund was released to the Society. This made possible a program of special aid for the churches most affected by the drouth. The need was greatest in North and South Dakota, Wyoming, Colorado, Iowa, and Nebraska. In the course of the drouth seventeen churches in South Dakota were assisted, fifteen in North Dakota, five in Wyoming, and seven in Colorado. This special fund could not be used in Iowa and Nebraska, but other means were found to help sixteen Nebraska churches and twenty-six Iowa churches. By 1938 about $20,000 had been sent to aid the churches in these six states, in addition to the money regularly provided for the work there.

This aid saved churches which otherwise could not have had pastoral leadership, and it saved pastors who otherwise would have had no salaries. It was reported at that time that none of the churches of the area had been lost through the drouth. Many of them came back to self-support with the coming of rain and the consequent better times for the farmers. Others passed into the group of churches regularly needing aid as missionary churches. Farms had been given up and other changes in population had cut away the basis for self-support. In 1955 thirty of the churches which had been aided during the drouth were self-supporting. Eleven of them were referred to by the state secretary as being among the leading churches of the state. Nineteen of the churches continued to receive aid. Thirteen, however, had passed out of existence because of the decline of population. Fourteen, after being saved by the funds of the denomination, had gone over to the Conservative Fellowship.

Flood, Hurricane, and Fire

In January, 1937, an emergency arose in Ohio and Indiana. The flood of the Ohio River washed away or seriously damaged many churches in those states, and the members of those churches sustained such serious losses in their homes and businesses that they did not have their normal ability to rebuild their churches. The Society raised $9,365 through a special appeal to the churches of the convention, and in addition used $9,500 of its regular funds in providing aid. In addition to this, Indiana raised $5,452 and Ohio raised $4,090. These sums were handled through the respective state conventions. By these means the congregations were enabled to rebuild or repair their church edifices. When the churches were rebuilt, they were erected on higher land.

In the fall of 1938 a hurricane struck New England and seriously damaged many of the churches. Again the Society appealed to the churches of the convention, but the response this time was pitifully small. A hurricane is quickly over; it does not dominate the news of the nation for weeks, as a flood does, and therefore does not impress the people so much. The Home Mission Society, however, added $4,000 of its own funds to the offering, and a number of churches were aided to some extent.

In October, 1947, one of the worst fires in the history of Maine swept through a part of that state, destroying churches and parsonages along with much other property. Some pastors lost everything they possessed, as did also many of their members. Dr. Mark Rich, secretary of the Department of Town and Country, and Rev. C. Harry Atkinson, secretary of the Department of Edifice Funds and Building Counsel, immediately joined the state secretary in a study of the needs of the situation. They agreed that at least $17,500 was needed. It did not seem possible to make a special appeal at that time. However, the Baptist

World Relief Committee donated funds to aid the pastors, and the Society provided grants and loans for rebuilding parsonages and churches.

In 1951 floods destroyed a number of Baptist churches in Kansas. The Home Mission Society proposed to the Woman's American Baptist Home Mission Society and to The Board of Education and Publication (the other two agencies which share in the proceeds of the America for Christ offering) that 10 per cent of the offering that year be used for the relief of these churches, together with some other funds to be provided by the Society. These grants were to be covered by contingent mortgages, with the understanding that the churches as soon as they were able, would repay the amounts they had borrowed. As such money was repaid, it would be set apart by the Home Mission Society as an Emergency Church Reconstruction Fund, to be used in a similar way in future emergencies. The Societies agreed and provided about $35,000 from the America for Christ offering. The Home Mission Society not only added to this amount from its own funds, but also made advances out of its funds while the offering was being collected, so that the churches could proceed with their rebuilding without delay. Regular Edifice Funds were used to supplement these gifts.

During the depression at least two city Societies were saved from disaster, in part at least, by aid from the Home Mission Society, and several states came through with less disastrous results to their work than they would otherwise have suffered had not the Home Mission Society come to their assistance.

Help for Distressed Peoples

After World War II there arose the problem of rehabilitating the people in parts of Europe and Japan. The Church of the Brethren started a movement called Heifers for Relief. They appealed to their people to give bred heifers to be sent to Europe to re-establish the herds there. When the Home Mission Society, with the cooperation of others, presented this matter to the churches of the Northern Baptist Convention, they responded generously. A collection center was established at Green Lake and by 1948 three hundred and fifty-eight heifers had been contributed by Baptists, and fifty-four more, given by others, wore the Baptist ear tag. These animals were sent with those from the other denominations, and were distributed according to the need without regard to church relationship. Instead of heifers, goats were collected and shipped to Japan.

Another project at the close of World War II was the aid given in resettling displaced persons in this country. Many people from the Baltic States, and some from other countries, were in Germany at the close of the war and dared not go back to their old homes because of the reprisals they knew the Russians would exact. Germany was already overcrowded and without food or work for her own people. The hope of these displaced persons was that they might settle in some friendly country. Congress passed laws permitting a large number of them to enter this country. It was necessary, however, for each person to have a sponsor who would guarantee him a job, a place to live, and transportation from the port of entry—in short, one who would take general responsibility for him. Appeals were immediately made to the churches to obtain these "assurances," and the Home Mission Society accepted a major responsibility in promoting this cause.

For the first several months the work went slowly; people were hesitant about taking on such responsibilities. Meanwhile, the time set by the law was running out. Then arrangements were made by which a responsible church organization was allowed to give a "blanket assurance" for a large number, and to get the individual assurances later. Church World Service, the interchurch agency that was handling the matter, apportioned the number needed among the cooperating denominations and asked The American Baptist Home Mission Society to give a blanket assurance for twelve hundred persons. This meant that the Society must find persons who would give individual assurances for that number. It was a tremendous undertaking, but the staff, after careful consideration, decided that with full cooperation from the states and cities, it could be done and that the Society should accept the challenge. The proposal was presented to the Board of Managers and they agreed to it, if the state and city secretaries would give full cooperation. Accordingly, on July 27, 1949, the matter was presented to a meeting of city, state, and national executives at Green Lake. After considering all that was involved, that group voted unanimously to give full cooperation, and the blanket assurance for twelve hundred persons was sent July 29, 1949.

All members of the Society's staff were to do what they could to secure the individual assurances, but Dr. M. E. Bratcher, the West Coast representative; Rev. R. Dean Goodwin, secretary of Public Relations; and Rev. Jobu Yasamura, field worker in the Department of Cities, were assigned to give their time almost entirely to this undertaking. The Christian Friendliness workers of the Woman's Society also gave much of their time to it. Quotas were apportioned among the states and cities, and each state and city secretary accepted responsibility for his quota. Everyone did what he could, and the people in the churches responded to the appeal. As a result of this cooperative effort, the Society was able to send in its twelve hundred assurances by January 13, 1950, the first of the larger denominations to fill its allotment. Assurances continued to come in. Twenty-five of the states reached or exceeded their quotas, some by a large number; and practically every city reached or passed its goal.

After this there came the task of settling the Volks Deutsch; that is, the people of German ancestry who had lived in Poland or neighboring areas for many generations, and who had been forced to leave by the agreements reached at the close of the war. Since Germany was too overcrowded to keep them, friendly nations gave homes to many of them. American Baptists, under the leadership of the Home Mission Society, provided for more than their proportionate share.

These are the major instances during the twenty-five years under consideration in which the Society has carried out relief undertakings, either as aid to the churches or to groups in distress. There have been many others of lesser importance. One of the regular services of the Society is to come to the aid of the local agencies in time of need. Because there is no department which has responsibility for such relief undertakings, when any such need arises the work is assigned where it seems most naturally to belong or where it can be cared for most effectively.

XV

Undergirding the Work

ALL GREAT ENTERPRISES OF THE CHURCH are dependent on two things: persons to do the work, and money to support them and to provide the equipment which they need. From the human point of view, these are basic requirements, and every missionary agency must have some means of securing them. Public relations, therefore, is the lifeblood of any organization that depends on the contributions of the public for the support of its work, and that must enlist workers on the basis, not of financial advantage, but of personal devotion to a cause. Only persons vitally interested in missionary work will give their lives to it and their money to support it. But persons will be vitally interested in a cause only when they are well informed concerning it.

The American Baptist Home Mission Society, therefore, like other missionary agencies, uses every available means to keep the people of the churches informed about the work and its needs. To do this, it operates in the closest relationship with the Council on Missionary Cooperation, which has as one of its responsibilities the task of maintaining the interest of the churches in the entire work of the denomination. The main task of the Council, which is composed of representatives of the various interests of the denomination, is to raise the unified budget by which the many activities of the Convention are supported. A large proportion of its effort must go toward arousing the concern of the people. However, the Council has so many and such varied things to present to the denomination that no one of them can be presented in adequate detail. Each agency, therefore, is under

202

compulsion to provide the churches with explicit information about its undertakings. This, however, must be done in close cooperation with the Council on Missionary Cooperation and its program of publicity.

The department of the Home Mission Society through which interest is cultivated was known in 1932 as the Department of Publicity, Literature, and Research. Dr. Coe Hayne, the author of several books, many leaflets, and innumerable magazine articles, was the secretary of the department. Upon his retirement in 1944, he was succeeded by Rev. R. Dean Goodwin, and the name of the department was changed to that of Public Relations. Mr. Goodwin came from the pastorate of the Baptist Temple in Dorchester, Mass. He was a graduate of Newton Theological Institution, and had held pastorates in Nebraska and San Francisco as well as in New England. Thus he came to the Society with a wide acquaintance throughout the denomination. He did very effective work until September 1, 1951, when he resigned to serve the Council on Missionary Cooperation. He was succeeded by Rev. Clifford G. Hansen, who had been director of Juvenile Protection for some time and so was familiar with the work of the Society, as well as with that of the denomination. A graduate of Colgate Rochester Divinity School, he came to the Society from the pastorate of the First Baptist Church, Milwaukee, Wis. His training, experience, and ability have made him an effective worker in this department.

Under Mr. Hansen's leadership the department worked through many channels. One was the production of literature to be distributed to the people in the churches. The department produced from six to nine major leaflets each year, averaging about 40,000 copies each. The issue of the one accompanying the annual Home Mission Study book ran to 60,000 copies, and it sometimes had to be reprinted. The National Council of American Baptist Women distributed 13,500 of these in their annual literature packet. Most of the leaflets printed were produced in conjunction with the Woman's Society.

Another phase of the literature program was the preparation of articles for the denominational press. These occasionally were written by the secretary, but more often were secured from missionaries, pastors, or lay persons who had a special message about some part of the work. Sometimes articles were offered to the denominational publications, *Crusader* or *Missions,* which at times asked for a news story on some particular subject. These publications gave excellent cooperation, and printed much material about the work of the Society. The *Watchman-Examiner,* while not an official organ of the denomination, gave excellent cooperation and gladly printed news items sent to it.

Two periodicals were published. *Home Mission Digest* was first published by the two Societies in 1943. It was in the usual "Digest" form, had about 150 pages, carried articles of human interest, and was illustrated. It was published every two years. In 1949 the Associated Home Mission Agencies took over this publication so that the work of all of the agencies might be presented in it, and that all might have a voice in formulating its policies. An editorial committee was appointed for each issue, but the actual work of assembling the material and producing the booklet remained with the Departments of Public Relations of the two national Societies. In 1954 it was decided to make the publication an annual. The issue ran to about 12,500 copies and usually was sold out. It was a "priced" publication, for it was entirely too costly for free distribution.

The second periodical published was the *Pastor's Round Table,* issued five times a year. This was for pastors only, and was sent to them without cost. It was not a promotional organ, but simply a medium for the exchange of methods and plans. Perhaps because it was an attempt to serve them rather than to secure support for the Society, it was greatly appreciated and widely read. It afforded a means by which the Executive Secretary might send messages to the pastors; it also carried in each issue some excellent devotional material written by Dr. Charles S. Detweiler.

The story of home mission work was told also by the speakers which the Society provided for conventions, associations, and churches. This was known as "deputation work." The most acceptable of these speakers were "live missionaries," the demand for whom was greater than could be supplied with fairness to the work. Because the real task of the missionaries was to do missionary work, rather than speak in churches, the Society was justified in withdrawing them from their fields of labor and sending them out to speak in churches only to the extent that their addresses would secure added financial support for the work. All of the secretaries gave a great deal of time to such speaking. Sometimes laymen or women who had visited some field would speak in the churches of what they had seen and of their impression of its value. Probably they were the most effective speakers, for the people felt that they were disinterested witnesses. Although the appointments for such speakers were commonly made by the Council on Missionary Cooperation, the Department of Public Relations of the Society had a great deal to do with finding these speakers and preparing them for their particular appointments. The secretary of the department himself took large part in such service.

Some special types of deputation work have arisen in recent years. In 1954 the two Boards held a joint meeting in Chicago to which they brought an unusually large number of missionaries. During the week, missionaries, board members, and secretaries all spoke in the churches throughout the city. One evening was given to a city-wide rally in a downtown center.

Another variation was a week chosen by a city or state, when a large number of missionaries, both home and foreign, were brought together and sent to all the churches in the area. Michigan, in 1954, had the help of a team of between fifty and sixty missionaries, which made it possible for every church in the state to be visited by at least one missionary. New York city did a similar thing in January, 1956. Oregon has done the same. These different types of deputation work were a systematic effort to acquaint the church people with the missionaries and what they were doing. These special approaches have met with so good a response that they are likely to be used more frequently in the future.

At the sessions of the American Baptist Convention this department had two major tasks, to say nothing of many lesser ones. The first was responsibility for the home mission program in the Convention. Although the program set forth the work of the entire group of Home Mission Agencies, it fell to this department to build that program, secure the speakers, assemble the materials needed, and see that all went according to plan. This was no small undertaking, but it was of tremendous significance in acquainting the people with the work. The Convention usually afforded sufficient time for a satisfactory presentation, and the delegates looked forward to this part of the program.

Another large task was the preparation and manning of the booths in the exhibit hall at the Convention. Each department that had a booth carried the responsibility for setting it up and operating it, but the Department of Public Relations was responsible for securing from the denomination the space required, allotting it to the causes to be presented, and, while helping all the others, had full responsibility for the general booth. Thousands of people visited these booths each year, hundreds of conferences were held, and thousands of pieces of literature were distributed—all matters of great importance.

The Department of Public Relations also has shared in the Home Mission presentation at the conference held each year at Green Lake for all the second-year men and women in the various seminaries. This is known as the Conference for Seminary Middlers, and it is planned by the Board of Education. This conference, begun before the denomination had obtained Green Lake, at first was held under great difficulties, but it proved its worth even under those limitations. When Green Lake became available, the conference really came into its own. It was extended to five days, with the students from all the seminaries brought together at one time, instead of being divided into three groups as previously had been done. There were no distractions of a surrounding city to take the students away from the program and the whole atmosphere was helpful to the purpose of the conference. Under the present plan each agency has time to present its work, and there is ample time for the students to ask any questions they desire. They are encouraged to voice freely any concerns or doubts that may be in their minds, and each secretary does his best to answer frankly and in friendly spirit any questions or criticisms that arise. Students from different schools have become acquainted with each other and with the secretaries. Such friendships last through the years and are a tremendous force in maintaining the unity of the denomination.

Another duty of the secretary of this department has been to serve as financial counselor to home mission institutions when they were raising funds for buildings or other capital projects. This service, begun in 1955, has large possibilities of usefulness.

By 1950 the great improvement in travel conditions had made it easy for members of the churches to visit the mission fields in Latin America and in Alaska. Tours previously had been conducted under various auspices, but more and more it has fallen to the secretary of Public Relations to assume responsibility for them. The tours are valuable to the Society because the more that pastors and lay people can see of the work, the greater will be their devotion to it.

The integration of the work of the two Home Mission Societies in 1955 brought considerable change in this department. Each Society had a Department of Public Relations and their work was closely parallel. In the process of integration, the work of the two departments was combined and then redistributed along functional lines. A new Department of Publications and Communications was established, with Miss Helen C. Schmitz of the staff of the Woman's Society as secretary. This department, as its name indicates, was made responsible for literature, advertising, publications, and related matters. Rev. Clifford

G. Hansen of the General Society's staff was made secretary of the Department of Public Relations and was "responsible for the interpretation of the program, plans, and needs of the Societies to the constituency." This interpretation of the program, it was further stated, was to include "personal presentations, exhibits, program presentations, audio-visual presentations, and personal interviews." Each department represents both Societies through the united Boards.

A new task added to the Department of Public Relations was the supervision of the Western and Midwestern field representatives. These men were using all means available to them to enlist the members of the churches in the support of home missions, and until that time they had been under the personal direction of the Executive Secretary of the General Society. It seemed better, in the process of integration, to place them under the direction of the secretary of Public Relations.

A new publication was established in the department of Publications and Communications, a house organ named *Memo from 164*. It is sent to all the workers in the home mission field, to all secretaries in the denomination, and to all others who might have an interest in it. It carries information about the plans and operation of the Societies, gives news items about the missionaries, and seeks to bring home mission workers more closely together through a greater knowledge of the total work being carried on.

Enlisting Workers

The efforts of the two departments described above have been directed largely toward securing adequate support for the work. But the greatest financial support is valueless unless there are missionaries. The money must function through persons. The Home Mission Society, however, had never employed a secretary whose principal function was to enlist workers. When a missionary was needed, the secretary responsible for the work simply hunted up some person who could fill the place. In 1946 this matter was discussed by the Central Committee of the Associated Home Mission Agencies. The general desire was that such a secretary should be appointed, that he should be related to the Central Committee, and that he should serve all the Home Mission Agencies. It was soon concluded, however, that he must be related administratively to one agency, and that the Home Mission Society was the one that could best accept this responsibility. When it came to the matter of financing such a department, since the Associated Home Mission Agencies were in no position to do it, it was decided that The American Baptist Publication Society, the Woman's American Baptist Home Mission Society, and The American Baptist Home Mission Society should supply funds for the project in proportions that seemed just and practical to them. The Home Mission Society assumed the larger proportion.

About the time that this arrangement was being made, the work of the Christian Ministry to Service Personnel was becoming less demanding. It was planned, therefore, that Rev. Ernest C. Witham, secretary of that department, should divide his time between the two departments. Later, his duties as Personnel Secretary came to require all of his time; consequently, the Christian Ministry to Service Personnel was transferred to Rev. Joseph H. Heartberg, secretary of the Department of Town and Country. As Secretary of Personnel, Mr. Witham served the Woman's Society, the Publication Society, the state conventions, and the city societies, as well as the Home Mission Society. He worked in conference with a committee appointed by the Associated Home Mission Agencies, but administratively he was related to the Home Mission Society. The other supporting agencies paid their portion of the cost to that Society.

The Personnel Secretary gave the major portion of his time to enlisting young people for the church vocations, particularly in the fields of home missions and Christian education. In this he worked in close cooperation with the Candidate Secretary of the Foreign Societies. Frequently the two men visited college campuses and held joint conferences. Reference of interested persons by one secretary to the other was standard practice and of common occurrence. Contact with the young people was made through visits to colleges, through the university pastors, through high schools and the preparatory schools of the denomination, through meetings of youth held by the Baptist Youth Fellowship at Green Lake, through the state camps and assemblies, and in every other way possible. By 1956 the secretary had assembled a file of approximately fifteen hundred young people who had expressed an interest in the church vocations and might be interested in home mission work or Christian education. He kept in touch with them through general letters sent out from time to time and also by correspondence with individuals. Many of these young people will be placed in some form of home mission service or Christian education.

In both fields, positions were sometimes filled from the ranks of those already in the ministry who might be interested in entering another type of service. The Personnel Secretary kept a file of all such persons of whom he learned, and corresponded with them. He visited state ministers' conferences, state conventions, and associations to present to the ministers the need for such workers and to meet those who might have some such interest. By 1956 he had built a file of approximately two hundred persons with whom he kept in touch.

Two or three times a year the Personnel Secretary sent to all Home Mission executives a list of these possibilities, together with an account of their qualifications and particular interests. If an executive was interested in any of them, he wrote to the Personnel Secretary who furnished him with all the available information. On the other hand, if an executive needed a person to fill a certain position, he could write to the Personnel Secretary who, from his file, would make suggestions. This department has rendered well a much needed service.

This department also has helped to recruit young people for the summer service projects which had come into being during this period. These summer projects have now become an important part of the denomination's program. In them, a group of young people give their services during the summer months to some Christian work. They serve largely at their own expense, but where necessary they may receive some financial support from one of the denominational agencies. They are then sent to some home mission field where they work under the direction of the missionaries. Several groups have been sent out each year, and they have rendered worth-while service. This work has been carried on in cooperation with the Baptist Youth Fellowship.

The Society, through various departments, also appointed students for work during their summer vacations. These appointees were likely to be young men who were preparing for the ministry or at least were considering it. Usually they were sent to an established field where there was a permanent missionary. Occasionally they were used to explore a new field or to make the first beginnings of a new work. They were paid a sufficient amount to cover their expenses and give them something toward the cost of the next year in school. The Personnel Department assisted in the recruitment of these students.

This department also helped in securing Baptist Youth Fellowship interns. These interns were young people who on or before graduation from college gave a year of service on a strictly subsistence basis. They were attached to the staff of a State Convention or a City Society and devoted their time to strengthening the work of the Baptist Youth Fellowships in that area. There have been a number of these interns each year.

The fact that the department was engaged in such work led to placing the secretary of the department on several committees and boards in cooperation with other agencies. He is a member of the denomination's Commission on the Ministry, which seeks in various ways to interest more young men in the ministry as their life work. Life Service Sunday is observed by the denomination each year to bring the claims of the ministry and especially of the mission fields before the young people of the churches. The Personnel Secretary is a member of the committee which promotes that Sunday and is responsible for the Home Mission phase of the program.

He also serves as a member of the Youth Work Committee of the Baptist Youth Fellowship, of the Board of Directors of the Student Volunteer Movement, and of the Committee on Personnel of the Division of Home Missions of the National Council of the Churches of Christ in the U.S.A.

This department has not only discovered workers for home missions and Christian education, but has brought before the public the demand for personnel in the church vocations. It has made both young people and parents aware of the needs for such service and of the rewarding life which such service offers. Thus it has served not only the home mission agencies, but also the entire Christian cause.

The integration of the work of the two Societies has made no change in the work of this department. It already was serving both Societies, and the secretary was a member of both staffs.

XVI

Developing Relationships

THE AMERICAN BAPTIST HOME MISSION SOCIETY was the third national organization to be formed by Baptists in America.[1] Like the two organized earlier (the American Baptist Foreign Mission Society and The American Baptist Publication Society), membership was on the basis of support given to its work; delegates to its annual meeting were sent only by churches that had contributed. Each of these organizations was an independent corporation, but they held their annual meetings at the same time and place. Each Board of Managers was responsible to its annual meeting, and the delegates to that meeting were responsible to no other body. When the Northern Baptist Convention was organized, this situation was continued; and each Society held its annual meeting at the time of the Convention. Through the years the Convention has widened the scope of its activities, and the annual meetings of the Societies have become little more than meetings for the election of officers and the observance of the technical formalities required by law. The independence of the Societies is limited by the Convention. This was indicated when the two Home Mission Societies and the two Foreign Mission Societies prepared to integrate their work. Approval for integration was first voted by the Convention, and only then did the annual meetings of the Societies vote to adopt the plan. The delegates to the Convention are delegates to the annual meeting of each Society, and in this way the Boards of Managers of the Societies have become to all intents and pur-

[1] It is interesting to note that it is the only one of the three that continues under the name given it at its formation. The designation "American," adopted by this Society, later was adopted by the Woman's Societies, and finally by the Convention itself.

213

poses Boards of the Convention. At the annual meetings of each Society no actions are taken except those required to maintain the legal competence of its Board of Managers.

All the business of the Society is in the hands of the Board of Managers, which determines policies, appoints the missionaries, and directs financial matters. The integration of the work of the two Societies was authorized by their annual meetings, but the detailed plans for integration were formulated by the Boards of Managers.

The Board of Managers of the Home Mission Society organizes itself into departments for handling the work. For each department there is a committee composed of members of the Board. The committee's responsibility is to bring its recommendations to the Board of Managers, and its actions become effective only when they have been adopted by that Board. Each committee is served by an employed officer or secretary who has a twofold responsibility: he is responsible for carrying out the actions of the Board that pertain to his department; he is responsible also for bringing to the committee's attention the matters that call for action and for advising the committee as to the suitable action to be taken. The committee will follow his recommendations only when it believes them to be wise, just as the Board will adopt the committee's recommendations only when it believes them to be wise. However, the fact that the secretary is in constant touch with the field and gives close attention to the work adds weight to his advice.

The Executive Secretary and the Treasurer are related to the total work of the Society. The former, with responsibility for administering all of the affairs of the Society, works with the Executive Committee on which each departmental committee is represented by its chairman. By this means he is related to all of the committees. He is also the chairman of the Headquarters Council, which consists of the entire staff. He is responsible for bringing to the Executive Committee, and through it to the Board of Managers, all problems related to the Society as a whole, all matters having to do with the internal health of the organization, and all matters of general policy that require the Board's attention. He is also responsible for securing financial support for the work.

The Treasurer is the administrative officer of the Finance Committee. The investment of permanent funds is handled by that committee. It is the Treasurer's responsibility to see that funds are expended by the departments only in accordance with the vote of the Board of Managers. Every department turns to him for advice on business and legal matters. In many cases he and the Executive Secretary function together as general officers related to all departments.

Thus, the authority is vested in the Board of Managers and its committees. The effectiveness of each officer depends entirely on the measure of confidence which the Board and the related committee come to have in him. A thoroughly trusted secretary carries a heavy responsibility.

Changes in officers in each department have been noted in the account of that department. The office of Executive Secretary was vacant in 1932. The writer of this account, Rev. G. Pitt Beers, then pastor of the First Baptist Church of Paterson, N. J., was called as Executive Secretary in 1934 and took office on October 1 of that year. He continued in the office until he retired April 30, 1953.

Dr. Theron Chastain, pastor of the First Baptist Church of Phoenix, Ariz., was called as Associate Executive Secretary in 1952 and began his work September 1 of that year. He became Executive Secretary on May 1, 1953. Between that date and 1956 he has led the campaign for Churches for New Frontiers, and has had an important part in the integration of the two Home Mission Societies. In this latter achievement he has brought to a happy solution an issue that had agitated the denomination for half a century.

In 1932 Mr. Samuel Bryant was Treasurer of the Society. He had held that office since 1919, and had been a member of the Board of Managers for four years prior to that time. He and Mrs. Bryant had made substantial personal contributions to Home Mission work, and for several years he served as Treasurer without salary. He continued in that office until his death September 21, 1938.

He was succeeded in office by Mr. S. E. Hening, who had had long experience in Y.M.C.A. work. He continued in office until August 31, 1946, when he resigned. During his administration the Board of Managers largely liquidated the real estate that had come into its hands during the depression through the inability of mortgagors to repay loans made to them from the permanent funds of the Society.

Mr. William H. Rhoades, of Toledo, Ohio, was next called as Treasurer and began his work April 1, 1947. His training had been in law and he was experienced in the handling of corporations, estates, and real estate. He came to the Society from his service in the Army in World War II, in which he had attained the rank of lieutenant colonel. During his administration he has rendered an outstanding service. The moving of the offices to a building owned by the Society was made under his leadership. This move, made in 1951, brought the two Home Mission Societies together in the same building for the first time in their history. His knowledge of the affairs of the denomination has made him a helpful counselor in all departments. He became the Treasurer for the Woman's Society also, when Miss Edna R. Howe resigned in 1952.

With the Treasurer is associated an Assistant Treasurer. In 1932 this office was held by Mrs. H. Estelle Hendry. During the period between Mr. Bryant's death and Mr. Hening's election she carried the responsibility of the Treasurer's office. She resigned December 31, 1942, and was succeeded by Mr. Harry Kummann, who had been in the Treasurer's office since 1919. He carried the responsibility of the Treasurer's office during the period between the resignation of Mr. Hening and the election of Mr. Rhoades. His term of service with the Society was the longest given by anyone who was in the Headquarters office in 1956 and probably has been exceeded by very few during the Society's history.

When the work of the two Societies was integrated, the Executive Secretary, the Treasurer, and the Assistant Treasurer continued in their respective offices that they might serve the integrated Societies.

In the early years of the depression the Society, as explained above, had come into possession of a number of pieces of real estate. Mr. Alvah Jacobus was employed for a time in superintending these properties. Then a real estate department was set up, with Mr. Abner F. Bowling, Jr., in charge. Soon Mr. Jacobus closed his service with the Society, and Mr. Harry E. Bailey was brought in to assist Mr. Bowling. He had been a member of the Board of Managers and of the Finance Committee for a number of years, and so was familiar with the problems involved. In addition, Mr. and Mrs. Bailey had been deeply interested in Home Mission work and had made substantial contributions to it. Mr. Bailey also had served as acting Assistant Treasurer from October 1 to December 31, 1942. After Mr. Bowling resigned, Mr. Bailey became head of the real estate department and Mr. Herbert Hubsch assisted him. When Mr. Bailey retired, Mr. Hubsch became head of the department. During this period the responsibility of this department was extended to include the management of the headquarters building, the servicing of all mortgage loans, and all insurance matters relating to the properties of the Society. Mr. Hubsch has rendered a valuable service in all of this.

The officers of the Society and the Board of Managers are elected by the Society at its annual meeting. The Board of Managers elects its own officers and appoints its own committees. Lists of those who have served the Society in this way during the past twenty-five years will be found in the Appendix. For these names and terms of service, see Appendix B, p. 249; Appendix C, p. 250; Appendix D, pp. 251-253.

In 1932 Miss Susan T. Keese, one of the office secretaries, was the recording secretary of the Board of Managers. She filled that office until May, 1938, when she was approaching her retirement. She was succeeded by Miss Elsie Larson, who was still in office in 1956. Miss Larson was secretary to the Executive Secretary and under his direction supervised the office staff. In the reorganization, Miss Larson was continued as the recording secretary of the integrated Boards.

The objective of all of this organization, of course, is to maintain missionaries on the home mission field and to enable them to do effective work. These workers are of three classes, according to the measure and directness of support by the Society. One group is made up mostly of those in Christian Centers, bilingual churches, church extension projects, and similar types of work. They are supported jointly by the Society and the state convention or city mission society. The selection of these workers is made jointly, but the work is administered by the local agency. The Society sends its share of the support to the local agency which pays the worker his entire salary. This provision aids the administrative control of the local agency, but frequently leaves the missionary and the local church people with very little awareness of the part taken by the national society. A second group includes the missionaries to Latin America, most of those to the Indians, the general workers, the area directors of evangelism, and others with similar responsibilities; these are supported entirely by the Society. They are appointed by action of the Board of Managers alone and are administered directly. A third group consists of the nationals working in Latin America. The Society shares in their support through a contribution to the total budget of the mission in each country, but it does not select or appoint the individual workers.

Naturally the Society assumes the largest responsibility for those workers whom it selects and wholly supports. The group insurance plan, the retirement allowance plan, the plans for furloughs and sabbatical leaves—all are set up with this group in mind. As far as the plans apply to the other two groups, it is by adaptation, and in all cases is limited to the salary support provided by the Society.

The group insurance plan is calculated to meet only the funeral expenses and immediate needs of a dependent family. Very early the Society faced the situation of those who had come to retirement age, but who, because of the small salaries paid, had never been able to make any financial provision for such a time. A retirement allowance plan was set up with such workers in mind. The cost was borne entirely by the Society, which retained the right to change the plan or to discontinue it at its own discretion. When the pension plan of the Ministers and Missionaries Benefit Board had sufficiently entered into the thinking of the denomination, the Society placed in it, entirely at its own expense, all of the missionaries whom it wholly supported, and urged the jointly supported missionaries to go into it, agreeing to pay the portion of the cost that was based on the share of their salary which the Society paid. Because the denomination's pension plan did not provide for these low salaried workers as generously as the Society's plan did, the Board of Managers agreed to supplement the pension sufficiently to bring the allowance up to that provided in their own plan. These provisions accordingly were put into effect.

Furloughs have always been provided for the workers in Latin America and Alaska. Workers in the continental United States have been given vacations on the basis common for pastors. In the late 1940's, some of the missionaries made an urgent request for sabbatical leaves for study. The first Home Mission workers frequently had very limited training. Later, in the 1930's, the requirements were raised and full college and seminary training came to be expected. Better trained men appreciated the advantage of still further training and began to ask for sabbatical leaves for that purpose. At first these requests were met individually and without rules. It soon became apparent that there should be a definite basis for dealing with these requests. On

January 21, 1948, the Board of Managers adopted controlling regulations. This step was a further contribution to the higher standards of training for Home Mission workers. The regulations adopted were as follows:

REGULATIONS IN REGARD TO FURLOUGHS AND SABBATICAL LEAVE FOR SPECIAL STUDY FOR MISSIONARIES OF THE AMERICAN BAPTIST HOME MISSION SOCIETY

FOR MISSIONARIES IN THE STATES

An annual vacation of one month with full salary is authorized and shall be taken at the missionary's expense.

During the eighth consecutive year of full-time service a missionary receiving his entire salary from The American Baptist Home Mission Society may elect to spend one semester in further study under the following conditions:

1. This study shall be pursued in an institution approved by the Society.
2. The courses taken shall be related to his missionary service.
3. Courses shall be carried through to completion for regular credit.

A missionary on leave for study shall receive his full cash salary during the period agreed on for this purpose.

In the case of missionaries jointly supported with other agencies The American Baptist Home Mission Society will pay its share of the salary during such a semester of study provided satisfactory arrangements are made with the other agencies.

Special cases will receive special consideration.

FOR MISSIONARIES IN LATIN AMERICA AND ALASKA

An annual vacation of one month with full salary is authorized and shall be taken at the missionary's expense.

A furlough of six months shall be allowed every four years. Normally three months of this time shall be given to deputation work and the remainder to complete rest.

If on alternate furloughs the missionary desires to take a semester of advance study related to his work, the length and time of his furlough will be adjusted to make this possible.

Full cash salary will be paid during furloughs in either case. Rental allowances shall be adjusted in individual cases.

On regular furloughs transportation for the missionary, his wife and minor children dependent on him for support, from and back to the field will be met by the Society.

Special cases will receive special consideration both in regard to the need of furlough and opportunity for study.

Every missionary and his family on return to the States on furlough will have medical examinations, upon the basis of which the physical examiner will give those examined and the Board answers to the following three questions:

(a) Do they require any special treatment while on furlough?

(b) If so, what?

(c) Do the cases suggest the necessity of further medical examination toward the end of the furlough, to determine fitness for return to the field?

Unusual expenditures necessary because of treatment prescribed as a result of the examination will be taken under consideration by the Board.[1]

During the twenty-five-year period considered in this history, the standards of training and the support of missionaries have steadily risen. The work to be done grows more and more demanding, and the Society has steadily advanced to meet these demands. However, with the amount of money provided by the churches, the number of missionaries has never been so large as the work called for, and the support of these missionaries has never been wholly adequate. Consequently, the planning of the Board of Managers has been a constant process of deciding the level of support the Board was justified in giving in view of the available funds and the many unmet needs. There was no absolute standard by which such a decision could be made. Whatever the Board of Managers might decide, some persons would feel that the Board had neglected work that should have been done, and others would declare that the support of the missionaries should have been more generous. The Board of Managers endeavored to maintain as even a balance as possible between these two conflicting ways of thinking.

[1] Following the integration of the two Home Mission Societies the Board of Managers adopted new policies on furloughs and study leaves combining advantages from both Societies.

Relationships Within the Denomination

This fifth quarter century of the Society's history has witnessed many adjustments in the Society's relationship to other Home Mission agencies. When The American Baptist Home Mission Society was organized in 1832, there were only nine state conventions, of which Indiana, organized the same year as the Society, was the farthest west. The American Baptist Publication Society had been organized eight years before. The Woman's American Baptist Home Mission Society did not come into existence for another forty-five years. The Home Mission Society and the Publication Society, therefore, were the only agencies of the denomination through which the entire area west of Indiana could be evangelized. (Organizations like those in Massachusetts and New York had done some pioneer work, but very little of it had been west of Indiana; and as the Home Mission Society developed its work, they soon confined their efforts to their own areas and became state conventions.) The trend of the Publication Society was toward its present specialization in publications and Christian education. In the early decades, and until recently, the Publication Society conducted an active colporter work. In addition to distributing literature, the colporters were zealous evangelists. They established many Sunday schools and churches.

The missionaries of the Home Mission Society were sent specifically to evangelize and establish churches, but they also distributed Bibles and other Christian literature, and founded Sunday schools. Thus the two Societies were doing much the same work, but in each there was a growing tendency toward its present function. The story of the adjustment between these two Societies was told in Chapter VII.

At the same time that relationships between these two national societies were being worked out, the state conventions were increasing in number, and standard city mission societies were being organized in the larger metropolitan areas. The Home

Mission Society was active in promoting both developments. As soon as the pioneer work of the missionaries had produced a few churches, the Society encouraged them to form a state convention and to begin taking the leadership in the further evangelization of their own state. The churches, at first, were without experience in directing such an undertaking, but the missionaries counseled with them and helped them develop plans for further extension of the work. There was then no general plan for financial support such as came into being later. Because the amount of money this small group of churches could contribute was entirely inadequate for what needed to be done, the Home Mission Society provided most of the money. It also aided by sending workers from the older states. Many of the best known pastors in the Northern Baptist Convention in the early years of the twentieth century gained their first experience on the home mission field.

As the churches increased in number and strength, the state convention became stronger and took over more of the work. As this occurred, the Home Mission Society transferred its efforts to other areas not so far developed, and later to other types of service which had begun to demand attention. This shifting of control and support inevitably led to differences of opinion which could not always be immediately settled to the satisfaction of all parties, even though the friendliest relationships existed. Some means was needed for reaching equitable adjustments.

While the state conventions were developing, some of the cities in the United States had grown very large. The crowding together of masses of people, the mingling of many races with widely different religious and cultural backgrounds, the concentration of poverty in certain areas, the deterioration of property in the older sections of the city, and the rise of delinquency and crime, combined to produce a set of totally new problems for the churches. Furthermore, the amount of work needing to be done in such a city was great enough to require the full time of at least one secretary and frequently of a staff. This demand for highly specialized investigation, together with the size of the task, led to the organization of the standard city societies in cities which had at least a half million population each, and an adequate budget to maintain at least one full-time secretary. These city societies were independent organizations and functioned much as did the state conventions. In some states the relationship between the state convention and the city society was entirely friendly and cooperative. In other states there was a strong difference of opinion as to what the relationship should be. There were debates also as to the amount and kind of support which the Home Mission Society should give to the work of the city societies.

By 1932 the Woman's American Baptist Home Mission Society had come to have much the same problems in its relations with the state conventions and the city societies. Sometimes questions arose between the two national societies, usually as to their relationship to local projects in which both were involved.

It was necessary to find some means by which these problems could be solved. For a long time conferences of various kinds were held, sometimes informally and sometimes formally between groups of agencies. For a number of years at the midyear meetings of the Council on Missionary Cooperation (under its various names), the Home Mission Society entertained at dinner the executives of the other home mission agencies and used these opportunities for discussing the general problem and the specific issues that grew out of it. Out of these dinners and conferences there finally grew in 1925 an informal organization named the Associated Baptist Home Mission Agencies. It met once a year at the time of the midyear meetings, and functioned between times through a small Central Committee on which the three national agencies,[1] the state conventions as a group, and the city societies as a group, were represented. All of these agencies contributed to the treasury of the organization in varying amounts according to their ability, but the budget was small. The only expense of the organization was for meetings of the

---

[1] The third national agency was The American Baptist Publication Society.

Central Committee, for stationery and postage, and occasionally for bringing a speaker to the annual meeting. In 1933 this organization was formally recognized by the Northern Baptist Convention as a duly constituted advisory body.

Many procedures in the cooperative support of projects have been worked out by the Associated Home Mission Agencies. It has been agreed: that the administration of local projects shall be in the hands of the state convention or the city society, and the national societies shall work through the local agency. That salaries provided by the national societies for cooperatively supported workers shall be paid through the local agency, not directly. That no cooperatively supported worker shall be chosen, even informally, until approved by all parties contributing to the support. That the national societies shall not support the general program of any state convention or city society, but shall appropriate definite amounts to specific workers or projects.

The Associated Home Mission Agencies has fully justified its existence. When questions arise, as they do from time to time, they do not become the acute problems that they formerly did, because there is this group to whom appeal can be made and through whom adjustments can be worked out.

Another great service which the Associated Home Mission Agencies has rendered is in studying the needs of the field and devising improved means for meeting them. In 1935 a series of conferences was held in which representatives of the national societies met with the state and city representatives to study the total home mission situation faced in each area. These conferences were held in Boston, Mass.; Binghamton, N. Y.; Toledo, Ohio; Sioux Falls, S. Dak.; Dubuque, Iowa; and Colorado Springs, Colo. Two days were spent in each conference discussing the needs of the field and what could be done to meet them within the limits of the greatly reduced financial resources of all the agencies. Out of these conferences came a cooperatively planned program which became the guide of all the agencies for several years.

Another approach has been made by bringing to the annual meeting of the Associated Home Mission Agencies speakers qualified to deal with particular situations. Out of the forum always conducted after such an address has come a better understanding of the task confronting the agencies.

At first the Associated Home Mission Agencies had a very small Central Committee which met only twice a year, one of those meetings being a short breakfast conference at the time of the annual meeting of the Agencies. As the Agencies faced the new responsibilities growing out of World War II, there arose a conviction that there was need for more united planning and action in the home mission field. Accordingly, after long study, it was agreed that this should be brought about through a greatly strengthened Central Committee. It was decided that the committee should be considerably enlarged, and that the membership should be so distributed as to come from all parts of the convention; and that it should hold at least one meeting each year of at least two days' length at a time apart from the American Baptist Convention or the midyear meetings, so that the members could give themselves to a serious study of the problems faced. It was hoped that they might give more definite direction to specific projects, such as the Rural Church Convocation, workers' training conferences, and the editing of the *Home Mission Digest*. Since all of this called for greatly increased expenditures, the Agencies voted that each organization should be assessed in proportion to its undesignated income from the unified budget. This was the final test of the feasibility of the whole plan, and it was well met. Almost all of the organizations paid their allotment the first year and the rest did so later. Thus was launched the greater Associated Home Mission Agencies.

Since the Central Committee has been enlarged, the Associated Home Mission Agencies has taken on several new responsibilities. It has assumed the planning and direction of the Training Conferences for Workers. There are conferences for Christian Center workers, bilingual pastors, Spanish-speaking pastors,

Japanese-American pastors, Educational Center workers, and other groups. Each of these conferences has grown out of a sense of need to confer with others confronting the same problems. Through the exchange of plans and programs, all present became better fitted for their tasks. At times, speakers from the outside who could lend understanding to a particular phase of the problem were secured to lead the discussion. By this means the workers steadily grew in their ability to serve their cause.

Most of these workers' conferences started in a rather informal way under the leadership of the Home Mission Society. The Woman's Society shared in them when it had a part in the project. The states and cities were vitally interested and soon took an active part in promoting them.

The Associated Home Mission Agencies also promotes and finances the Rural Convocations at Green Lake. The first of these was held in 1951, and proved so successful that the Central Committee made plans for others at regular intervals, upon recommendations by the Commission on Rural Advance. Another was held in 1954, and at the time of this writing, quadrennial conferences have been decided upon, beginning in 1959. The secretary of the Department of Town and Country of the Home Mission Society gives executive leadership.

In addition to the activities already outlined, the Associated Home Mission Agencies fosters the home mission program at the American Baptist Convention and a booth in the exhibit hall, publishes *Home Mission Digest,* and sponsors the work of the Personnel Secretary. More and more this organization is becoming the effective agency of Baptist cooperation in the home mission field.

The Larger Fellowship

The American Baptist Home Mission Society has taken an active part in all of the movements for closer cooperation between the denominations in its field of work. When the Federal Council of Churches was organized in 1908, the Home Mission

Society took an active part in the proceedings, and through the
years it has participated in all of the Council's activities that per-
tained to Home Missions. The part taken by the Society in the
evangelistic program has been recounted in Chapter XI. It has
also participated in the work of the Federal Council, through the
Home Missions Council, in the fields of comity and of the rural
church.

Naturally the greatest interest of the Society has been in
the Home Missions Council. The Society, in 1908, gave leadership in organizing the Home Missions Council of North America,
and has been active in it through all of its history. The Society
has shared in the financial support of this Council, and its officers
have carried a full share of the work. Their leadership is constantly felt in the formulation of plans and policies. During the
twenty-five years under consideration, the Council has made
two major adjustments in its relations to other organizations. In
1940 the Home Missions Council of North America and the
Council of Women for Home Missions united in a single organization under the name of the Home Missions Council. In 1951
the Home Missions Council united with other national interdenominational councils to form the National Council of the
Churches of Christ in the U.S.A. The Home Mission Society
shared fully in bringing about both unions. It has been represented on the General Board of the National Council of Churches
from the beginning.

Early in the development in the West, the Society worked
with other denominations to organize a State Home Missions
Council in each of the states. This was the organization through
which home mission problems and questions of comity could
be worked out. In the years since 1932, these councils have
given place to state councils of churches, organized for a broader
program but including all of the activities of the older organization.

The Home Mission Society has cooperated with other interdenominational organizations wherever they were working in the

same fields. The Society's relation to the Committee on Cooperation in Latin America has been described in Chapter XII. The work with other denominations in Heifers for Relief and also in the settlement of displaced persons has also been described. These individual cases of cooperation are simply expressions of a spirit that underlay all that the Society did. Winning North America for Christ was the goal, and the Society was ready to cooperate with all who were working to that end.

Integration of the Two National Societies

The most dramatic development within the Society in this period has been the integration of the work of the General Society and that of the Woman's Society under one Board of Managers and one staff. There had been widespread agitation for this for many years. Whenever a conference on Home Missions in any church in the American Baptist Convention was opened to questions, one that was almost sure to be asked was, "Why are there two Home Mission Societies?" The answer, historically, was easy to give. It could be explained that usually (with exceptions on both sides) the General Society employed men while the Woman's Society employed women. It also could be shown that the two Societies planned and worked very closely together. But these answers never fully satisfied the questioner. There had been agitation for uniting the two societies for many years. Several moves looking toward this end had been made in the Northern Baptist Convention, but none of them had been successful.

It was clearly recognized, however, by many in both organizations that their separate work was not justified under present-day conditions and that a change should be made. There had been a great deal of joint planning, and it was common for the two Boards of Managers to meet together for discussion. Members of the staffs who worked in the same field constantly conferred. In 1946 the Woman's Society suggested that the work of both Societies in Latin America be administered by Dr. Wilbur Larson, secretary of the Department of Latin America of the

General Society and that he become an officer of both Societies. This arrangement proved to be very satisfactory. In the same year, when the Associated Home Mission Agencies voted to appoint a personnel secretary, Mr. Witham became an appointee of both of the Home Mission Societies, as well as of the Associated Home Mission Agencies. In 1952, when Miss Edna Howe resigned as treasurer of the Woman's Society, arrangements were made for William H. Rhoades, treasurer of the General Society to become treasurer of the Woman's Society as well. In both of these cases the officer's financial relations were with the General Society alone, and the Woman's Society paid to the General Society an agreed amount toward salary and office costs. It will be noted that in each case the work was united only in the person employed. Each Board still directed the officer in regard to its own affairs. This arrangement, however, was a definite step forward.

In the fall of 1953, active negotiations were begun for the "integration" of the two Boards of Managers and their work. This was finally brought about May 19, 1955, by the vote of the annual meetings of the two Societies at the sessions of the American Baptist Convention at Atlantic City, N. J. The plans had been thoroughly worked out in advance, so that the integrated operation had actually begun May 1, the beginning of the fiscal year. All were confident that the annual meetings would approve the proposed plan, and the vote justified their confidence. It was unanimous.

The Societies have maintained their separate legal existence so as to avoid any legal complications that might possibly arise. Each holds an annual meeting and elects officers of the Society and a Board of Managers. The same persons are elected to both Boards, so that they can function as a single Board for both Societies. All of the departments formerly maintained by the two Societies were continued. Since some of them had changed responsibilities, three new departments were established. One new department was that of Alaska, Indian Work, and Schools in the

United States. To it was assigned the work of both Societies in Alaska, formerly administered in the General Society by the Department of Cities; and the work among Indians, including Bacone College and Murrow Children's Home, formerly administered in the General Society by the Department of Town and Country, and the Negro schools in the South supported by the Woman's Society, and the Baptist Missionary Training School in Chicago. Miss Dorothy O. Bucklin, a secretary on the staff of the Woman's Society, was made secretary.

As already explained, both Societies had Departments of Public Relations, with activities which were closely parallel. Accordingly, the work of the two departments was combined, then redistributed along functional lines. A new department—namely, Publications and Communications—was established, to which was assigned the work in the office. Miss Helen C. Schmitz, a secretary on the staff of the Woman's Society, was made secretary. Another new department—that of Public Relations—was given the work on the field and the supervision of the two field representatives. Rev. Clifford G. Hansen, a secretary on the staff of the General Society, was made secretary of that department.[1]

A department of Special Services was established, and Mrs. Milo E. Wenger, former Executive Secretary of the Woman's Society, was made secretary. This department was made responsible for certain specifically defined liaison relationships. It was to represent Home Mission interests in local churches and in city, state, and national groups. A by-law of the Board of Managers states: "The secretary of Special Services shall be a woman. She shall be designated by the Boards as the official woman representative of the Society, to present the general Home Missions viewpoint in denominational and interdenominational circles." Aside from these cases, each secretary continued in the position formerly held, but administered the work of both Societies in that field.

[1] For a fuller statement, see pages 203-208.

This plan of unification satisfied a public demand of long standing. The Societies have not expected that this integration of the work would bring any considerable financial saving. It has, however, simplified administration on the field and has clarified relationships in the minds of the church people.

As has been shown, this quarter of a century has been one of great changes in both the organization and the work of the Society. A healthy condition has been clearly demonstrated by the Society's ability to make these adjustments and to meet effectively the demands of the new day. The Society, therefore, can face the future with confidence and courage.

XVII

North America for Christ

THE TWENTY-FIVE-YEAR PERIOD in the history of The American Baptist Home Mission Society under consideration was one of turbulence and confusion. When it began, the country was passing through the greatest depression it had ever endured. As a result of that depression, the government assumed a new attitude toward human welfare, and labor acquired powers it never before had possessed. During that quarter of a century a world war and the Korean war were fought; throughout the closing years of the period the "cold war" held the nations of the world in its grip. Humanity had been on the move as never before. It had been, indeed, a turbulent time.

Achievement Amid Turmoil

In the midst of all that turmoil, Home Mission work steadily advanced. Work already begun was strengthened. New paths of service were discovered, and many old activities took on new phases.

A general program for training workers was developed. Three to five Schools for Rural Pastors, each from two to four weeks in length, are now conducted each year at the Rural Church Center. One of these is interdenominational. The training program for Christian Center workers at Brooks House is filling a long-felt need. Although still not adequate, it marks a real advance and is capable of much further development. A regular plan has been instituted for sabbatical leaves for further study. The annual or biennial conferences for bilingual pastors and kindred groups of workers are now conducted for training

233

as well as for program planning. Training and planning are mingled also in the conferences for the state directors of rural work and for the area directors of evangelism. At the same time that this program of training was being developed, the educational requirements for the workers of the Home Mission Society were steadily raised. Today, home missionaries, as a whole, are better trained for their tasks than ever before.

Much new work was started during this period. Juvenile protection grew out of the alarming increase of juvenile delinquency during the war. The work with service personnel was the outgrowth of earlier beginnings, but it has grown greatly both in character and in extent. It has become a continuing program, rather than an emergency measure. The Rural Church Center at Green Lake was new, not only in its establishment, but also in the type of service rendered. The Baptist Rural Convocation was an adaptation of an interdenominational movement, and it has brought help to many whom the earlier movement had not reached. Church extension, which was the chief home mission activity in the earlier years, had practically ceased in 1932. By 1940 it again had become a major responsibility, and on a far greater scale than ever before. New methods were developed rapidly to meet the demands of changed situations. The work with homes and hospitals, a totally fresh approach to a long-felt need, has proved of great assistance to the denomination's philanthropic institutions. The work of the Personnel Department was new in home missions, although other agencies had used similar methods before. It not only recruited home missionaries, but also increased the number of young people who were preparing for the church vocations. Although the first Educational Center was started in Harlem prior to 1932, its program was perfected in this period, and other Centers were established in cities where the concentration of Negroes made such work desirable. The adaptation of this method to a state-wide situation was a new development. The appointment of state directors of town and country work was begun in this period. A few workers had used that title at an earlier time, but they had not done the type of work which the title came to signify in this period. The introduction of the Christian Center among the Indians was a new adaptation of an old program. The entire enterprise in Alaska was a new undertaking for the General Society.

The Missions Conference at the American Baptist Assembly, Green Lake, Wis., is another development which has come to have great significance in the missionary life of the denomination. It is one of the few national conferences which have been held every year since the American Baptist Assembly opened in 1944. It is planned by the four national Mission Societies, with the chairmanship alternating among them. It brings together outstanding missionary speakers from the United States and abroad and Bible scholars who open the Scriptures by skilled interpretation. The Missions Conference gives to the capacity audience which is always in attendance an opportunity to meet their own missionaries and also national converts from their own mission fields, and this is done in an open, friendly fashion which is not possible at any other time or in any other way. The delegates carry the missionary enthusiasm back to their churches.

In this quarter century there was a considerable increase in the amount of time which the Board of Managers gave to the program. In 1932 the Board met for one day six times a year; the committees met in the morning and the Board in the afternoon, usually concluding its work before four o'clock. Later the time was extended to two days. One list of committees met on the morning of the first day and another list of committees met on the afternoon of that day. Since most members of the Board were on two committees, they were in committee sessions all day. Usually there was a dinner meeting on the evening of the first day, frequently with the Board of Managers of the Woman's Society. The following day was given entirely to the meeting of the Board. Although two of the six Board meetings of the year were replaced with meetings of the Executive Committee, the total number of hours given to the work by most of the members was more than doubled. This increase of time made possible a much more careful consideration of important matters.[1]

During this period the Society bought a headquarters building to be occupied by the two Societies. Bringing them together in one building has helped cooperative planning and the spirit of unity. This building gave each of the Societies more adequate quarters than it had before. The move also proved profitable financially. In a period of rapidly rising rents, the Societies stabilized their costs at a relatively low level.

Satisfactory progress was made in finances. There were no spectacular additions to the funds of the Society, but the funds increased steadily, and the income of the Society for the conduct of its work was higher than ever before. The World Emergency Fund, under various names, provided the Society with nearly a million dollars of extra money to be used in current operations. The World Mission Crusade brought the Society more than one million dollars, most of which was expended on property or other nonrecurring items. The Edifice Funds in 1932 amounted to about $750,000. In 1956, when all the returns from the campaign for Churches for New Frontiers have been collected, the Edifice Funds will amount to nearly $4,500,000. The general financial situation is summarized in the fact that whereas the Society in 1932 had an accumulated operating deficit of $178,399, in 1956 there was no operating deficit but a substantial reserve with which to meet any emergency that might arise.

The Society has had an opportunity to do a special educational task in home missions owing to the inauguration of the two annual offerings which are a part of the Unified Budget. First proposed by the Finance Committee to the Convention in 1950, these have assumed an important place in the stewardship of individual Baptists. The World Fellowship offering, received in the fall, is for the work of Foreign Missions and the Ministers

[1] Following integration the schedule for meetings of the Board has been changed. There are three Board meetings a year with three sessions in each for business and one for a program of missionary addresses. Aside from these meetings the Executive Committee during the year has two meetings of three sessions each. Meetings of Department Committees continue as before.

and Missionaries Benefit Board. The America for Christ offering, received in the spring, is for the work of the Home Mission Societies and the Board of Education and Publication. It is the occasion for the visits of many missionaries to the churches and for an educational emphasis that begins with the children and extends through all age levels.

The experience of the denomination has shown the value of the form of organization which the American Baptist Convention has established for home mission work. At first the national society was the dominant body, but from the first it encouraged and aided the formation of state conventions. As the cities grew larger and their problems became more perplexing, the national society encouraged the formation of city societies also. Sometimes there has been a tendency to overstress the importance of one or the other. However, this period has clearly demonstrated the value of close cooperation between local and general agencies. Basic problems are never purely local, but must be understood in terms of their impact on the total work of the Christian church. On the other hand, these problems must always be dealt with in the local area. When the local and the national agencies work together closely, the best results can be achieved for the whole.

This cooperation of the national agency with the local agency takes many different forms. Sometimes the role of the national society is to study general problems and bring the results of the study to the attention of the local agency. Sometimes it is to discover the varied forms which the problem assumes in different areas, and to report the experience of each agency in dealing with it.

Sometimes the national agency coordinates and reinforces the activities of the local agencies in meeting a local need, as was done in the matter of Churches for New Frontiers. The need was felt at various points and eventually became evident everywhere. Very few states and cities could have handled their own problems. A national approach made it possible to strengthen the denomination at all points and to minister to the unchurched masses everywhere. Only by a national approach was it possible to bring the matter to the attention of the entire denomination, thereby enabling the churches to see the full significance of it and make the response that was needed.

That many problems of local areas affect the entire convention was made clear in the matter of service personnel. When a military camp or other installation was near a given church, that church might or might not be able to provide the needed ministry; but the young men and women were from many parts of the country, and their welfare was a concern of all the homes from which they came. The national agency was able to help the local people discover the most effective ways of ministering to the young people, and it also could furnish financial assistance.

The national agency usually has taken the lead in experimentation and pioneering ventures. When new problems arise, the way to solve them is not certain. Someone must risk the failures of an experimental approach. This fact became evident with the coming of great numbers of Negroes into the northern cities. Because they were not an unevangelized people, they soon formed their own churches. Their chief difficulty was the unpreparedness of their leadership for the new and unfamiliar situation. No one knew the remedy. The experiment with the Educational Center required the willingness to try new things and a readiness to recognize the failures, to discard them, to save what was promising, and so to work out a solution. Although this experiment necessarily was made by a local agency in its own area, the national agency gave aid to the experiment throughout. The Society later recommended this approach wherever a like need arose, and it encouraged and aided the local agencies to put the plan into use.

There are certain service functions that must be carried on by a unit larger than the local ones. For example, few states or cities can have edifice funds adequate to meet their requirements. Moreover, the needs in any given area are not uniform through the years. It must be possible to supply funds where they are needed at the moment. Besides, few local units could afford to maintain trained personnel to handle building counsel; even those who could afford it have seldom felt it profitable. Yet both funds and personnel must be available when needed. Three men on the staff of the Home Mission Society, trained in giving building counsel, have served both the convention and the local areas better than would have been possible on the basis of the employment of a man in each state and city.

The same has been true in evangelism. It was not possible to maintain a full-time specialized worker in each state and city, but by making a well-trained and able man available to a group of agencies, all were better served than they would have been by a man attached to a local unit, who gave only a part of his time, frequently a minor part, to evangelism.

The national agency can also move funds and workers with reasonable dispatch into situations of special need. In the emergencies of fire, flood, and drouth which have been recounted in earlier chapters, the national agency has been able to come to the assistance of the local bodies. Its aid was never entirely adequate, for the resources of the national society are never entirely adequate, but at least it met the situation in some measure and its help was quickly sent.

Since the cooperation of the local agencies is wholly voluntary, it is sometimes delayed and sometimes ineffective. The experience of this period, however, has clearly demonstrated the effectiveness of the system of local and national agencies cooperating freely and in good will.

Facing the Future

In the onward march of the kingdom of God, each achievement becomes a foundation stone on which a greater achievement can rest. These twenty-five years have built on the century that went before, and they in turn now form the foundation on which the future will be built.

The task that was most obvious and most urgent in 1956 was that of evangelizing and gathering into churches the moving masses of unchurched Americans. The villages that had become cities, the small cities that had become large ones, and the sprawling edges of the older cities all required attention at once. There were literally thousands of communities of large size that had no churches. There were vast areas around the growing cities that would never be evangelized or adequately served through the existing churches. They were too far away and had no contact with or relation to the new community. But in it babies were being born, children were growing up, young people were entering into the responsibilities of adulthood and citizenship. They would become increasingly pagan unless the church performed her task well. Although the resources, both of money and of workers, were sadly inadequate, the churches needed to make the best possible use of them. For the nation to be evangelized, it had to be provided with churches.

The ill will between the various races has clamored for attention. No other failure has so much damaged America's status in the world. No other surviving pagan attitude has so much hampered America's world-wide Christian mission. The decisions of the U. S. Supreme Court in 1955 and 1956 have made this a crucial time for all the denominational agencies, and above all for the Christian church. What is done quickly will have double value, because the racial situation is at the center of the world's attention as never before. The church cannot afford to be anywhere but in the forefront of this undertaking. By every possible means home mission agencies must give themselves to wiping out every expression of unfairness or inequality between the various races in America. Local churches must welcome all members who come in a common loyalty to Christ. Christian Centers must help all who have need and who will receive their ministry. Every agency must serve all whom it can reach.

The needs of the deteriorating areas of the inner city have not been met in any adequate way. Only sporadic thrusts into it have been made. There, the masses of the people, for the most part, have no contact with the church or interest in it. There, poverty is at its worst, crime is concentrated, and juvenile delinquency is increasing. The churches have made little impression on these crowded masses. The Christian Centers are the most effective agency Baptists have, and some of them have done excellent work. But their number is pitifully small, and many are inadequately staffed. Occasionally a church has undertaken a program adapted to the changed community and has welcomed into its membership the mingled peoples around it, but too often the church has thought only of drawing from a distance a congregation of its "own kind." This futile policy frequently has been followed until the church has become so weak that it can no longer serve its community. Then it has appealed to the home mission agencies, whose resources were entirely inadequate to meet such needs. Moreover, these needs should have been met by the local church in the first place. Some strategy was needed for ministering to these deteriorating areas. Otherwise, as the cities increased in number and size, the nation would become more and more unchurched and paganized.

Two needs were seen in the rural areas. The farm population was declining as a result of the increased size of the farms and the use of more and larger farm machinery. But over thirty million people were there, and the church needed to find a way to be a vital force in their lives. In the nonfarm rural areas, the population was growing. Sometimes the people were gathered about an industry in that community. Sometimes they lived in the country and commuted to their work in the nearby city. Sometimes they had full-time jobs and did only a little gardening. Among all these people there was need for the church to become much more effective than it usually has been.

Both of these situations were in the purview of the Rural Convocations, the Rural Church Center, and the Department of Town and Country. No single formula would solve all of the problems. The solution of the problems depended mainly on persons who had the creative imagination and the consecration to devote themselves wholeheartedly to the task.

The challenge in Latin America was for an advance along all lines. Haiti, which had been so fruitful evangelistically, greatly needed more and better schools, and a rapid advance in medical work. With the development of these two services, Haiti could rapidly become an evangelical country. In all of the Latin-American fields the doors were wide open to advance as rapidly as American Baptists could furnish the workers and give them the means with which to do their work. The key to advance on each field lay at two points. The first was the training of a national leadership. Evangelical religion, to be generally accepted, must come to a nation through its own people. The schools needed to be strengthened so that they could adequately train the Christians for this work. The second was the support of these leaders. They needed help, if they were to secure the necessary buildings and equipment. In the course of time, this would become their own task and American Baptists could then turn their attention to other fields, but the only way to achieve that objective was by training leaders and giving them sufficient support to enable them to do their work.

Basic to all of these objectives is a passion in all of the churches to reach the masses of the people for Christ. There is always too great a readiness on the part of each church to think only in terms of its own prosperity. Until American Baptists come to think in terms of the millions of people who have not been led to Christ and who do not know how rich and satisfying life can be in Him, they will not fulfill the destiny for which God called them into being. Paul's ambition, "in order that I may reap some harvest among you as well as among the rest" (Rom. 1:13), must become the passion of every Christian. We have a great responsibility for the intellectual who is blinded to the meaning of life by his self-sufficient pride, for the prosperous man who fancies that in the attainment of many things he can satisfy his soul and know the full meaning of life, for the laborer who sees no meaning in his toil, and for the one whose hands are raised against society and who has never learned that brotherhood and cooperation are essential to human life.

The constant peril of the churches is that by seeking to save their lives they may lose them. They need to learn that only as they throw themselves with a glorious abandon into a completely devoted quest for all people within their reach can they save their own souls. The churches are entrusted with "the ministry of reconciliation" and the "message of reconciliation" (2 Cor. 5:18-19). Only as they fulfill this ministry and bear this message to all who are within their reach, and through their missionary outreach to this entire country and to all countries of the world, can they attain their true life as Christian churches. We, as Christians, must learn that we must "suffer with him in order that we may also be glorified with him" (Rom. 8:17). The cross is not for Christ alone.

Appendix A

The First One Hundred Years[1]

On an April day in 1832 the "General Missionary Convention of the Baptist Denomination in the United States for Foreign Missions" recessed its sessions in Oliver Street Baptist Meeting House in New York city to allow some friends of home missions to call a meeting in the Mulberry Street Church of that city in order that they might consider a matter which they thought to be imperative; namely, the setting up of an organization to spread the gospel *within* the United States. So it was that on the 27th day of April, 1832, the dreams of John Mason Peck and Jonathan Going came true, and The American Baptist Home Mission Society came into being. Later the Executive Board phrased the reason for the Society's existence in meaningful, picturesque words: "To encourage efficiently all local efforts for supplying the destitute with the preaching of the gospel, and not in the least to interfere with or disturb them." It added this statement: "One leading object in the establishment of the Society has been to combine in one sacred brotherhood all the friends of home missions throughout the United States." There was need, too, to make it clear to those Baptists who were insisting upon local autonomy that the new Society was not assuming any ecclesiastical authority: "The General Society claims to be but the servant of the churches."

Looking back on those first one hundred years, it appears that much of the expansion of Christianity on this continent came through the ministry of the Society's missionaries to the pioneer frontiersmen, to the Indians, to the Negro (often referred to as "the recently freed man"), and to the newly arrived immigrant. Furthermore, the Society had recognized on the day of its organization that no country can expect to become Christian when its neighbors do not know Christ, and accordingly it had taken the whole of North America as the scene for its endeavors.

[1] Because the reader may not have access to a copy of *A Century of Faith*, written by Dr. Charles L. White, giving a detailed account of the organization of The American Baptist Home Mission Society and its many services during the first one hundred years of its history, it has been thought wise to include here as an appendix this brief summary of those years. It was prepared especially for this book by Mrs. Milo E. Wenger, Secretary of Special Services, for The American Baptist Home Mission Boards.

244

The latter part of the first century saw the beginning of the work out-side the borders of the United States.

The exact number of local Baptist churches over the United States that owe their existence to the Home Mission Society will never be known, but it is estimated that the proportion may be four out of five. Early missionaries forded rivers, rode horseback, and slept on beds of pine needles to make such churches possible. Later, they rode the rails in "Chapel Cars," and residents of western towns in the early part of the twentieth century watched the coming of "the church on wheels." And so the number of churches grew.

Neither will it ever be known how many thousands of Negroes received an education and a knowledge of Jesus Christ, their Lord, through the many educational institutions established in the south by the Society and the Woman's Societies. Being a group to whom educa-tion even in its simplest form had been denied, the Negroes grasped eagerly at the opportunity for learning, as well as at the opportunity for training for service in the Christian church. The records of those years tell of the desire on the part of those so recently freed to carry the gospel even into Africa! To a cynical world that today sometimes asks what was done for the American Negro by those who helped to make his release possible, one answer is that strong denominational home mission bodies poured millions of dollars into work on his behalf. Baptists were among the foremost of these, and today we are thankful for the keen insight and determination shown by our forebears.

"As the motto of this Society is *North America for Christ,* I should say, and I think, that means the Indian, too." Those were the words of a young Cherokee as he spoke on the occasion of the fiftieth year observance of the Society in 1882. The Society had recognized this responsibility when it accepted in 1865 the trust from the Missionary Union (formerly the Convention referred to above) for the Indian work in the United States. Great men emerged in those years. Their recogni-tion of the need for education, which led to the establishment of Bacone College, was given praise by this same young Indian when he said, "A Christian school among the Indians is one of the most powerful agencies for educating and Christianizing them that we could have." He went on to say, "The Indian is the original inhabitant of this continent and the work of this Society should be to aid them." The Indian work soon spanned the continent. It extended from New York to Oklahoma, to Montana, to Nevada, to Arizona, and to California.

Meanwhile the population of the country, between 1860 and 1880, had grown from thirty to fifty millions. Liberal homestead laws, extension of railroads, development of rich farming lands, and industrial expansion had attracted large groups of immigrants from practically all of the countries of Europe. During a period corresponding approximately to the Society's first one hundred years, 1830 to 1930, the total immigration was 37,762,012. Again, the responsibility was not neglected. Before many years had elapsed, the Society's missionaries were at work among twenty-six different language groups. Almost without exception the missionaries were members of the same nationality as those to whom they ministered. They protected the newly arrived immigrants from exploitation, contended for their rights in labor relations, assisted in language difficulties, prevented sabotage and violence, encouraged young people to seek an education, and, most important of all, they influenced the immigrants spiritually. Today, the many in the American Baptist Convention's ministry and lay leadership who have come from bilingual backgrounds are a constant reminder of the influence of those faithful missionaries. The establishment of Christian Centers by the two Mission Societies in the early years of the twentieth century was an achievement of Baptist originality and showed a desire to meet every need of the city dweller.

The fact that missionaries of the Society reached Puerto Rico and Cuba in 1899, only two weeks after the American flag was raised over San Juan, is again proof of the foresightedness of the Society's leaders who now saw their obligation for the Christianizing of the Islands, even as they had seen their obligation for Mexico in 1870. Later they were to extend the work still farther on the North American continent by going into El Salvador, Nicaragua, and Haiti. In those countries there was need for word of a personal Christ, for tender nurture of souls new in the Kingdom, for physical healing, and for training that the converts might be able to carry on the work themselves, teaching in their own schools, preaching in their own pulpits, doctoring and nursing their own people. The perspective which one hundred and twenty-five years gives, shows how well these measures have been accomplished; for the strength, consecration and devotion of Christians south of the border is an example to everyone who visits them.

Throughout this one-hundred-year scene run two main threads: evangelism and cooperation. There has been no time in the Society's existence that has not been marked by the bringing of men and women to know Jesus Christ. The first missionaries knew that to be their greatest privilege, as do those of today. In 1906 two evangelists journeyed across the nation, holding conferences on evangelism with pastors everywhere. As a result there was cooperative denominational evangelism shared in by State Conventions and City Societies. This was a forerunner of the establishment of the department of evangelism in 1919, when the services of a national secretary and state and area workers became available to local churches and pastors. Through the years two-by-two calling, New Testament fashion, has resulted in hundreds of workers reaching the unchurched. A youth evangelist of the Baptist young people, an evangelist to the laboring groups, and a social evangelism to sick and convalescent patients were a part of the services in those early years.

Fifteen state conventions were organized prior to the Society. As new ones were developed they were often, in the beginning, auxiliary to the Society. The Jubilee report of the Board in 1882 made this comment: "There seems to be the need today pre-eminently of a Society which shall afford opportunity for the fraternal interchange of views about the great and manifold work which God has given us to do." The Associated Home Mission Agencies gave that answer years later and opened the way for planning together in a way that was not possible during the first 50 or 75 years.

Local woman's mission societies began their support of the Home Mission Society as soon as it came into being. Through individual gifts, through the use of mite boxes, and by becoming life members of the Society, women gave of their means for the support of missionaries. Although the White Cross program known by all women today was not begun until 1919, as early as 1849 the annual report published explicit directions respecting the sending of material goods. There was conference with the national Woman's Societies after their organization in 1877, and after 1909 with the unified group, the Woman's American Baptist Home Mission Society. Missionaries of each Society worked together on fields in complete cooperation.

Not only within the Baptist family but also farther afield cooperation was displayed. After 1907 the Society bore its full share in the important work of the Federal Council of the Churches of Christ in America. In the formation of the Home Missions Council in 1908, the Society took a leading part. It helped to form the Committee of Cooperation in Latin America.

Throughout those first years the work of the Society never became static. Nor is it static now. For in this moving land of ours there is always room for change and there is always need for change. The "destitute" was the one who was in the minds of the founders. Those destitute of the gospel have been in the minds of all those who have followed. Terminology may change, but people and their needs are the same; and the Home Mission Society with its co-workers constantly is in the midst of new situations, studying and praying that such means may be used as shall result in a wide-spread proclamation of Christ as Lord of all.

Appendix B

Presidents of The American Baptist Home Mission Society
1932-1957

1932-33	H. Theodore Sorg, Newark, N. J.
1933-34	Rev. Rivington D. Lord, Brooklyn, N. Y.
1934-35	Rev. Rivington D. Lord, Brooklyn, N. Y.
1935-36	Rev. Rivington D. Lord, Brooklyn, N. Y.
1936-37	Rev. Rivington D. Lord, Brooklyn, N. Y.
1937-38	Rev. Rivington D. Lord, Brooklyn, N. Y.
1938-39	Rev. Rivington D. Lord, Brooklyn, N. Y.
1939-40	Ernest E. Rogers, New London, Conn.
1940-41	Ernest E. Rogers, New London, Conn.
1941-42	Ernest E. Rogers, New London, Conn.
1942-43	Rev. Charles H. Heimsath, Evanston, Ill.
1943-44	Rev. Charles H. Heimsath, Evanston, Ill.
1944-45	Harry A. Gilman, Boston, Mass.
1945-46	Harry A. Gilman, Boston, Mass.
1946-47	Rev. Gordon Palmer, St. Davids, Pa.
1947-48	Rev. Sidney W. Powell, Boston, Mass.
1948-49	Rev. Sidney W. Powell, Boston, Mass.
1949-50	Theodore B. Clausen, Trumansburg, N. Y.
1950-51	John R. Gray, Waukesha, Wis.
1951-52	John R. Gray, Waukesha, Wis.
1952-53	Rev. Kenneth L. Maxwell, Hartford, Conn.
1953-54	Frank A. Nelson, Racine, Wis.
1954-55	Rev. Edwin T. Dahlberg, St. Louis, Mo.

Since Integration

1955-56	Rev. Clarence W. Cranford, Washington, D. C.
1956-57	Rev. Clarence W. Cranford, Washington, D. C.

Appendix C

Chairmen of the Board of Managers, The American Baptist Home Mission Society
1932-1957

1932-33	Rev. Rivington D. Lord, Brooklyn, N. Y.
1933-34	Rev. Albert W. Beaven, Rochester, N. Y.
1934-35	Rev. Albert W. Beaven, Rochester, N. Y.
1935-36	Rev. Albert W. Beaven, Rochester, N. Y.
1936-37	Rev. Albert W. Beaven, Rochester, N. Y.
1937-38	Rev. Albert W. Beaven, Rochester, N. Y.
1938-39	Rev. Albert W. Beaven, Rochester, N. Y.
1939-40	Rev. Albert W. Beaven, Rochester, N. Y.
1940-41	Rev. Albert W. Beaven, Rochester, N. Y.
1941-42	Ernest E. Rogers, New London, Conn.
1942-43	Rev. Albert W. Beaven, Rochester, N. Y.
1943-44	Theodore B. Clausen, Trumansburg, N. Y.
1944-45	Theodore B. Clausen, Trumansburg, N. Y.
1945-46	Theodore B. Clausen, Trumansburg, N. Y.
1946-47	Theodore B. Clausen, Trumansburg, N. Y.
1947-48	Theodore B. Clausen, Trumansburg, N. Y.
1948-49	Theodore B. Clausen, Trumansburg, N. Y.
1949-50	Rev. Warner R. Cole, Detroit, Mich.
1950-51	Rev. Warner R. Cole, Detroit, Mich.
1951-52	Theodore B. Clausen, Trumansburg, N. Y.
1952-53	Theodore B. Clausen, Trumansburg, N. Y.
1953-54	Theodore B. Clausen, Trumansburg, N. Y.
1954-55	Theodore B. Clausen, Trumansburg, N. Y.
1955-56	Rev. Isaac Higginbotham, Wollaston, Mass.
1956-57	Rev. Isaac Higginbotham, Wollaston, Mass.

Appendix D

Board Members, The American Baptist Home Mission Society
1932-1955

The following list, arranged alphabetically, includes the names of those Board Members who were in service in 1932, the beginning of the last quarter century, and their successors until 1955, when the Board became integrated with the Board of the Woman's American Baptist Home Mission Society.

George L. Allin, 1927-
Rev. Alfred Williams Anthony, 1923-1934
Rev. Ambrose M. Bailey, 1933-1937
Harry E. Bailey, 1928-1938
Rev. David K. Barnwell, 1932-1934
Rev. Omar Barth, 1952-
Rev. Richard S. Beal, 1931-1942
Rev. Albert W. Beavan, 1929-1943
Rev. G. Pitt Beers, 1934, (Executive Secretary, 1934-1953)
Rev. Edwin A. Bell, 1938-1939
H. C. Bickford, 1936-1946
Rev. William O. Breedlove, 1952-
C. I. Cady, 1941-1953
A. M. Calvin, 1954-
Rev. Harold B. Camp, 1932-1937
Rev. Carlton G. Christensen, 1953-1956
Herbert B. Clark, 1919-1936
Rev. George A. Clarke, 1933-1936
Theodore B. Clausen, 1939-1949 (President, 1949-1950), 1951-
Rev. F. G. Codd, 1942-1951
Rev. Warner R. Cole, 1941-1951
Rev. Clarence W. Cranford, 1943-1954
Rev. Gilmer Cross, 1950-1951
Rev. Edwin T. Dahlberg, (President, 1954-1955); 1955-
Rev. Fred Dean, 1946-
Rev. Austen K. deBlois, 1922-1937

251

H. E. Drake, 1952-
Duncan Dunbar, 1934-
Rev. R. N. Dutton, 1949-1955
Richard Edie, 1924-1935
Rev. Roger W. Floyd, 1951-
Mrs. Robert Ford, 1949-1956
Rev. John F. Fraser, 1928-1933
F. W. Freeman, 1930-1932
Rev. J. Harold Gamble, 1935-1938
Wendell Gangwish, 1948-1954
Harry A. Gilman, 1930-1944, (President, 1944-1946); 1946-1952
William J. Grippin, 1904-1942
Rev. H. O. Gronseth, 1951-
Rev. Lewis M. Hale, 1942-1952
William B. Hale, 1913-1934
Rev. J. Lester Harnish, (Vice-president, 1953-1954); 1954-
Rev. Charles H. Heimsath, 1933-1942, (President, 1942-1944); 1944-
    1947
Rev. Isaac Higginbotham, (Vice-president, 1954-1955); 1955-
Rev. Angus C. Hull, Jr., 1947-1952
Rev. Harold V. Jensen, 1938-1948
Clinton C. Johnson, 1946-
Chester J. Jump, 1953-
Rev. G. K. Keegan, 1948-1950
Norman Keim, 1952-1955
James L. Kraft, 1944-1947
L. R. Landfear, 1936-1946
Rev. Frederick Lent, 1918-1935
Rev. Rivington D. Lord, 1911-1933
Willfred O. Mauck, 1939-1943
Rev. Kenneth L. Maxwell, (Vice-president, 1951-1952; President, 1952-
    1953)
Rev. Charles R. McBride, 1938-1946
Rev. G. D. McClelland, 1947-1951
Rev. Philetus H. McDowell, 1921-1941
Clarence Meadows, 1947-1950
H. D. Millar, 1933-1945
Rev. Robert A. Moore, 1951-1954
Rev. Robert H. Moorman, 1939-1948
Frank A. Nelson, (Vice-president, 1952-1953; President, 1953-1954;
    President, A.B.C., 1954-1955)

John Nuveen, Jr., 1946-1947
Mrs. I. H. O'Harra, 1922-1937
Mrs. R. E. Olds, 1926-1935
Rev. Verner I. Olson, 1940-1950
Rev. Gordon Palmer, 1930-1946, (President, 1946-1947); 1947-
Rev. Norman W. Paullin, 1950-1956
Roland W. Peterson, 1950-
Rev. Sidney W. Powell, 1938-1947, (President, 1947-1949)
Rev. Homer P. Rainey, 1934-1939
Howard L. Roach, 1946-1949
Omer Robbins, 1949-1952
Ernest E. Rogers, 1919-1939
Rev. Wilbour E. Saunders, 1935-1944
Max Schimpf, 1914-1941
Rev. Avery A. Shaw, 1915-1933
Rev. C. Elroy Shikles, 1949-
Mrs. F. W. Skoog, 1948-
Rev. William R. Sloman, 1935-1938
Rev. John Bunyan Smith, 1937-1944
Rev. Ondon P. Stairs, 1952-
Rev. Frank M. Swaffield, 1926-1935
Mrs. B. C. Tandy, 1937-1940
Rev. John W. Thomas, 1946-1947
R. M. Thompson, 1944-1953
Mrs. Alberta V. Torbet, 1950-1956
Mrs. L. C. Trent, 1940-1950
Rev. Clifton H. Walcott, 1940-1950
Rev. Vance Webster, 1942-1949
C. F. Wheaton, 1935-1955
Rev. Howard C. Whitcomb, 1929-1940
A. F. Williams, 1947-1949; 1950-1956
John J. Wittmer, 1943-1951
Mrs. Nathan R. Wood, 1937-1948
Rev. Whitney S. K. Yeaple, 1934-1940
Rev. Wayland Zwayer, 1936-1946

Index

Abella, Pedro, 124.
Adams, Earl F., 12.
Age of the Great Depression (Wechter), 17, 21.
Alaska, work in, 85 ff.
Alaska, Indian Work, and Schools in the United States, Department of, 33, 78, 89, 103, 114, 230.
Allin, George L., 251.
Alton, Ill., 12.
Amenia, N. Y., 12.
America for Christ offering, 237.
American Baptist Assembly, 93, 167, 192, 235.
American Baptist Convention, 8, 36, 61, 96, 110, 191, 206, 230.
American Baptist Home Mission Society, organized, 213, 222, 245; Executive Committee of, 235; officers of, 214 f.; Board of Managers of, 214; cooperation of, 37, 110, 121, 129, 130, 207, 227; Headquarters Council of, 43, 214.
American Baptist Publication Society, 94, 99, 173, 176, 207, 222, 236.
American Bible Society, 122.
Anadarko, Okla., 104, 107.
Anchorage, Alaska, 88.
Anderson, Frank L., 66.
Andrews, Emery E., 74.
Anthony, Alfred Williams, 251.
Antunez, Joaquin, 118.
Arizona Baptist Convention, 105.
Associated Home Mission Agencies, 95, 207, 225 ff., 247.
Atkinson, C. Harry, 89, 187, 197.
Atlanta University, 31.

Babcock, Rufus, 13.
Bacone, Almon C., 109.
Bacone College, 32, 33, 104, 109 ff., 111, 231, 245.
Bacone singers, 111.
Bailey, Ambrose M., 217, 251.
Bailey, Mr. and Mrs. Harry E., 251.
Baptist, The, 11.
Baptist Missionary Training School, Chicago, 78, 231.
Baptist Rural Convocation, 96.
Baptist Youth Fellowships, 211.
Barnes, L. C., 142.
Barnwell, David K., 251.
Barranquitas Academy, Puerto Rico, 133, 136 ff.
Barrio, 134.
Barth, Omar, 251.
Bartlett, C. Eugene, 42.
Beal, Richard S., 251.
Beaven, Albert W., 250, 251.
Beers, G. Pitt, 28, 215, 251.
Bell, Edwin A., 251.
Benedict College, 31.
Beynon, Lee J., 42.
Bible Study Hours, 174.
Biblical Basis for Evangelism (Dahlberg), 178, 179.
Bickford, H. C., 251.
Bilingual work, 64.
Birch, Mr. and Mrs. A. O., 136.
Blankenship, Lois, 173, 174.
"Blanket assurance," 197.
Board of Promotion, Northern Baptist Convention, 11.
Bowling, Jr., Abner F., 217.
Bradford County, Pa., 172.
Bratcher, M. E., 35, 37, 200.
Breedlove, William O., 251.
Brenner, Robert D., 154.

254

Brewer, George H., 146.
Britton, Amos, 152.
Brooks, Charles A., 28.
Brooks House, 27, 77, 79, 233.
Brown, Edwin R., 68.
Bryant, Samuel, 215.
Bucklin, Dorothy, 89, 114, 231.
Budget, 25, 70, 236; for Latin America, 116.
Bureau of Indian Affairs, 113, 114.
Butler, Floyd L., 100.

Cady, C. I., 251.
Caguas, Puerto Rico, 118.
Calabar College, 119.
Calvin, A. M., 251.
Camaguey, Cuba, Province of, 126, 129.
Camp, Harold B., 251.
Camp Okalona, 48.
Candidate Secretary of Foreign Societies, 209.
Caraballo, Justino, 137.
Carr, Ruth, 144.
Carson Indian School, 106.
Casanella, J. Mario, 127.
Catlos, Edward, 65, 187.
Catskill, N. Y., 14.
Cattaraugus Reservation, N. Y., 12, 108, 109.
Cedarholm, Jason E., 143, 145.
Centennial Sunday, 14.
Century of Faith, A (White), 7, 14, 67, 158, 183, 245.
Chapel Cars, 98, 245.
Chaplains, 194; General Commission on, 34, 42; World War II, 36, 38.
Chaplains' Fellowship, Institutional, 194.
Chapman, Percy T., 143.
Chastain, Theron, 8, 55, 215.
Chicago Baptist Institute, 84.
Chicago Conference, 174.
Children's Homes, 189, 191.
Chinese, Work among, 70 ff.
Chipman, Edward E., 187.

Christensen, Carleton G., 251.
Christian Centers, 27, 77, 191, 235, 241.
Christian Centers, Director of, 79.
Christian Commission in Camp and Defense Communities, 37.
Christian Friendliness, 114, 200.
Christian Growth and Development, 178.
Christian Life Crusade, 176.
Christian Ministry to Service Personnel, 35, 40, 209.
Chronicles of America Series, 17.
Chuck, James, 70.
Chung Mei Home, 71 ff.
Church Edifice Fund, 183, 236.
Church Extension, Department of, 56, 187.
Churches for New Frontiers, 55, 186, 237.
Church World Service, 199.
Cienfuegos, Cuba, 131.
Cities, Department of, 29, 40, 51, 65, 78, 88, 100.
Clark, Herbert B., 251.
Clarke, George A., 251.
Clausen, Bernard C., 12.
Clausen, Theodore B., 249, 250, 251.
Clinton Fund, 169.
Clovis, Calif., 104, 107.
Codd, F. G., 251.
Cole, Warner R., 250, 251.
Colegio Bautista, Nicaragua, 151 ff.
Colegios Internacionales, Cuba, 117, 118, 127, 128, 131.
Colporters, 97 ff., 222.
Comity agreement in Puerto Rico, 129.
Commission on Rural Advance, 95.
Commission on the Ministry, 211.
Committee on Cooperation in Latin America, 121, 247.
Conscientious objectors, 39.
Conservative Baptists, 166.
Conaway, Mrs. A. M., 136.

255

Cooperation in Latin America, Committee on, 121, 247.
Cooperative Field Research, 64.
Cordova, Alaska, 87.
Council on Missionary Cooperation, 203, 205.
Council on World Evangelization, 168.
Crain, Margaret L., 174.
Cranford, Clarence W., 42, 249, 251.
Cress, G. Clifford, 11.
Cross, Gilmer, 251.
Crow Agency, Mont., 107.
Crusade for Christ, 177.
Crusader, 203.
Cuba, Baptist Convention, 117, 124 ff., 129, 140; churches, number of, 132; contributions of churches in, 117; Council of Churches in, 131; Curriculum building conference in, 131; Roman Catholic opposition in, 128.
Cummings, Oliver deWolf, 175.

Dahl, J. B., 86.
Dahlberg, Edwin T., 179, 249, 251.
Dean, Fred, 251.
de Blois, Austin K., 14, 251.
Delaware Avenue Church, Buffalo, N. Y., 12.
Denver Christian Center, 114.
Deputation work, 205.
Detroit Baptist Training School, 84.
Detweiler, Charles A., 33.
Detweiler, C. S., 110, 140, 144, 164, 204.
Detweiler, J. F., 68.
"Diary of the Covered Wagon" (Cress), 13.
Dinsmore, C. M., 184, 187.
Diriomo, Nicaragua, 148.
Displaced persons, 199.
Dixon, Robert W., 140, 146.
Dixon, Thomas F. F., 143, 145.
Dixon, Wesley, 185.
Dolan, Edwin, 110.

Dorram, Charles B., 13.
Douglas, H. Paul, 64.
Drake, H. E., 252.
Drouth, The Great, 195.
Dugger, Ray, 175.
Dunbar, Duncan, 252.
Dutton, R. N., 252.

Earl, George, 190.
Edie, Richard, 252.
Edifice Funds, 186, 236.
Edifice Funds and Building Council, Department of, 27, 89, 184, 187.
Educational Centers, 81 ff., 234.
Education, Department of, 27, 32.
Eight O'clock Fellowship of Prayer, 178.
El Cresto, Cuba, 117, 127.
El Salvador, 142 ff.; Baptist Convention, 145; churches, number of, 145; contributions, 145.
Engel, Millicent, 163.
Evangelism, Department of, 124, 164, 166, 167, 169, 181.
Evangelistic Conference, 167.
Evangelizing Our Constituency, 178.
Evangelizing the Unchurched, 178.
Evelyn Briggs Cranska Memorial Hospital, 147, 153.

Farm income, 19.
Faulkner, Harold W., 17.
Federal Council of Churches, 37, 64, 166, 227, 247.
Fehl, Samuel, 175.
Felton, Ralph, 129.
Fire relief, 197.
Fish, Laura, 138.
Fisher, Franklin A., 84.
Five Year Plan, 177.
Fleischman, Conrad, 60.
Flood relief, 197.
Floyd, Roger W., 252.
Ford, Mrs. Robert, 252.
Fordham, Forrest B., 175.

Fort Wayne, Ind., 12.
Fraser, John F., 252.
Freeman, F. W., 252.
Frerichs, Robert T., 94, 102.
From Versailles to the New Deal (Faulkner), 17.
Fujin Home, 76.
Furloughs, regulations of, 220.
Furman, Richard, 102.

Gamble, J. Howard, 252.
Gangwish, Wendell, 252.
Geary, Okla., 108.
General Education Board, 31.
German Conference, 63.
Germans, 60.
Getz, Roger, 112.
Gilman, Harry A., 249, 252.
Gleiss, H. C., 84.
Going, Jonathan, 14.
Goodwin, R. Dean, 177, 200, 203.
Gordon, William J., 105.
Grace, chapel car, 99.
Gray, John R., 249.
Great Depression, 23; in Latin America, 115.
Green Lake, Wis., 47, 54, 64, 93, 95, 99, 101, 120, 167, 192, 198, 206, 235.
Grippin, William J., 252.
Gronseth, H. O., 252.
Group Insurance Plan, 219.
Guatajiagua, El Salvador, 145.
Gutierrez, Angel Luis, 138.

Haiti, 117; American Baptist Mission, 126; Baptist Convention, 126, 156; growth, 154 ff.; medical program, 162; number of churches in Cuba, 131; twenty-fifth anniversary, 158.
Hale, Lewis M., 252.
Hale, William B., 252.
Hall, Rosa O., certificate, 90.
Hansen, Clifford G., 47, 203, 207.
Harlan, Rolvix, 90.
Harnish, J. Lester, 252.

Hatler, Mrs. Grace, 144.
Hayne, Coe, 11, 183, 203.
Hayne, Don, 12.
Heartberg, Joseph H., 40, 101, 209.
Heifers for Relief, 137, 198.
Heimsath, Charles H., 249, 252.
Hendry, Mrs. Estelle, 216.
Heneise, Mr. and Mrs. Harold K., 161, 162.
Hening, S. E., 216.
Hestines, John M., 79.
Hickey, James, 121.
Higginbotham, Isaac, 250, 252.
Hill, Horatio S., 83.
Hinche, Haiti, 157.
Hippolite, Lucius, 158.
Hoiland, Richard, 177.
Home Mission Agencies, 206.
Home Mission Council, 228, 247.
Home Mission Digest, 203.
Home Mission Society, see American Baptist Home Mission Society.
Homes and Hospitals, Association of, 190 f.; Board of, 189; Commission on, 190; Committee on, 190; Department of, 189; National Conference on, 192.
Homes for the Aged, 189, 191.
Hospitals, 191.
Howe, Edna R., 216, 230.
Hubsch, Herbert, 217.
Hull, Angus C., 252.
Hurricane relief, 197.

Immanuel, chapel car, 99.
Indians, 244; education of, 109; largest groups of, 113; number on reservations, 114.
Inner city, 240.
Institutional Chaplains' Fellowship, 194.
Integration of the two societies, 8, 33, 89, 103, 114, 194, 207, 213, 221, 229 ff.
Interdenominational centers, 41.

257

International Seminary, East Orange, N. J., 33.

Jackson, Perry L., 106.
Jacobus, Alvah, 217.
Janssen, Lawrence H., 47.
Japanese-Americans, 74.
Japanese, work with, 73 ff.
Jensen, Harold V., 252.
Jervis, Clifford W., 101.
Jett, Mrs. Ida, 12.
Johns, Vernon, 83.
Johnson, Clinton C., 252.
Johnson, C. Oscar, 44.
Johnson, Ralph M., 55.
Jubilee report, 247.
Judd, W. L., 158.
Judson Memorial Church, 77.
Jump, Chester J., 252.
Junior Citizens Camps, 48.
Juvenile Protection, 45, 47, 48, 191.

Katherine House, 77.
Keams Canyon, Ariz., 104, 107.
Keech, Finley, 54.
Keech, William, 143, 146.
Keegan, G. K., 252.
Keese, Susan T., 218.
Keim, Norman, 252.
Kelly, C. Stanford, 156.
Kester, Harvey, 42.
Ketchum, Inc., 112.
Killian, John C., 99.
King, T. D., 185.
Klinck, C. Dwight, 79.
Kodiak, Alaska, 85 ff.; Children's Home, 85.
Kontz, Emil, 47, 64.
Kraft, James B., 252.
Kummann, Harry, 216.

Lackey, John, 12.
Landfear, L. R., 252.
Larson, Elsie, 218, 229.
Larson, Wilbur, 110.
Latin America, American Baptists in, 115 ff.; budget, 116; contributions from, 116; Department of, 229; Depression in, 116; evangelism in, 116; ministry to, 120.
Latin American fields, 242.
Lawrence, Matthew, 13.
Lee, Mabel, 70.
Lent, Frederick, 66, 252.
Life Service Sunday, 211.
Limbe, Haiti, Theological Seminary in, 161.
Lincoln, Dorothy, 154.
Litchfield, Conn., 13.
Litsey, Harold J., 185.
Livingston, Benjamin, 164, 171.
Lord, Rivington D., 249, 250, 252.
Lord's Acre plan, 92.
Loughhead, H. C., 94.
Loveridge, Arthur F., 105.

Madras Conference, 120.
Madsen, Paul O., 48, 56, 89.
Maldonado, Ruth, 138.
Managua, Nicaragua, First Church of, 120, 149; Seminary in, 153 ff.
Marc, Eli, 158.
Marc, Ruben, 158; educational program of, 159 f.
Masaya, Nicaragua, 152.
Matanzas, Cuba, 129.
Matthews, Jr., Hubert C., 107.
Mauck, Wilfred O., 252.
Maxwell, Kenneth L., 249, 252.
May, Howard E., 87.
McBride, C. R., 94, 252.
McClelland, G. D., 252.
McCormick, H. P., 140.
McCullough, W. J., 175.
McCutcheon, Evalina, 144.
McDonald, Osgoode H., 189.
McDowell, Philetus H., 252.
Meadows, Clarence, 252.
Meadows, F. L., 122.
Mejia, Rudolfo, 152.
Memo from 164, 208.
Memoir of John Mason Peck, edited by Rufus Babcock, 13.
Memorial and Pioneer Programs, 14.

Mercado, Luis Fidel, 118, 138.
Mergal, Angel, 139.
Merrill, George E., 183.
Merrill, Thomas W., 12.
Mexican Baptist Convention, 117.
Mexicans in Southwest, 67.
Mexico, Ministry in, 121 ff.
Mexico City, First Church of, 120, 123.
Millar, H. D., 252.
Miller, Stanley, 137.
Minimum Salary Plan, 96.
Ministers and Missionaries Benefit Board, 11, 194, 219.
Ministry, Commission on, 211.
Missionaries, 218, 245; salaries of, 116.
Missionary Cooperation, Council on, 203, 205.
Mission of the Church, The, 96.
Missions, Conference, 235; Department of, 29, 88.
Missions, 13, 183, 203.
Mitchell, Mrs. Sarah C., 12.
Monterrey, Mexico, church at, 122.
Moore, Robert A., 252.
Moorman, Robert H., 252.
Morales, Adam, 68, 69.
Morales, Benjamin, 69.
Moravians, 142.
Morehouse College, 30.
Morikawa, Jitsuo, 76, 77, 182.
Morony, Gregory S., 86.
Moseley, H. R., 124.
Murrow Indian Orphans' Home (Murrow Children's Home), 32, 33, 104, 112, 231.
Murrow, J. S., 112.
Myer, Everett B., 122.

Nallinger, Otto, 102.
National Council of the Churches of Christ in the U.S.A., 228; Foreign Missions, Division of, 121; Home Missions, Division of, 212.
National Ministers' Council, 167.

National Planning Conference, 95, 96.
Nationals, in El Salvador, 147; in Latin America, 117, 218; salaries of, 116.
Negroes, concentration of, 81, 234; education of, 30, 231; migration of, 81; missionaries to, 244.
Neil, Samuel G., 99.
Nelson, Frank A., 249, 252.
Nelson, Reuben E., 55.
Nelson, Samuel F., 68.
New Friends for Christ, 175.
Nicaragua, 146; Baptist Convention, 147, 149, 150, 153; contributions of, 154.
Nisei, 74 ff.
"North America for Christ," 7, 115, 245.
Northern Baptist Convention, 8, 11, 14, 30, 38, 40, 61, 92, 165, 169, 213.
Norwegian Baptist Conference, 63.
Nuveen, Jr., John, 253.

O'Harra, Mrs. I. H., 253.
Ojedo, Alejandro Trevino, 118.
Oklahoma State Board of Education, 112.
Olds, Mrs. R. E., 253.
Olsen, Mabel, 105.
Olson, Verner I., 253.
Oriente, Cuba, 129.
Osborn, Charles R., 107.
Outstations, 139.
Ouzinkie, Alaska, 85.
Owl, David, 12, 108, 109.

Palmer, Gordon, 113, 249, 253.
Parajon, Arturo, 118, 147, 149.
Pastor's Round Table, 204.
Paul, Thomas, 158.
Paullin, Norman W., 253.
Peck, John Mason, 12, 14; *Peck, John Mason* (Lawrence), 13; *Peck, John Mason and One Hundred Years of Missions* (de Blois

259

and Barnes), 13; *Peck, Memoir of John Mason* (edited by Babcock), 13.
Pentecostals, 67; in Puerto Rico, 133.
Pepper, Clayton A., 102.
Personnel Department, 234; personnel secretary, 209.
Peterson, Ronald W., 253.
Pixley, John S., 154.
Poling, Daniel A., 175.
Population, growth of, 23, 245; movement of, 49, 58.
Port-au-Prince, Haiti, First Church of, 116, 120, 157; anniversary of, 120.
Poston, Ariz., 104.
Postwar Planning Commission, 43, 45.
Powell, Sidney W., 177, 179, 249, 253.
Printed Page Evangelism, 168, 181.
Promotion, Director of, 29.
Publications and Communications, Department of, 206, 207, 231.
Publicity, Literature, and Research, Department of, 203.
Public Relations, Department of, 204, 205, 206, 207.
Puebla, Mexico, First Church at, 120.
Puerto Rico, Baptist Convention, 133, 137; comity agreement in, 136; number of Puerto Ricans in New York, 67; work in, 117, 136.
Puerto Rico Evangelico, 136.

Racial antagonism, 240.
Rainey, Homer P., 253.
Rainy Mountain, Ariz., 107.
Ramerez-Ruiz, Donato R., 123.
Raney, J. Lester, 108.
Rapp, Edward D., 47.
Realengo Diez y Ocho, Cuba, 125.
Reddin, Estoy, 144.
Red Stone, Okla., 107.

Regular Baptists, 166.
Rehabilitation, Europe, Japan, 198 ff.
Reno, Nev., 104.
Retirement allowance plan, 219.
Rhoades, Jr., E. H., 43.
Rhoades, William H., 216, 230.
Rich, Mark, 91, 101, 197.
Richmond, Calif., 50.
Riley, Earl, 110.
Rio Piedras, Puerto Rico, 138.
Roach, Howard L., 253.
Robbins, Joseph C., 43, 253.
Robbins, Omer, 253.
Robinson, Edith, 160.
Robleto, Adolfo, 152.
Rock Springs Seminary, 13.
Rodriguez, Esteban, 152.
Rodriguez, Felix Castor, 140.
Rodriguez, Oscar, 117, 126, 131.
Rogers, Ernest E., 249, 253.
Roman Catholic immigrants, 165.
Roman Catholics, opposition of, in Cuba, 128; El Salvador, 145; Haiti, 163; Puerto Rico, 133.
Rosser, Pearl, 173, 174.
Routledge, Dr., 127.
Ruiz, Jose Maria, 147.
Rural Advance Commission, 95.
Rural and Indian Missions, Department of, 101.
Rural Church Center, 94, 99, 101, 120, 233, 241.
Rural Convocations, 227, 234, 241.
Rural Life Sunday, 90.

Sabbatical leave, regulations of, 220.
Saddle Mountain, Okla., 106.
Santa Ana, El Salvador, First Church, 120, 143.
Santiago, Cuba, church at, 120, 124, 130, 131.
Santurce, Puerto Rico, First Church of, 120.
Saunders, Wilbour E., 253.
Schimpf, Max, 253.
Schmitz, Helen C., 207.

Schools for Rural Pastors, 233.
Scott, Charles S., 146.
Sears, Charles H., 168, 189.
Seminary Middlers, Conference of, 206.
Shaw, Avery A., 253.
Shearman, Evan J., 177.
Shepherd, Charles R., 70.
Sherman, Jeannie, 101.
Shikles, C. Elroy, 253.
Shock, Harold D., 106.
Shongo, Barry E., 108.
Shupbach, T. H., 127.
Shurtleff College, 12.
Silva, Alfredo, 152.
Skoog, Mrs. F. W., 253.
Sloman, William R., 253.
Smart, George W., 106.
Smit, Pieter, 174.
Smith, Ellsworth, 29, 91.
Smith, Frank A., 29, 88.
Smith, H. M., 84.
Smith, John Bunyan, 253.
Smith, Luther Wesley, 44, 172, 177.
Smith, Marc Jack, 110.
Smith, Paul, 175.
Social Security, 22.
Social Service and Rural Community Work, 90.
Sorg, H. Theodore, 249.
Spanish-American Seminary, Los Angeles, 33, 67, 68, 69, 123.
Spanish-speaking work, 66.
Special Services, Department of, 231.
Spelman College, Atlanta, Ga., 31.
Stairs, Ondon P., 253.
Standard for the Rural Church, 96.
Steiger, Robert, 76.
Stewart, Nev., 106.
Stickler, Lolita, 105.
Student Volunteer Movement, 212.
Stump, John S., 184.
Sundt, Edwin E., 90.
Swaffield, Frank M., 253.
Swedish Conference, 63.

Tandy, Mrs. B. C., 253.
Ten Day Cooperative Crusade, 178, 181.
Thomas, John W., 29, 40, 45, 74, 88, 253.
Thompson, Francis W., 111.
Thompson, R. M., 253.
Tibbets, Orlando, 123.
Tingley, Charles E., 184.
Titus, E. L., 76.
Todd, John G., 143.
Torbet, Mrs. Alberta V., 253.
Torbet, Robert G., 8.
Town and Country, Department of, 29, 77, 88, 92, 114, 227, 241.
Town and Country Fellowship, 92.
Trent, Mrs. L. C., 253.
Trueblood, Elton, 179.
Turkington, William, 11.

Unchuka, Okla., 112.
Uranium ore, 53.

Vanguard of the Caravans (Hayne), 13.
Virginia Union University, 31.
Volks Deutsch, 200.
Voodoo, in Haiti, 162.

Wadsworth, Lincoln B., 56, 90, 188.
Walcott, Clifton H., 253.
Walker, Ralph C., 42.
Walters, Ota G., 122.
Warner, W. A., 86.
Watchman-Examiner, 203.
Webber, Aaron F., 140.
Webster, Vance, 253.
Weeks, B. D., 110.
Welsh people, 60.
Wenger, Mrs. Milo E., 231, 244.
West Indies, 115.
West, Walter Richard, 111.
Westrup, Thomas, 122.
West Union Baptist Church, Oregon, 11, 13.
Wheaton, C. F., 253.

Whitcomb, Howard C., 253.
White, Charles L., 7, 14, 67, 158, 183, 245.
White Cross program, 247.
Wilkinson, R. N., 86.
Williams, A. F., 253.
Willis, Wilkin, 108.
Willkens, Fred. H., 81.
Wilson, D. A., 146.
Wilson, Gustavo, 152.
Wilson, Leonard D., 138, 146.
Winning the Children for Christ, 172, 173, 176.
Witham, Ernest C., 37, 40, 207.
Wittmer, John J., 253.
Woman's American Baptist Home Mission Society, 72, 78, 85, 89, 105, 106, 115, 117, 122, 130, 207, 221, 224, 247.
Wood, A. Groves, 155.
Wood, Mrs. Nathan R., 253.

Woodbury, Walter E., 29, 164, 170, 172.
World Emergency Fund, 35, 44, 46, 51, 236.
World Evangelization, Council on, 168 f.
World Fellowship Offering, 236.
World Mission Crusade, 43, 45, 53, 136.
World Relief Committee of Northern Baptist Convention, 117, 198.
World Sunday School Convention, 120, 131.

Yasamura, Jobu, 77, 200.
Yeaple, Whitney S. K., 253.
Yokefellows Group, 180.
Youth Work Committee, 212.

Zwayer, Wayland, 253.